Why Gender Matters in Southeast Asia Politics

Why Gender Matters in Southeast Asia Politics

R Verma

MD PUBLICATIONS PVT LTD
NEW DELHI
www.mdppl.com

Published by :

MD Publications Pvt Ltd
"MD House", 11, Darya Ganj,
New Delhi - 110 002
Phone : +91-11-45355555
E-mail : contact@mdppl.com
Website: www.mdppl.com

ISBN: 978-81-7533-359-8

Published and Printed by Mr. Pranav Gupta on behalf of **MD Publications Pvt Ltd** at Mohit Enterprises, Delhi.

PREFACE

Southeast Asian societies are witnessing a rapid social change due to the economic growth of this region and the tide of globalization. The aim of this session is to discuss the variety and universality of the changes in gender roles in this region on empirical ground. Four papers are all from a joint research project on this topic conducted in six societies in this region: China, Thailand, Singapore, Taiwan, Korea and Japan.

While many scholars of gender and gender studies have looked at the ways in which gender is practiced in Southeast Asia, a region that has long been pointed to by scholars as an area where women have 'relatively high status,' gendered transnationalism demands greater attention. The need for critical examination of issues such as displacement, deterritorialization, and globalized political movements is imperative, as more and more people in Southeast Asia are contending with these issues on a daily basis.

Historians of Southeast Asia have begun to consider the history of women and gender relatively recently, even though the complementary relationship between men and women has long been cited as a regional characteristic. In the last twenty years or so the field has witnessed some important advances, most notably in the study of the twentieth century but also in the preceding periods as well. Generalizations advanced in the past are now being refined through a number of new case studies.

The concept of "gender pluralism" to analyze historical and ethnographic material bearing on Southeast Asia since early modern times. Deployment of this concept in the context of an analysis that approaches transgenderism as an optic through which to view such pluralism entails an intervention against the grain of much writing on gender and sexuality. This intervention involves an interpretive framework conducive to the comparative historical investigation of culturally interlocked domains that are often separated or ignored in scholarly accounts, as occurs when "gender" is construed as a code word for "women" and is thus stripped of much of its significance before research has begun or when transgender practices or certain modalities of sexuality are examined in relative isolation from other salient components of the more encompassing sex/gender and cultural-political systems of which they are a part.

It is argued that for this region and period transgenderism provides a valuable window on gender pluralism partly because the vicissitudes of transgendering are broadly indexical of the greater formalization and segregation of gender roles, the distancing of women from sources of power and prestige, the attenuated range of legitimacy concerning things erotic and sexual, and the constriction of pluralistic gender sensibilities as a whole.

I am very grateful to Mr. Pranav Gupta, Director of MD Publications Pvt Ltd, New Delhi, for his kind cooperation and support for this book.

R Verma

Contents

	Preface	*v*
1.	Why Gender Matters in Southeast Asia Politics: An Introduction	1
2.	Women in Elected Office: Global Under Representation	35
3.	Women, Citizenship and the Politics in Philippines	89
4.	Community-based Movements of Japanese Women	139
5.	The State of Gender in the Sathya Sai Baba Movement in Malaysia	155
6.	Gender and Religious Legitimacy in Thailand	171
7.	Consciousness-raising Among and Beyond Women's Movement Activists in China	223
	Bibliography	287
	Index	291

1

Why Gender matters in Southeast Asia Politics

An Introduction

The image of women in South Asian novels has undergone a change in the last three decades. Throughout this period, women writers have moved away from traditional enduring, self-sacrificing women toward conflicted female characters searching for identity. The interests of women writers have changed with South Asian society and its relationship with the West. This trend in writings by South Asian women clearly appears if one compares the images of suffering women in Kamala Markandaya's Nectar in a Sieve and Meera Mahadevan's Shulamith to recent subversions and expansions of the traditional image in works by Chitra Fernando, Anita Desai, Kamala Das, Sara Suleri, and Anees Jung.

In contrast to the main women characters in Markandaya's Nectar in a Sieve and Mahadevan's Shulamith, female characters in the 1980s assert themselves and defy marriage and family strictures. Chitra Fernando's collection of short stories Three Women, like Anita Desai's In Custody, portray women who want their individual worth realized and attempt to break through the suffering that traditional society offers them. The most recent books, of the last three years (1986-1988), explore an educated woman's search for identity and meaning in autobiographical form, as in Kamala Das' *My Story* or in Sara

Suleri's *Meatless Days*, or combining autobiographical and ethnographic form, as in Anees Jung's *Unveiling India: A Woman's Journey*.

Traditionally, marriage for women-except in certain matriarchal tribes in the south that remained unaffected by the Aryan invasion that began in 1500 B.C.E. has entailed a most submissive feminine role. Although a woman ideally had power as a mother, as a wife she submitted to her husband and his family. Only recently have South Asian women in the dominant patriarchal tradition started to question aspects of this role, or decided against marriage altogether. In Image of Woman in the Indo-Anglian Novel, Meena Shirwadkar claims that, following the changes in Indian society, novels have started to progress from depicting women characters solely as epitomes of suffering, womanly virtue to portraying more complex, real characters.

Tradition, transition and modernity are the stages through which the woman in Indo-Anglian novel is passing. The image of traditional woman, the Sita Savitri type, was at once, easy and popular. In India, with its strong bent for tradition, woman was expected mainly to live for others than for herself because "others" controlled and moulded the social structure. Even woman in life and literature herself voluntarily surrendered to the ideal of self-sacrifice. Modern woman, in life, has been trying to throw off the burden of inhibitions she has carried for ages. Yet, a woman on way [sic] to liberation, trying to be free from inhibitions, is rarely seen in Indo-Anglian literature.

Shirwadkar's study, published in 1979, criticizes a literary tradition still overshadowed by the traditional, suffering ideal of womanhood. This ideal has persisted in culture permeated by religious images of virtuous goddesses devoted to their husbands. The Hindu goddesses Sita and Savitri still exist as powerful cultural ideals of women in South Asia. Both images tell women to devote themselves to their husbands to extremes of endurance, loyalty, and self-sacrifice.

As Susan S. Wadley explains, [The god] Rama's wife Sita exemplifies the behaviour of the proper Hindu wife, devotedly following her husband into forest exile for twelve years, and eventually, after being kidnapped for a time by the evil Ravanawhom Rama finally destroys, proving her wifely virtue by placing herself on a lighted pyre. Throughout North India, the women yearly worship Savitri, a goddess whose renown emanates from her extreme devotion to her husband, through which she saves him from the god of death. The story of Savitri is held up as a prime example of the lengths to which a wife should go in aiding her husband. The good wife saves her husband from death, follows him anywhere, proves her virtue, remains under his control and gives him her power. ["Women and the Hindu Tradition," in Women in India (New Delhi: Manohar, 1986), 122-123]

Meena Shirwadkar finds that the representation of women in Indo-Anglian literature fulfils this ideal of suffering devotion, which she calls the Pativrata tradition. She argues that "a graded change" has occurred, however, in Indo-Anglian fiction. "The early novels show the wife in her traditional role, mainly as a house-wife and child-bearer, and the writers are preoccupied with her suffering," she claims. Later novels, in contrast, show "the wives to suffer more because of the incompatibility between her individuality and awareness of herself and the traditional views of her husband and her in-laws".

From women who endure namelessly fulfilling the ideal of the devoted wife-goddess, South Asian fiction by women has progressed to a conflicted yet liberating naming of one's one experience and that of other women. Although Easterners and Westerners can debate South Asia's traditional valuation of suffering, both must value the latest developments in South Asian women's writing. These women authors incorporate their experience in both worlds in an attempt to make new, empowering image for women. As Anees Jung points out: "Where the two experiences meet lies a revelation, and a story." Recent writers' stories realize both the diversity of women and the diversity within each woman. Rather than limiting the lives of women to one ideal, they push the ideal towards the full expression of each woman's potential.

According to a recent report (IPU 1999:25), only 14 per cent of parliamentarians in Asia and just under 14 per cent in the Pacific are women. In the last decade, interest in women's participation in politics in the Asia–Pacific region has focused on three main issues: why more women should become involved in politics and decision making at all levels; how more women can enter and survive in politics; and how women can make a difference in the quality of political decision making.

NETWORKING AND INSTITUTION BUILDING

Although various women's groups in Asia–Pacific have been engaged in the struggle to promote women's political roles since the end of the nineteenth century, the movement really gained momentum in developing countries only in the last ten years. In 1990, UNESCO wanted to present the output of a research project on Women in Politics. At the suggestion of UNIFEM, which provided co-funding, UNESCO and UNIFEM brought together non government organisation (NGO) women activists and women politicians to provide an appropriate forum. The participants soon began to network and strategize on the future of women in politics in the Asia–Pacific region.

An obvious requirement was the creation of mechanisms, and ultimately institutions, that could assist women struggling to survive in politics, and others seeking to enter, to share their experiences and learn from one another. Two years later, in 1992, Netherlands funding enabled a few of these women to meet in Manila, where they decided to form a Women in Politics network. An important characteristic of the group was the fact that several were already actively engaged in politics, while others had the kind of administrative and management experience that would be invaluable in establishing and maintaining institutions.

The outcome of the meeting was the incorporation in the Philippines in 1992 of the Center for Asia–Pacific Women in Politics (CAPWIP). CAPWIP began with good regional coverage from its 13 board members, representing Australia, Japan, Korea, Pakistan, Papua New Guinea, Philippines, Singapore, Thailand and the USA. In 1996, the board decided to add two representatives from each sub-region, to be nominated by the CAPWIP sub-regional focal points. In June 1994, CAPWIP organised the First Asia-Pacific Congress of Women in Politics.

Held in Manila in the week after the regional preparatory committee for the Fourth World Conference on Women, the congress represented a sharpening and focusing of ideas widely debated by governments and NGOs throughout the region during the preceding months. Twenty-one countries and territories were represented by the 241 participants drawn from academia, government and politics at all levels, NGOs and community groups. Following the success of this first congress, the CAPWIP regional network initiated sub-regional workshops. In South Asia, Chandni Joshi (UNIFEM Regional Programme Adviser) and Ranjana Kumari (Director of the Center for Social Research (CSR) in New Delhi) organised a Women in Politics Workshop for the sub-region, held in Kathmandu later in 1994.

That workshop named CSR as the CAPWIP focal point in the region and set up a loosely structured council that is now a fully fledged network: the South Asian Committee for Political Empowerment of Women (SACPEW), with CSR as its secretariat. A later meeting of SACPEW in Sri Lanka approved publication of a newsletter, the addition of 30 new organisational members, and a plan for regular national and South Asian conferences and meetings, research and leadership training.

In East Asia, the Korean Institute for Women and Politics (KIWP), chaired by Dr Jung- Sook Kim, became the sub-regional focal point. It organised the First East Asia Congress of Women in Politics in Huairou, China, during the 1995 NGO Forum. Although logistical difficulties and the lack of a common language have hampered activities at the sub-regional level, the individual countries of East Asia have been enthusiastic members of the regional network. KIWP hosted a regional meeting in December 1996 on Quality of Life in the Asia-Pacific Region & the Role of Women Political Leaders, while in September 1997 Taipei hosted the Fourth Asia-Pacific Congress on Women in Politics.

The Women in Politics Pacific Centre (WIPPaC) grew out of the experience of Pacific participants in the First Asia-Pacific Congress. CAPWIP and the UNIFEM Pacific office, with funding from AusAID and the Australian national UNIFEM committee, initiated the First Regional Women Leaders Congress in the Pacific, held in July 1995.

A total of 26 women and 4 men, representing 15 Pacific Island countries, attended the four-day congress on Effective Governance and Transformative Politics and decided to form WIPPaC as an informal networking group, with UNIFEM Pacific acting as the secretariat. The Pacific network is now among the most active of the sub-regions in the CAPWIP network, having organised sub-regional WIPPaC congresses in 1995 and 1996, and regional training programmes in 1997, 1998 and 1999, and hosted the Third Asia-Pacific Congress on Women in Politics in November 1996.

GLOBAL NETWORKING

From the outset, the group that established CAPWIP saw the potential value of global networks. In 1994, they took advantage of the 1994 Taipei Global Summit on Women's Leadership in Politics which brought together women from both regional and global networks. This group agreed to work towards the formation of a global network and to meet again at the preparatory committee for the Beijing World Conference to be held in New York in March 1995.

The Fourth World Conference on Women provided an ideal opportunity for the various networks to meet and strategise at minimum cost. During the NGO Forum in Huairou, four regional congresses were organised by GLOBALNET and CAPWIP: the First European-North American Congress of Women in Politics; the Second Asia-Pacific Congress of Women in Politics; the First Latin American-Caribbean Congress on Women in Politics; and the First Western Asia Congress of Women in Politics.

Finally, on a wet and rather miserable 6 September in 1995 in Huairou, the First Global Congress of Women in Politics was held to receive the reports of the respective regional congresses and to share visions, plans and strategies. Agreeing that a global network was needed, the congress decided on a second global congress in 1997, again with CAPWIP as the interim secretariat. The Second Global Congress of Women in Politics was originally scheduled for February 1998 in New Delhi. Somewhat ironically, the Indian national elections the same month forced relocation to the Philippines. Rescheduled to August 1998 in Makati and organised by the Global Network of Women in Politics, this congress was hosted by the Women in Politics Institute, Philippines, with CAPWIP as secretariat, UNIFEM as sponsor and the Asian Development Bank as co-sponsor. At the conclusion of the meeting, new officers were elected and a new secretariat designated in Africa.

In some ways, the history of the CAPWIP congresses and associated meetings documents the story of the development of ideas about women's roles in politics and good governance in the developing countries of Asia–Pacific. One of CAPWIP's first activities was political leadership training, organised in partnership with the Global Summit in Bangkok in 1993. Among the participants were delegates from China, Malaysia, the Pacific, the Philippines, Singapore, Thailand and Vietnam. It was here, after a session on power, that the group, prompted by Kanwaljit Soin, a nominated MP in Singapore, began to ask themselves: 'What kind of politics should women promote?'

This question produced the second theme of the First Asia–Pacific Congress on Women in Politics: Why Women? What Politics? Participants were challenged to define why women needed to become actively engaged in politics and to identify the kind of politics that they wanted to practice. Dr Rounaq Jahan, of Columbia University, emphasised that women must enter politics in order to bring about major changes in their lives because the political arena is where mainstream decisions are made. The congress also agreed that only women can really understand and articulate women's needs and specific gender issues, that only they can provide a women's perspective on all issues. For their concerns to be met effectively, therefore, women must be directly represented as a group in the political process.

The answer to this question was clear in principle: women should make a difference. However, the details of what kind of difference were less clear. The general expectation was that women's involvement would improve standards of governance. Kanwaljit Soin referred to a 1991 Australian survey which found that 54 per cent of those surveyed believed that women entering politics were motivated by altruistic and community welfare concerns, compared with only 13 per cent for men. By contrast, 64 per cent thought men were motivated by personal interest and power, compared with only 11 per cent for women.

Rounaq Jahan also argued that women are better equipped to be transformative because of their role as outsiders, bringing in new kinds of values. Khunying Supatra Masdit, an active Thai politician since 1979, emphasised that, for her, politics should not be corrupt, should serve people's rather than personal interests and should be action-oriented. The congress also described some characteristics of political processes that improve women's prospects for success. Rounaq Jahan noted that it was particularly difficult for women to enter the winner-take-all American and British models of parliamentary democracy, while European experiences suggested that women candidates are more likely to succeed in systems based on proportional representation.

TRANSFORMATIVE POLITICS

Although the term 'transformative politics' emerged during the First Asia–Pacific Congress, that meeting did not focus very directly on the nature of the transformation that women were expected to bring about. The vision of politics that participants presented in the workshops was rather idealistic, emphasizing empowering, community- oriented, 'clean and honest' and participatory governance, in contrast to the traditional 'power over,' capital-oriented, corrupt and top–down models of politics that were identified with traditional 'masculine' and 'transactional' politics.

In the heady atmosphere leading up to the Beijing Conference, there was a feeling that women would be 'better', less corrupt and more socially oriented than men. Thus, the workshop sessions focused mainly on practical measures to help women enter and succeed in politics through training, mentoring, the education of women voters, networking, and so on. At Beijing, some prominent women politicians made it clear that getting into politics was barely the first step. Once there, it had proved extremely difficult-in some cases, impossible-for them, however strongly motivated, to make a difference.

Certainly, few would be considered transformative in terms of the definitions that had emerged from the regional Asia–Pacific congresses. Thus, later regional and sub-regional congresses began to address the challenge from a more realistic perspective that focused on political structures and mechanisms. Even when successfully elected, women almost invariably remain part of a tiny minority on women's issues or in advocating a women's perspective on mainstream issues. However strongly they promote their issues and perspectives, most find little or no support and are forced to take up more mainstream positions and issues in order to have any impact in their chosen field. Thus, voters often find that the women they elected do not 'make a difference'.

This may be reflected in a backlash in the vote for these or other women at subsequent elections. In such a hostile environment, the women politicians who survive in the longer term are likely to be those who push their party's rather than a women's agenda and who conform to the standards and views of the (masculine) mainstream. The third and fourth congresses adopted a more analytical approach to the themes, respectively, of The Power of the Women's Electorate and Transforming Politics. At the Third Asia–Pacific Congress of Women in Politics, in Fiji in 1996, Marilyn Waring shared her experiences as a young parliamentarian in New Zealand.

Her sobering paper highlighted the gender biases and outright discrimination that women could anticipate in politics, even in a developed Western context. This congress emphasised the importance of building an informed and aware body of women electors who both understand and are able to articulate their issues as women. Women electors are not only the key to getting women into parliament but are also an essential mechanism that can empower women politicians to 'make a difference'. Margaret Shields, another former New Zealand MP, related how women politicians in the NZ Labour Party seeking a more liberal abortion policy against the tide of male party opinion had surveyed women party members.

Their survey showed that the men's understanding of women electors' views was almost completely the opposite of women's actual opinions, and this enabled the women politicians to persuade their male colleagues to change their vote. An aware and vocal body of women in all electorates, including those of male politicians, can enable the voices of even a minority of women politicians to be heard-and respected-in the parliament by their male colleagues.

When women MPs express an opinion, whether on a women-specific issue or on a general issue from a women's perspective, male MPs will be obliged to take note if they realize that many women in their own electorates share these views. Thus, an active women's electorate can be a powerful force facilitating women's role in transforming politics. The third and fourth congresses also moved towards recognising the importance of women as electors in ensuring another important plank of a transformative political agenda: those women politicians should be accountable to their constituents.

Women in the region were no longer so sure that women politicians would remain 'better' than men. Many examples suggested that women could also be tainted by the money and power of traditional politics. Given a better understanding of how difficult it would be for women politicians to actually stick to their transformative platforms, the congresses looked for mechanisms both to support women politicians and to hold them accountable. Here, the role of women's NGOs was seen as critical in developing countries. In the absence of well-developed political parties, women's NGOs and community groups can provide a rallying point, facilitate analysis and identification of women's issues, identify and help to train potential candidates, provide support during and, for those women who are successful, after election campaigns, and demand that those elected remain responsive and accountable to their electorates.

Has all this activity and networking produced concrete results? In a number of countries in the region, Women in Politics networks have been involved in gains in women's representation in politics. In India and elsewhere in South Asia, affirmative action has brought an unprecedented number of women into local politics. The Women in Politics networks, together with many other women's NGOs, have been involved in a massive training effort to assist these women to represent their sisters effectively. Changes in the political systems in the Philippines and Thailand have encouraged more women to stand for election, supported by NGO members of the Women in Politics networks.

In the Philippines, a women's political party, Abanse Pinay, successfully contested and won a seat under the new system of representation for special interest groups. The Filipina members of CAPWIP were active in the campaign and the former president of the Global Women in Politics Network now chairs this party. In Fiji, a concerted campaign by women's groups across party lines, led by WIPPaC, saw eight women successfully elected and five of them enter the new cabinet, one in the position of deputy prime minister. Thus, at the end of the twentieth century, women made quantitative gains in participation in politics in the Asia-Pacific region.

Women's groups and women in politics networks have been working hard to put into effect their vision of transformative politics for the new millennium. In several cases, the gains were associated with changes in political systems. In others, effective training and networking enabled women to gain a place at the table in traditional political systems. In developing countries, in particular, the extent to which these quantitative gains can be translated into qualitative improvements in good governance will not depend on women's innate qualities as politicians.

Rather, it will depend on the success of the women's movement in developing a strong and aware women's electorate to support women candidates, while at the same time holding them accountable for promoting women's issues and women's perspectives on all issues. International efforts to address gender inequality have largely emphasized education as a means of achieving women's empowerment. Education serves as the conduit by which women, long rooted in the private sphere, move into the public sphere and assert themselves on an equal basis with men.

As a springboard to employment and economic independence, advocates say, education provides the critical foundation from which further empowerment flows. The rhetoric of female empowerment focuses on the individual empowerment, and in doing so, neglects the issue of women in power. While women have experienced significant gains in literacy and educational attainment, their representation among heads of state and members of Parliament remains low in comparison to their population share.

The absence of female leadership is common to countries all over the world, despite a nation's level of economic development and near-universal consensus on women's political rights. The question then arises as to whether women's education facilitates their political empowerment. On the one hand, education presents an access point to the political elite. On the other hand, access may not be enough to win political office, as many other issues determine candidacy and election.

Women's empowerment through education mainly relies on endogenous change to achieve greater equality between men and women. In this context, endogenous change equips women with the requisite skills to engineer their independence, but does not interfere with their surrounding environment. Exogenous change, then, would call for policy intervention and the restructuring of incentives to bring about gender equality. These two approaches complement each other in certain respects, but there has been less action with regard to exogenous change in recent years.

The international focus on women's political rights following World War II resulted in a wave of government recognition of these rights all over the world; since then, the endogenous change approach has dominated international discussion of gender inequality. Politics, however, may be one realm in which further exogenous change is necessary. I will argue that gender equality in political representation cannot be achieved by relying solely on past efforts to confer political rights and current efforts to increase women's educational attainment.

Policy interventions to restructure the incentives within the political environment are necessary to increase women's political representation. I will focus on reserved seats for women in national parliaments, and argue that while such measures are politically controversial, they are effective in combating gender inequality in politics and achieving higher proportions of female legislators.

Institutions and incentives determine women's share of power, and so endogenous change can only take women so far. The equitable distribution of political power between the two sexes cannot be achieved without the examination and revision of societal structures. Gender Inequality as an International Policy Issue Gender inequality was not established as an international policy issue until the latter half of the 20th century. Prior to the United Nations its focus on human rights, women had few channels through which to seek redress of their equality-related grievances. Between the start of the 20th century and World War II, most Asian nations were under colonial or authoritarian rule.

Women's rights were hardly a priority to governments based on the subjugation of an entire population group. The establishment of the United Nations and its emphasis on human rights ushered in new opportunities to address gender inequality. The United Nations established its Commission on the Status of Women in 1946 and the General Assembly passed the Convention on the Political Rights of Women in 1951. While the existence of the Commission and subsequent conventions brought attention to gender inequality around the world, these mechanisms did not guarantee action. In the era of development following decolonization, it was assumed that development would benefit everyone equally.

When it became clear that development policies were in fact perpetuating gender inequality, advocates, development practitioners and scholars rallied to fight for the mainstreaming of gender into development. Thus, the field of women in development was born. This section will give historical context to the field of women in development. I will outline the evolution of the field by discussing the theories it sought to debunk and the achievements in legitimacy enjoyed by the field's advocates. I will also discuss current efforts to address gender inequality led by multinational organizations like the United Nations and the World Bank.

Finally, I will trace the field's theoretical origins to explain why the emphasis on addressing gender inequality internationally is through social and economic channels rather than through political and legal means. Women in Development: The History of a Movement International development policy was a product of post-war reconstruction and decolonization. As new countries were formed, many states sought international legitimacy through membership in the United Nations. By 1961, the number of member nations had doubled, only sixteen years after the establishment of the UN (United Nations 2005).

The majority of new member nations who joined the UN during this period were former colonies of Britain and Belgium on the African continent. Because so many of these nations were struggling to establish themselves, they appealed to the United Nations for assistance. Thus, as the focus of the UN shifted toward the economic needs of the majority of its member states, development policy moved from a question of national infrastructure to the international policy agenda. In 1961, the United Nations launched its First Development Decade, setting forth guidelines for development policy which emphasized industrialization and economic infrastructure.

Concentration on macroeconomic projects reflected the influence of modernization theory, which purported that industrialization would bring greater affluence to all parties involved. According to modernization theory, then, the main priority of development planning should be to build and strengthen the economic infrastructure which would spur and sustain economic growth. Poverty reduction was a secondary goal which would be achieved indirectly, once economic growth had stabilized. As the Decade progressed, a debate ensued over whether the policies of the First Development Decade were achieving their desired goals.

The UN had mobilized many of its agencies and other international organizations to concentrate on macro-development in postcolonial countries, which resulted in an infusion of funds to countries without proper infrastructure to distribute them effectively. Inequality worsened under these conditions, exacting a significant human cost and prompting disapproval for development initiatives. A 1963 UN resolution tied economic and social issues together, thus laying the foundation for a more human-centered development approach which would evolve through the next few decades.

Critics of early development policy not only questioned the overall efficacy of development projects, but also protested the role of development policy in reinforcing and worsening the subordination of women. Gender inequality was not a part of the initial development agenda; the policies of the First Development Decade made no specific mention of women. Women's activists, advocates, and scholars mobilized to ensure that gender inequality would be an integral component of the next Development Decade's policies, giving form to the women in development (WID) movement.

WID advocates faced practical and philosophical challenges in expanding the development agenda to include women. Many people believe then, and still believe today, that it is "natural" for women to perform domestic labor while men earn wages for their work their outside the home. WID activists thus had to raise consciousness about the internalized ideas which perpetuated gender inequality before it could address the insidious effect such beliefs had on women's lives.

In 1970, Ester Boserup published *Woman's Role in Economic Development*, a critical work which would be embraced by the women in development movement. Boserup argued that in changing industrial societies, women faced further marginalization rather than increased freedom. The introduction of new agricultural technologies in developing countries leads to greater yields, shifting agriculture from the subsistence level to market production. Labor specialization became inevitable in order maximize efficiency of production.

If specialization is decided upon comparative advantage, those who have greater decision- making power, autonomy and higher levels of education will assume authority over market activities. In most societies around the world, culture and tradition dictate that these individuals are men. Thus, Boserup writes, "The process of increasing specialization of labor is accompanied by an increasing hierarchization of the labor force and a gradual adaptation of the sex distribution of work". Gender is thus inherent to the decision rule for who performs what tasks.

Allocating responsibilities by sex may not be undesirable if viewed only in the context of comparative advantage. The concept of comparative advantage, one of the foundations of modern economic theory and a basic tent for international trade, argues for labor specialization according to strengths in ability and access to resources. Thus, if one producer, whether it be one firm, one group of people, or a nation, has an advantage in one area, then that producer should specialize in that area.

If we believe that women have an advantage in performing household duties and raising children because of their reproductive capacities, then comparative advantage would dictate that women should capitalize on their strengths and concentrate in the domestic "field." Thus, comparative advantage finds no conflict with the concentration of men in wage labor activities outside the home and women in domestic labor inside the home, often referred to as the public-private dichotomy, so long as both parties are capitalizing on each of their strengths. However, comparative advantage is not a useful criterion to explain why we should blindly accept women's relegation to the domestic sphere.

Comparative advantage assumes that both parties are capitalizing on their economic strengths in order to reap economic gains. Women's labor in the home, however, is often unpaid. In the public-private dichotomy then, males earn wages while women do not, creating the dependency of one party on the other. Dependency constrains one's freedom to live one's life in the manner she sees fit. Furthermore, gains made from economic activity are not only associated with material worth, but also individual and societal worthiness.

Those with more material resources enjoy greater power and authority over those with less. Thus, women are not only subordinate in the home to their wage-earning husbands, but also subordinate in society as a group for their lack of independent economic resources. The public-private dichotomy carries deleterious consequences for women's agency and well-being. When a woman's place in society is tied only to her reproductive capacity, there exist few incentives to justify equal allocation of resources between sons and daughters.

A daughter is a "lost investment." The deprivation of resources to girls is most acutely witnessed among the poor. The public-private dichotomy thus explains in part why girls are educated at rates far less than boys, why women's literacy falls behind men's, and why sex ratios in certain areas fall drastically below the norm of 1.022 women to men. Critics of early development policy protested that without specific attention to gender inequality, women would derive little benefit from development initiatives. The ignorance of gender in development planning elevated national debates on women's issues to the international level.

Women's labor, never deemed productive on the national level, was now internationally denigrated by virtue of its exclusion from international assessments of GDP. Women's agency, often limited due to local and national cultural contexts, was now internationally constrained due to development planning's treatment of women as welfare recipients instead of potential agents who could engineer their own empowerment. WID advocates argued that international development planning was founded upon gender bias and it effectively sanctioned gender inequality.

They sought redress of this bias through the disaggregation of national statistics by gender, the inclusion of women's domestic labor in national economic indicators, and policies which would empower women as agents rather than perpetuate women's dependency. The 1970s presented a more favorable climate to the women in development movement. The Second Development Decade followed up on the 1963 UN resolution on economic and social issues by calling for development which concentrated on basic human needs.

Human-oriented development created an opportunity for attention to women's needs as individuals which had not been present before. WID advocates won legitimacy when the UN's Second Development Strategy encouraged the full integration of women into development in 1970. Yet challenges would continue to face the movement. In 1972, the Interregional Meeting of Experts on the Integration of Women, which included Ester Boserup, generated recommendations for statistical studies on women's employment and the inclusion of women's work in manpower statistics.

This small victory was ultimately turned into defeat when the recommendations were not implemented. By 1974, offices for integrating women into development programs had been set up in the US and in various international organizations such as the World Bank and UNESCO. Advocates for gender equality worldwide won an important victory with the UN's declaration of the year 1975 as International Women's Year. The UN had resisted holding an international conference on women's issues until 1972, when International Women's Year was proclaimed for 1975.

The 1975 conference, held in Mexico City, legitimized the international women's movement by elevating women's issues to visible international debate. All UN member nations were required to send representatives to the conference. Though the original theme of the conference had focused on equality before the law, development issues were added to the conference's agenda, signaling recognition and wider endorsement of the WID platform.

The Mexico City Conference set a chain of events in motion, ensuring international attention to gender inequality would not wane once the conference ended. As an outcome of the conference, UN agencies began to disaggregate statistics by sex, realizing one of WID's main priorities (UN 1991). The conference also resulted in the declaration of the UN Decade for Women from 1976-1985. The Decade was intended to sustain momentum from International Women's Year and follow up on the goals that had been set in Mexico City.

Two more conferences on women were planned for 1980 and 1985, at the Decade's midpoint and conclusion. The UN also created the Voluntary Fund for the Decade of Women, an agency directed to assist in the implementation of the goals and policies resulting from the Decade's three conferences. Originally formed as a temporary instrument, the General Assembly voted in 1981 to extend the Fund's tenure beyond the Decade. In 1984, the Voluntary Fund was renamed the United Nations Development Fund for Women (UNIFEM) and placed under the organizational umbrella of the United Nations Development Program (UNDP).

The 1990s saw solidification of the human development paradigm and new indicators with which to measure gender inequality and women's progress. The United Nations published its first Human Development Report in 1990 which introduced the Human Development Index (HDI). The Human Development Index measured a number of development indicators for UN member countries, and then ranked countries according to how well they "performed" on these indicators.

The 1995 Report focused specifically on gender and human development, and introduced two gender-related indicators by which to measure countries. The gender-related development indicator (GDI) accounted for gender inequality's penalty on development by reducing a country's HDI score and re-ranking countries according to its GDI score. The other indicator, the gender empowerment measure (GEM), measured women's ability to wield decision-making power and authority in a given country. These indicators signified progress but have their limits.

Though these measures have been instrumental in describing trends across regions, they treat gender inequality as a constant within a country. General trends may be useful to compare one country to another, but the GDI cannot be used as a definitive measure of gender inequality for countries where there is a great deal of variation in gender equality within the country, as it is in India. Another conference on women was held in 1995, ten years after the Decade on Women had ended. The 1995 Beijing Conference focused on "Action for Equality, Development and Peace."

As with past conferences, the Beijing conference was well attended by representatives from UN member states, and women all over the world came to attend the parallel NGO Forum on Women, where activists traded strategies and shared stories of their work. The Beijing Conference resulted in the signing of the Beijing Platform, which is up for review this year in 2005. The signing of the Millennium Declaration and the development of the Millennium Development Goals in

2000 confirmed that gender equality had been mainstreamed into international goal-setting.

The Millennium Development Goals provided a set of development targets for UN member countries to reach by 2015. Gender equality was institutionalized as one of the eight goals, and while the goal itself discussed political, economic, and educational dimensions, the target was limited to the elimination of gender disparity in primary and secondary education by 2015. WID: Changes in Approach Though women in development began with the narrow focus of eliminating gender bias in development policy, the goals of the movement have since grown.

Today, WID stands for the larger eradication of gender inequality and is sometimes taken as shorthand for representation of all international efforts to advance women's equality. The movement's theoretical evolution has largely paralleled the expansion of the human development paradigm, but with some differences. One significant change in WID thinking has been the shift in emphasis from women's well-being to women's agency. Though there is substantial intersection between these two concepts, it is important to recognize the areas where they do not overlap, and the resulting implications for development policy.

Well-being is tied to a person's capability to enjoy a life of worth. In *Development as Freedom*, Sen argues that the most basic capabilities are tied to basic human functioning: "Among the basic capabilities are the ability to lead a long life in good health, be well-nourished, educated, housed and adequately clothed and integrated into the community". The advantage of well-being is its ease of measurement, as well-being statistics are standard in national surveys: life expectancy, mortality rates, education rates, etc.

The disadvantage of the well-being approach, however, is that it is not always clear how to conceptualize gender equality in this dimension. For example, while gender parity in education lends itself well to measurement, gender parity in life expectancy and mortality is less evident. Klasen argues that gender differences in outcomes do not necessarily reflect lower well-being for those who have the lower outcome. Klasen notes that the gap in life expectancy between men and women is due to higher rates of male abuse of nicotine and alcohol and more dangerous traffic and workplace behavior.

If males reduce their life expectancy out of their own actions and thus their preferences, should we simply accept that women will always live longer than men? Conversely, if women allocate more food to their children than to themselves and experience malnourishment, should we try to change these behaviors if they are acting on their own preferences? In the well-being approach, it is unclear how to target what behaviors for change when one is only examining outcomes.

Another disadvantage to the well-being approach corresponds with early criticism by WID advocates, that early development policy treated women as welfare recipients rather than independent actors. Well-being is a condition that one possesses or does not. The focus on well-being may dictate greater public welfare programs to provide housing or cash grants to allow women to buy more food but it does not challenge the gender bias inherent in development policy by treating women as passive actors. Well-being does not necessarily lead to empowerment on its own.

Agency, however, challenges the public-private dichotomy by viewing individuals as "a member of the public and as a participant in economic, social and political actions". From this line of thinking, women already belong to the public sphere and can be empowered to use this position to enhance their own lives. In addition to challenging gender bias, the concept of agency can be used to strengthen regard for women's well-being. Additionally, Klasen writes, "...evidence shows that greater female political representation, particularly at the local level, improve public policy favoring female well-being".

Women with formal political authority, then, stand in a position to improve women's quality of life. Agency, however, is not easily measured and so necessitates reliance on proxy indicators. Because empowerment is not an easily quantifiable concept, no proxy truly captures female empowerment in both the public and the private realms. Many of the indicators currently used to judge women's agency, such as the GEM, measure the number of women in national legislatures or professional workplaces with decision-making authority.

These indicators are biased toward formal authority at the highest levels-women's ability to exercise influence over others, rather than the exercise of influence over their own lives. If women create the most positive change for other women at local levels of political power, as Klasen argues, then measures of empowerment which look only at the national level provide a limited view of women's agency and the gains women are bringing about.

Furthermore, such indicators are biased toward women in better socioeconomic circumstances, who have access to better job opportunities and political power through better education and strong family connections. Thus, empowerment indicators may reflect female empowerment as well as they does socioeconomic privilege. Due to gender inequality's complex nature and its intersection with class and race issues, no indicator will perfectly capture the total space of gender inequality. Thus, it is important to use more than one indicator, as the UN does with the GDI and GEM, and recognize how the well-being and agency approaches complement each other.

Just as agency can reinforce women's well-being, women's well-being can create the foundation for greater female empowerment. Women and girls who are well-nourished and educated have a better opportunity to become employed outside the home and thus can derive the most benefit from an independent income. Sen believes that individual empowerment derives from economic freedom: those with economic freedom increase their opportunities to pursue other freedoms, while those without stable incomes and harsh workplace conditions are vulnerable to their financial need.

Economic freedom for women, then, can be achieved through both the agency and well-being approaches to development. Women's poverty and economic vulnerability underscores many aspects of women's societal subordination. Women are expected to labor in the home for no wages, rendering marriage an economic necessity. When women enter the paid labor force, the jobs open to uneducated women pay low wages and are largely concentrated in the domestic service sector.

Lack of economic freedom has led many women to sell their bodies for sex and suffer public disrepute, abuse from pimps and clients, and the threat of sexually transmitted disease. These grim consequences for women lead to underinvestment in girls' development, continuing the cycle of gender inequality. WID hypothesizes that improvements in women's abilities to earn income, then, can break the cycle.

A greater range of economic opportunities for women will align the incentives to invest in girls' education, the equal allocation of resources to girls in the home, and the ability to choose jobs which do not jeopardize one's health or one's dignity. In turn, women experience gains in agency, as their earnings afford them an improved bargaining position in the home and greater liberty in controlling their own lives.

LIMITS OF ITS PRIORITIZATION

According to Keohane, any strategy to reduce gender inequality must focus on the empowerment of women. Keohane argues that in order to correct systematic discrimination against women, one must infiltrate the structures which perpetuate gender inequality and change the incentives: Political power is at the heart of both incentive systems and norms. Empowered people create incentive systems, typically to advantage themselves and people like them, and build normative structures that suit their own beliefs and practices.

If these systems generate inequality through gender differentiation, only the empowerment of people with different interests, and different subjective values, is likely to change their systematic bias. Empowerment is therefore at the heart of any strategies to reduce gender inequality. WID focuses on changing economic incentives, so that underinvestment in women and girls will no longer occur. However, WID assumes that a successful realignment of economic incentives will have spillover effects in other dimensions of gender inequality.

In WID's view, once women are economically empowered, they have more standing to exercise political authority and demand their legal rights. The history of WID shows that legal and political inequalities were downplayed in order to focus on women's economic means. During the Decade of Women, WID advocates successfully pushed for greater attention to women's economic vulnerability, arguing that economic power would carry a greater impact on women's equality than unenforceable laws and legal norms which strengthen women's legal and political rights. Thus, WID overwhelmingly focuses on women's economic rights, presuming that social and political empowerment will follow once women are established as economic independents.

It is unclear, however, that women's economic rights alone are sufficient to realign incentives so that gender inequality is addressed in dimensions other than economics. In emphasizing economic development over exercise of political rights, WID favors the improvement of women's status through endogenous means rather than exogenous ones. The inherent paradox, however, is that WID needs a supportive political environment to thrive. This is so for two reasons. First, any economic gains that women make must be supported by firm ownership rights which allow women to own and inherit property.

Without accompanying ownership rights, women have no authority over their earnings and thus few incentives to educate themselves in order to access better-paying work opportunities. Secondly, WID policies can hardly benefit women if they are not implemented in the first place. WID policies stand a better chance of endorsement and implementation with more women in positions of government authority. However, WID delays substantive political authority for women into the future, after they have established themselves economically.

If WID policies do not have a supportive political environment, the scope of the policies may not be as broad as advocates originally hoped, thus slowing the realization of women's economic empowerment and delaying women's political empowerment further into the future. This paradox potentially explains why the movement has been criticized for having made more gains in research and goal-setting than in substantive policy changes.

Tinker and Jaquette noted as early as 1987 that where women in development was concerned, "it has been easier to get outside funds for studies than it has been to influence mainstream development planning". Keohane points out that while WID may have won the intellectual battle over gender mainstreaming in development, actual implementation has yet to follow. Though offices on women in development have been established in many countries, the mere existence of the office is not sufficient to ensure it can perform its mandate effectively.

Offices need to possess both funds and power, which they often does not. In his discussion of multilateral organizations and gender mainstreaming, Keohane compares the annual budgets of the World Bank and the IMF to that of UNIFEM. The budgets of the two leading multilateral development organizations were found to be significantly higher than that of UNIFEM: The World Bank's budget in 2004 was about $25 billion, almost 700 times greater than UNIFEM's 2002 budget of $36 million while the IMF's budget for its main development programs was $2 billion, about 50 times greater than UNIFEM.

With funding levels so low, it is hard to imagine that gender mainstreaming is implemented to the extent necessary to be able to address the many strands of gender inequality facing women today. The United Nations and other international organizations have been instrumental in bringing attention to gender inequality around the world, but these organizations lack a mechanism to force countries to meet its targets for progress. Thus, while UN organizations can track improvement or regression in gender equality indicators, it cannot incentivize the reduction of gender inequality for its member countries.

Additionally, targets and goals like the gender equality Millennium Development Goal favor a one-size fits all approach to addressing women's issues. The current MDG addressing gender equality uses an indicator to track progress comprised of the following: ratio of girls to boys in primary, secondary and tertiary education; ratio of literate females to males of 15-to-24 year olds; share of women in wage employment in the non-agricultural sector; and proportion of seats held by women in national parliaments.

The goal of the gender equality MDG, however, is limited to the realization of gender parity in primary and secondary school enrollments. This target is largely irrelevant to countries with near-perfect parity in school enrollments and one-hundred per cent literacy, such as Japan and the United States (UN 2000). Thus, these countries take little direction from international organizations on the subject of gender equality, making the debate on women's issues entirely internal to that country's political scene. The efficacy of WID depends in part on the socioeconomic circumstances of the group of women it is aiming to serve.

Where the well-being of women is low because of poverty and lack of access to education, WID stands to bring great gains. Women who fall in the middle of the socioeconomic distribution have both well-being issues and agency issues that can still be successfully redressed through economic means. However, for women in well-developed countries who fall towards the top of the socioeconomic distribution, their gender equality concerns largely have to do with political and legal agency, rather than economic agency.

Following the logic of the WID model, women in these circumstances are equipped to exercise political authority, since they do not have to worry about "lower-order" well-being needs. Examination of female representation in national legislatures shows us that under representation is an equal opportunity phenomenon, regardless of whether the country is developed or developing. This empirical evidence leads us to question the supposed direct connection between economic empowerment and political agency. In Asia, though all countries allow women the right to vote and the right to hold office, no national legislature is close to 50% female.

The question, then, is one of performance rather than the existence of the right itself. While the term "women in development" implies that this model best applies to women in developing countries, its influence on international debate about gender inequality cannot be ignored. WID's core notion that greater female political agency follows from economic empowerment deflects attention away from issues of female political agency, neglecting a dimension in need of improvement around the world. The fact of WID's legacy is that most international discussion of gender inequality concentrates on economic matters, employing a laissez-faire attitude to gender inequality in the political sphere. Once a country has established political rights for women, it is largely left to its own devices to ensure that women have the opportunity to exercise those rights.

THE LINCHPIN OF GLOBAL POLICY ADDRESSING GENDER

In laying out the history of WID and how its evolution has shaped current discussions of gender equality at the level of multilateral institutions. Considering the emphasis on endogenous means of advancing women's status, it makes sense that the international community would rally around female education as a potent means of empowerment.

By understanding the limits of WID in addressing gender inequality, one also understands that concentrating efforts on female education, a critical component of the WID approach, also carries its own limits. In developing countries where education was a privilege of the wealthy, universal access to education equips individuals with basic skills necessary for advancement and creates the illusion that a level playing field for men and women is possible. However, gender inequality is also shaped by cultural, social and political contexts that education alone cannot address.

The "gender, education and development discourse," as Heward calls it, began its heyday in the 1990s as an offshoot of WID. What sounds like a broad policy area in reality focuses mainly on the goals of gender parity in school enrollments and increasing women's literacy. Girls' education was touted for its benefits to reduce fertility, thereby aiding population control in areas where poverty was great and birth rates were high. In 1993, chief economist at the World Bank Larry Summers declared that girls' education "may well be the highest-return investment available in the developing world".

A 1994 policy paper from the World Bank pinned female education as the factor that could turn the "vicious cycle" of women's subordination into a "virtuous cycle" of female empowerment. US First Lady Hillary Clinton made a widely publicized speech in March of 1995, praising American investment in girls' education as a means of "reducing poverty by lowering fertility, improving child health and raising women's incomes from the labor market". Such lofty pronouncements reflected the optimism of the international community in promoting female education.

A growing body of literature has found that women's education enacts positive outcomes for the health of both mothers and children. A comparative study of nearly 300 districts in India showed that women's education and employment were the two most important factors in reducing fertility rates. Other studies commissioned by the World Bank corroborate this finding and also link the mother's education to the health of her children. Such outcomes are essential to advancing the well-being and agency of both mother and child.

In having fewer children, a woman is better able to pursue work outside the home and be less burdened with child care. The mother is also able to concentrate more resources per child than she would with a greater number of children, resulting in better well-being outcomes for children early on. The relaxation of the economic constraint through smaller family size can then lay the foundation for a more just allocation of resources within the home, leading to less underinvest-ment in daughters.

Female education, then, provides a means of addressing women's well-being and agency in more than one generation. Studies also linked female education to a country's economic growth, showing that gender inequality in education exacted costs in the public sphere as well. A 1993 study by King and Hill corroborated past studies in finding that the level of women's education had a strong positive effect on a country's GNP.

King and Hill also found that the ratio of female-to-male enrollment in primary and secondary education also exacted an effect on GNP. A large gender gap reduced GNP to the extent that where the ratio of female-to-male enrollment was less that .75, that country's GNP would be 25% lower than that of other countries similar in all respects expect for having a smaller gender gap in education. A more recent study by Klasen confirmed that the relationship between gender inequality in education and economic growth still held.

With such potentially high returns in both the private and public spheres, it is no wonder that the international community has seized upon female education as a powerful antidote to gender inequality. The sole target of the Millennium Development Goal on gender inequality calls for gender parity in school enrollments by the year 2015, showing that the gender, education and development discourse has been embraced by the United Nations in addition to the World Bank.

However, the studies supporting this paradigm speak mainly to the situation of women in the least developed countries, rather than speaking to the situation of women all over the world. Women in developed countries have little to gain from this focus on gender parity in school enrollments. By the early 1990s, most countries in the developed world were approaching, or had already realized, 100% literacy for women and men. As for developed countries' school enrollments at the beginning of the 1990s, no ratio of female-to-male enrollment in primary education was lower than .90 in developed countries.

Most ratios of female-to-male enrollment in secondary education were also above .90. Thus, these studies on female education address a subset of countries where the gender gap in school enrollments is great and the birth rates are high, most of them in sub-Saharan Africa and South Asia. In the theory set forth by WID, education pertains to both women's well-being and agency. By advancing women's well-being, education can further women's agency. Education is a necessary building block for economic and political empowerment. As Borque and Warren point out, women in the developing world will exact little impact on national development priorities "until they are literate and have the basic arithmetic skills with which to analyze their political and economic systems".

In today's information age, Nussbaum writes, literacy is a prerequisite for effective political authority due to reliance on the internet and mass media for information and communication. However, whether female education directly leads to greater economic and political empowerment is a claim which necessitates further scrutiny. The specific returns from education with respect to agency are not clear. Education of women in developed countries has not eroded women's unemployment nor closed the earnings gap, nor has it resulted in greater numbers of women in national governments on its own.

In order to understand why education does not directly solve larger claims of gender inequality, it is helpful to first examine why some girls are not educated in the first place. The reasons explaining lack of investment in girls' education vary greatly, representing the many pressures which effectively lock in sex discrimination and perpetuate gender bias in future generations. King and Hill group the main reasons driving women's lack of education into four categories: financial costs, opportunity costs, psychic costs, and differential benefits.

Financial costs encompass the costs of school tuition and associated fees of books, transportation or uniforms. The inclusion of school tuition as a cost disregards whether public education is available. In order for education to be a worthwhile investment, it must be of some quality, and in some areas, private and/or religious education is the only type of education that parents may deem worthwhile for their children. King and Hill point out that out-of-pocket expenses for girls' schooling may be greater than those for boys.

Concerns for girls' physical and moral safety may lead some parents to determine that more costly means of transportation or boarding arrangements at the school are necessary. Without the means to pay for such arrangements, some parents will decide that schooling is not worth risking the safety and moral reputation of their daughters. These concerns reflect anxiety over girls' well-being as well as their potential for marriage. In cultures where tradition is strong, a girl's moral reputation influences her marriage prospects.

Damage to one's reputation can thus condemn a young woman to a grim future, as marriage is the only source of economic footing for many women around the world. Here, a family's current economic resources as well as the daughter's future are the constraints on girls' education. These constraints are built upon the differential treatment of girls and boys within the home and the view of women as economic dependents. Opportunity costs of female education account for what chores are left undone while girls are in school.

King and Hill argue that in most developing countries, women and girls complete the domestic activities essential to daily living such as cooking, fetching water and child care for the young. If girls are in school instead of attending to these chores, the welfare of the family suffers. Girls stay home from school in order to provide for the well- being of the family, inculcating them into domestic roles and responsibilities at an early age. In some cases, girls do not attend schools in order to enable their brothers to benefit from education.

The opportunity cost explanation, then, rests on the notion of a woman's proper place as in the home laboring on behalf of the family rather than herself. This notion rests upon the public-private dichotomy but is also dictated by culture. Psychic costs refer to the cultural penalties exacted upon a woman who is seen to have "too much" education. If a woman is too viewed as having too much education, she may be worth less in the marriage market.

As mentioned before, unmarried women in the developing world are not merely spinsters but women with little economic security. So the incentives may align in order to allow girls to be educated, but only up to a certain level so that future husbands will not be threatened by the intelligence of their prospective wives. Differential benefits of women's education affect not only the recipient of schooling but parents as well.

Parents, as the decision-makers to send children to school, weigh their own interests just as heavily as that of the daughter in question. What kind of work force will the daughter encounter? Due to labor segregation by sex, employment opportunities for women are often limited and earn lower wages than men. If the daughter's prospect of lifetime earnings pales in comparison to that of a prospective husband's, little incentive exists to educate the daughter.

If the culture is one where the daughter leaves the natal home upon marriage, parents may not reap any economic benefits from sending their daughters to school. If the incentives align so that a daughter's education is viewed as a luxury, rather than a necessity, then the daughter's education becomes expendable. If cultural, social and economic factors together determine whether a girl attends school, then Summers' model of the vicious cycle turning into the virtuous cycle treats gender inequality too simplistically.

The theory that an educated mother will allocate resources more justly within the household by virtue of her education does not take into account whether the environmental incentives have changed. When one accounts for the diversity of factors influencing girls' education, one realizes it is still possible for educated mothers to favor sons over daughters with regard to schooling and resource allocation. If the cultural system continues to dictate that parents rely on their sons for economic security in old age, the incentive for mothers (and fathers) to have sons and invest in them remains.

Borque and Warren echo Heward's call for sensitivity to the social, political and cultural contexts which determine the limits of female freedom. "Differentials in education reflect system-wide patterns of gender relations," Borque and Warren write, implying a need to recognize the systemic causes of gender inequality. Once one understands the interlocking origins of gender inequality, one also understands why policies aimed at closing the gender gap are insufficient to tackle the problem on a large scale and do not dispute that girls' education should be a priority of the international development community.

The education of girls should be valued not only for its potential effects in fertility and national economic growth, but also on grounds of human rights and equality. However, the goal of reducing the gender gap in school enrollments is taken as an internationally applicable, comprehensive measure to address gender inequality when it clearly has its limits in scope and effect. Focus on gender disparity in school enrollments in the poorest countries of sub-Saharan Africa and South Asia allows more developed countries to ignore their own issues of gender inequality because these issues have not been designated as international development goals.

The Millennium Development Goals have done a great deal for increasing awareness of women's issues, but its single target of parity in school enrollments neglects other important issues related to gender equality. In order for more comprehensive change to occur, international policy initiatives must somehow account for the social, political and cultural contexts which are critical to understanding and correcting gender inequality.

2

Women in Elected Office

Global Under Representation

While the Millennium Development Goal on gender equality lists the increase of women's political representation as a sub-goal, most attention to women's share of political authority occurs within nation. Women's political under representation, however, afflicts every country, regardless of its economic wealth or political system. Though women's political rights are formally recognized all over the world and codified into national constitutions, the global average of women's share in parliaments stands at a paltry 15.9%.

Just as early development thinkers believed that women's economic empowerment could be achieved through a natural progression of development phases, so there are theorists who believe women's political representation will increase once a nation has reached economic and political maturity. Such thinking presents important philosophical and practical issues. Women's political rights as codified in international agreements and national constitutions are not qualified in accordance with a nation's own economic and political development; these rights are human rights and thus, inalienable. One can also argue that gender balance in political representation is a signal of political maturity in itself.

Where does the philosophical threshold for a nation's maturity lie, and how many more rights violations must women suffer before they can take an active part in addressing the conditions which enable such violations to occur? More practically speaking, nations currently viewed as economically and politically mature still have not achieved gender parity in their national legislatures. The United States, arguably one of the most economically advanced and politically stable nations in the world, only has an average of 14.7% female representation among its two houses of Congress (IPU 2005).

Democracy is no guarantee for female representation either. A study performed by Lee and Clark (2000) found that following democratization in the former Soviet bloc and Latin American countries, the proportion of female legislators in each country fell. The same applies to Nigeria and Indonesia, where women's share of Parliament also fell following democratization. This evidence leads to the conclusion that neither development nor democracies are sufficient safeguards for women's political representation. Barriers other than economic development and political system are at work in keeping women's representation low.

These barriers then, cannot be effectively addressed or quickly dismantled by improvements in female education or labor force participation alone. Policy interventions by states are necessary in the short-term to ensure that women's political voices are no longer ignored. This section will examine women's under representation in political office, focusing mainly on women in national legislative bodies.

WOMEN'S POLITICAL RIGHTS AND REPRESENTATION

In the early days of the United Nations, international recognition of women's political rights was a top priority. In 1952, the UN passed the Convention on Political Rights of Women (UN 2005d). The convention protected women's rights to vote, run for publicly elected bodies, and hold political office. 118 Member nations ratified or acceded to the convention. These rights were reaffirmed in the 1979 Convention to Eliminate All Discrimination against Women (CEDAW); CEDAW required ratifying countries to submit country reports on the gender equality progress to the UN Secretary General and the Committee on CEDAW on a regular basis.

Only 71 nations have ratified CEDAW to date, considerably less than the number of nations which ratified the 1952 Convention. The lower number of ratifying nations is attributed to CEDAW's more controversial provisions, not its terms on women's political rights. The attention to women's political rights by the UN builds an international consensus for countries to recognize these rights. Because most countries now grant political rights to women, emphasis has shifted from women's voting rights to women's share of political authority.

The United Nations target for 30% minimum female representation in national parliaments has been in place for more than a decade. The United Nations Economic and Social Council (ECOSOC) had originally called on nations to meet the target by 1995. When the target was unmet by an overwhelming number of nations, it was reaffirmed at the 1995 Fourth World Conference on Women in Beijing. By 2002, however, only 11 out of 191 UN Member nations had achieved the 30% benchmark (UNIFEM 2002). Each of these countries had some type of quota provision for women's political representation.

Today, only 15 countries are above the 30% benchmark and the best-performing countries are concentrated in the Nordic region. (Sweden, Norway, Denmark, Finland, the Netherlands occupy spots two through six among the countries with the largest proportion of female legislators.) Together, the Nordic countries average 39.9% female representation in their parliaments. The Americas, the second-best performing group of countries, falls distantly behind at 18.7% female representation. Arab states, the worst-performing countries with regard to female political representation, exhibit a paltry 6.7% average of female legislators in their national parliaments.

A handful of countries have no women legislators whatsoever: Bahrain, the United Arab Emirates, Kuwait and

Micronesia, to name a few. Valuing Women's Formal Political Participation The fact that the overwhelming majority of nations are far from meeting the 30% benchmark of female political representation casts a grim outlook on the ultimate goal of women's equality. Women's absence from national legislatures signifies their lack of status as political equals. They may have the right to hold office, but the right itself is insufficient in empowering them to do so.

In 1992, the United Nations made the following statement on the distance between women's right to vote and women in elected office: "Nowhere in the situation of women is the gap between *de jure* and *de facto* equality so wide." Women's participation in government bodies should be valued on several grounds. First and foremost, participating in one's government and influencing the decisions which affects one's life is a human right.

As the Beijing Platform for Action reads: The Universal Declaration of Human Rights states that everyone has the right to take part in the Government of his/her country... Achieving the goal of equal participation of women and men in decision-making will provide a balance that more accurately reflects the composition of society and is needed in order to strengthen democracy and promote its proper functioning. Thus, the denial of the right of equal participation to women, whether through overt or covert means, violates something fundamental to the human condition and renders women vulnerable to the abuse of other rights.

One can also oppose the relative lack of women legislators on the grounds of equity. Women constitute almost half the population of every country, yet with so few women in government, women's interests are hardly represented in proportion to their population share. Women's underrepresentation in politics distances nearly half of the electorate from elected officials. Women who do not see themselves reflected in the body of political decision-making may find it easier to dismiss government as a legitimate route through which to seek redress of their grievances.

A vicious cycle then takes hold: the low proportion of women in public office lead the general population of females to conclude that the political world does not adequately allow women a voice, preventing further women candidates from seeking office. Women's underrepresentation in government is also an inefficient use of human resources and can potentially hinder the development of nations. A nation with few women in government cannot benefit from the talents and expertise of a significant sector of the population.

In contrast to the political realm, women have been making steady gains around the world in education and entering the paid labor force. Women's human capital has been rising; governments who do not take advantage on this important source of human capital incur a significant opportunity cost with respect to human talent. An extension of the human capital argument leads to the idea that women offer something unique to the political process.

The idea that women can have a transformative effect on politics refers to two ideas: first, that women can broaden political debate by bringing attention to more-neglected issues, and second, that women can change the very nature of the political process. Women in government, particularly women in local governments, tend to focus more on issues of well-being and the welfare of their communities. Female legislators are more likely to focus on healthcare, clean water, childcare and education. Women's influence in politics, then, can not only advance women's rights but the health of the society on a larger scale. It is also thought that women approach politics differently. Female public officials are said to emphasize more democratic approaches to government and transparency.

Women's participation in political decision-making can thus strengthen democracy by giving voice to a profoundly underrepresented group and furthering government accountability through open decision-making processes. A 1999 study by Dollar, Fisman and Gatti examined whether increased female participation in government reduced government corruption. The authors' examination of past literature showed that women had consistently been found to sacrifice material or personal gain for the common good, thus implying that women embodied the spirit of public service: serving for others rather than oneself.

The study performed several regressions on different samples of countries, ranging from n = 144 to n = 270 depending on the data available for certain specifications of different models. The study found that the proportion of women in government had a statistically significant effect in reducing corruption in the given country's government. This study would seemingly confirm the idea of women's transformative effect on politics. However, some aspects of the study cast its findings in doubt. The authors admitted that if a different indicator for corruption was used, the coefficient on women's share of parliament was not found to be statistically significant.

In the original specification, however, the authors used the measure of corruption most widely used in economic literature and also covered the widest range of standard corruption indices. The authors also fail to examine whether there exists a threshold for the effect of women's share of parliament on government corruption. It is possible, however, that few governments have a sufficient number of female legislators in order to examine whether above a certain threshold, female legislators behave just as their male counterparts do in conducting secret deals, taking bribes or accepting gifts. The question of women's transformative effect on politics thus warrants further research as this is an argument for women's political representation based on outcomes rather than rooted in fundamental principles such as equality or human rights.

Another reason to take caution when invoking the transformative effect argument is the potential to perpetuate stereotypes which cement gender bias. The view of women as natural public servants confirms the belief that women serve others rather than themselves, discounting the value of women's own needs. Women's difference from men should not exclude the possibility of women's difference from other women. Women are just as diverse as men and deserve to be viewed as such. Indeed, recognizing women's diversity was among the overarching goals of the Fourth World Conference for Women, which called on the global community to avoid stereotypes, "particularly those that make assumptions about male and female traits".

When traits such as self-sacrifice are mistakenly tied to the inherent nature of what it means to be male or female, efforts to further gender equality thus hit unmovable roadblocks. It is thus important to view women in the context of their societal place and the constraints they have historically faced. If women legislators tend to focus on democratic decision-making procedures and "clean politics," their efforts are likely motivated by the historical monopoly men have had on political decision-making rather than by an inherent preference for open governance.

Accordingly, if women are inclined to concentrate on social welfare issues such as education, health care, or child care, their interest in this area more likely grows out of society's demands on women as mothers and caregivers. By viewing gender as a societal construct rather than ascribing difference between males and females to biology, one avoids trapping women in a fixed state of inequality and marginalization. The danger of stereotyping remains, however, even when women's interests are seen in the context of social and cultural factors.

The hypothesis of women's transformative leadership carries a potential negative effect in the marginalization of women into "soft" issue areas once they assume political office. Only a handful of countries have chosen women to serve in foreign policy, finance, trade or defense sectors of government, the "hard" issue areas. Moving women leaders into such positions is critical as it completes the transition of women's isolation in the private, domestic sphere to the public sphere. Secretaries and ministers of foreign policy, trade, finance and defense are the public face of a nation in the international arena.

If women are concentrated in domestic issue areas, then their transition out of the private sphere has not been complete- they are still not accepted to represent the nation in the public sphere of international politics. Achieving greater numbers of women in political decision-making then, is not only important from a human rights perspective or the potential influence women could have on politics and public policy. A critical mass of women legislators is necessary in order to effectively combat the gender stereotyping that entrenches bias and inequality in cultures.

Though several recent examples of women leaders have combated the negative stereotypes against women, many are described as having to take on "masculine" traits to prove their worthiness and mettle in political battles. Powerful female politicians such as Golda Meir, Benazir Bhutto, Margaret Thatcher and Indira Gandhi all provide examples of women whose political careers clashed with the different stereotypes of women and politics. When more women join their ranks as political leaders, two results could occur: the nature of politics could soften, as predicted by the hypothesis of women's transformative effect, or the behaviors currently necessary to succeed in politics will become distanced from the masculine identity.

Women's political leadership can thus challenge the tradition of ascribing gender to certain traits, laying a foundation for greater gains in gender equality. Barriers to Women's Political Representation As mentioned, politically active women are essential to disbanding the stereotypes which further gender inequality, but overcoming these stereotypes to assume political office presents a significant challenge in itself. The expectation of behaviors, attitudes, and traits ascribed to men and women, referred to in feminist scholarship as gender ideology, excludes women from politics in a variety of ways.

The public-private dichotomy which dictates different economic roles for men and women also determines who can legitimately participate in political activity. Politics belongs to the public sphere and thus to males, and is not seen as a field that would or should interest women. Candidates for public office are rarely seen as altruists; each declaration of candidacy insinuates zealous ambition and desire for personal advancement. The stereotype of women's selflessness stands in opposition to the traits associated with political candidates. Women who run for office must stand outside the boundaries of the stereotype and risk sanction by community and culture if they pursue their own ambitions, particularly if they are perceived as doing so at the cost of others.

In challenging an incumbent officeholder, women challenge a gender ideology which does not afford women their own ambitions. Women themselves may have internalized the prevailing gender ideology and see themselves outside of the political sphere, discounting themselves as potential candidates before the electorate can The public-private dichotomy also places reason in the public sphere, emotion in the private sphere. The Enlightenment's emphasis on reason over emotion has devalued emotion with respect to reason, instituting rationality as the proper decision rule for difficult matters.

Men are associated with rationality and objectivity, whereas women are perceived as emotional and subjective. The extension of this aspect of gender ideology validates men's dominion over political decision-making. If the public values "impartiality and imperturbability" in its politicians, then the public's bias toward men in this dimension justifies the exclusion of women from positions of higher authority. In addition to psychological barriers to women in public office, gender ideology presents tangible obstacles as well. Women's care giving duties provide one example of an overt barrier.

If a woman's daily care giving responsibilities for children, elderly parents, or both are considerable, little time remains to devote to political activities. Political positions on the national level may require traveling between the home district and the nation's capital, an unpalatable choice for any primary caregiver, who are most often women. Mothers and public servants both have little control over the allocation of their time as their work is centered on the needs of others. If the demands of domesticity are incompatible with political office, then women, associated with domesticity, are also incompatible with political office.

It is critical to recognize that gender ideology is not a universal, overt thought system, but is revised in every culture. The general aspects of gender ideology presented here are particularized in each country based on economic, religious and social makeup. The exact effect of culture and gender bias in limiting women's political representation cannot be universally measured, at least not directly. Proxy variables are necessary in order to approximate the effect of culture and gender bias. Scholarly literature has often appealed to religion as one such proxy, as some religions tend to emphasize traditional gender roles more than others.

A 1987 study by Rule on the factors affecting women's political representation found that Catholicism exacted an important and statistically significant negative effect. Rule examined twenty-three industrialized countries; the exclusion of developing countries likely led to her choice of Catholicism as the only religious specification. Kenworthy and Malami updated Rule's analysis in 1999 by studying the factors which affected women's political representation in 146 nations. Their sample was overwhelmingly comprised of countries from the developing world and so they considered the effect of religions other than Catholicism.

Kenworthy and Malami confirmed Rule's finding on Catholicism and also found that Islam exacted a negative effect on women's political representation as well. Their third religion variable also produced a statistically significant negative effect, but this variable bundled many different religions together: African indigenous religions, Buddhism, Eastern Orthodoxy, Hinduism, Judaism, and countries with no dominant religion. The baseline category for these religion variables, all dummies, was Protestantism, which is thought to be more egalitarian with regard to gender. Kenworthy and Malami, however, do not specify how they assigned religions to each country, whether they looked at official religions or national survey data, and also do not control for the degree of conservatism or liberalism of the religion practiced within a country.

Furthermore, religion may not be an accurate cultural proxy for nations in East Asia, which often do not have an overriding national religious identity. Kenworthy and Malami's study, while useful in providing a starting point in accounting for culture, warrant further study of the question of culture, religion, and women's political representation. In theory, women's lack of education, professional experience, and income relative to men would also prevent women from assuming positions of political authority. Political candidates often must satisfy a certain set of conditions before receiving the support of a political party or mounting an independent campaign.

As political elites are often comprised of individuals with high levels of education, access to financial resources and personal networks in professional and political circles, candidates must meet these conditions in order to make a successful bid for office. For women who labor exclusively in the home and lack independent incomes, running for office is near impossible since they lack connections and funds. Education, then, is a critical point of access to the political elite. In addition to increasing women's awareness of their political and legal rights, education also makes formal political activism possible by enabling women to join the paid labor force.

Higher education is particularly crucial as it can track women into professional occupations. Many elected officials have previous backgrounds in law, education, or business. While a strong theoretical argument can be made for the effect of education and labor force participation upon women's political representation, scholars conflict on the precise effect of these factors. Rule (1987) found the level of women in higher education to be significant, but her limited sample of developed countries prevents the extension of these results in different contexts. Matland (1998) conducted a study of women's political representation using two samples, one of developed and developing countries.

He conducted separate regressions for both samples, finding that women's university education was not significant for either developed and developing countries. Women's labor force participation, however, was significant for developed countries. Matland's findings can potentially be attributed to the correlation between women's labor force participation and education. In the sample of developing countries, the low numbers of women in higher education may contribute to the lack of significance of this variable, as there may not be enough women in higher education to produce any kind of effect as of yet.

Kenworthy and Malami (1999) do not find either labor force participation or women's university education to be significant, calling into question whether these factors do indeed bar women from political representation. Like Matland's study, these findings could result from the sample being overwhelmingly comprised of developing countries. Kenworthy and Malami do conclude, however, that the share of women in professional occupations does have a statistically significant positive effect on women's political representation, contradicting earlier analyses by Norris (1985, 1987) which found no impact for the level of women in professional occupations.

The studies by Rule (1987), Matland (1998), and Kenworthy and Malami (1999) hint at a differential effect on women's political representation for developed and developing countries, implying that the economic condition of the country stands as a barrier to greater numbers of female legislators. Both the Matland and Kenworthy and Malami studies include a specification for development in their analyses. Matland creates a measure of development from a country's literacy level, consumption of oil barrels, and GDP adjusted for purchasing power parity.

In his analysis, development is a significant factor: the more developed a country is, the less of a political barrier imposed on women. In contrast, Kenworthy and Malami only use GDP to account for a country's development. Their study finds that development does not have an effect on women's political representation. One possible way to resolve the in congruencies between these two studies is to perform an analysis using the human development measures used by the UN, which neither study did. Currently, the United Nations sides with Kenworthy and Malami and states that no relationship exists between a country's level of development and the number of women in national parliaments.

Electoral Systems which Favor Women's Political Representation Given the many barriers women face with regard to holding public office, it seems nearly impossible for the proportion of women legislators to improve without commensurate improvements in women's overall societal status. However, certain electoral conditions do favor women's representation and can accelerate changes in the gender balance of legislatures. Local government, proportional representation systems, multimember districts and political quotas all provide favorable conditions for women's political empowerment.

There exist three general phases of the electoral process common to most countries around the world: recruitment, selection of candidates, and election. The barriers to women's political representation, discussed in the previous section, are influential at each stage. Each stage of the electoral process and the corresponding remedy or conditions which can increase women's share of elected offices. Recruitment refers to the determination of eligible candidates according to national criteria as well as the separation between those who are politically active and those who are not.

Gender ideology and care giving responsibilities may cause women to self-select out of the pool of the politically active. However, Drage (2003) suggests that women find it easier to integrate local government into their lives. Women's concerns related to domestic issues are often handled on the local levels and so their activism in local government can be seen as an extension of their duties as caregivers. With more positions available, local government is more accessible to women due to the number of opportunities to become involved. In some contexts, local office is apolitical, and thus women can run without the backing of a political party.

If campaigns are waged, costs are low as the scope of the campaign is limited. Because the position is located in the community, fewer conflicts between public service and family responsibilities exist, reducing the strength of an important barrier. Drage's hypothesis on women and local government is significant because local government can track officials into further positions of political authority. If women can prove their political worth in local governance, they are more likely to be recruited for public office at higher levels. However, if women enter local government precisely because doing so does not pose a conflict with their family responsibilities or the prevailing gender ideology, they may resist recruitment for office at higher levels of government when conflicts do arise.

Local government may prove to be fertile grounds for women's political empowerment, but its effect is limited if the underlying barriers to women's political representation go unchallenged. Thus, women's increased participation in local government cannot be viewed to dictate greater improvement in women's representation at higher levels. In order to effectively recruit women to positions at all levels of government, the prevailing gender ideology must change and a woman's care giving responsibilities must be shared. Once potential candidates have been recruited for public office, the selection phase differentiates who will be put up as a candidate and begins a campaign.

Again, gender biases play a role in winnowing candidates from the pool of the politically active. A female with fewer connections and resources stands at a disadvantage with respect to a male who is more likely to have well-established connections and more sizeable financial resources. Major political parties are interested in winning seats to strengthen the representation of the party, not necessarily to strengthen the representation of women or other marginalized groups. Their determination to win seats renders them averse to new tactics; parties are more likely to take a conservative approach to selecting a candidate and mounting a campaign.

Election is the final stage, where the selected candidates are put before the public. Rule writes, "[considerable evidence shows] that women are as likely to be elected as men in the constituencies they contest," negating the idea that the electorate is less likely to elect a woman when given the choice of a male candidate. If this is the case, then selection is the more crucial phase for women's political representation in comparison to election. The design of the electoral system influences the selection and election stages and thus can influence the number of women in political office. On the national legislature level, the proportional representation system is most favorable to women.

In proportional representation (PR), political parties compile a national list of candidates. Voters vote for the party, rather than a candidate, and the party is apportioned seats according to the share of votes won. The use of a party list emphasizes the values of the party rather than the values and reputation of an individual candidate. This can be beneficial to women as no tests of fitness for office based on gender can be mentally applied to female candidates by voters. More importantly, parties often add women to their party lists as a means of broadening their electoral appeal.

Few studies have contradicted Rule's original finding of the significance of proportional representation with regard to women's share of legislatures. While other studies have expanded on the effect of other variables, PR remains a consistent and important factor in determining the gender balance of parliaments. One notable study to contradict Rule was that of Matland (1998). In addition to accounting for women's labor force participation, and education in his analysis of women's political representation, Matland also tested whether proportional representation had a positive effect for women in office. Matland confirmed Rule's findings only for his sample of developed countries, not for developing countries.

A potential explanation for this result is the lack of sufficient variation in the dependent variable (proportion of women in national parliaments) in the sample of developing countries. Indeed, Kenworthy and Malami confirmed the significance of proportional representation for 146 countries, most of which were in the developing world. Kenworthy and Malami, however, name their variable "party list/multimember districts," which presents an expanded definition of PR. This expanded variable definition may have caused them to include countries that Matland would not have included.

Rule had also tried to account for multimember districts in her 1987 studies; finding the variable highly correlated with proportional representation, she dropped multimember districts from her specification. I will assume, then, that Kenworthy and Malami's expansion of the variable to include party lists and multimember districts is an improvement over Rule's analysis and confirms proportional representation as a significant determinant of women's political representation. Proportional representation is not a guarantee for women's parity in government, however.

This electoral system's effect in increasing the number of women in office depends on how women candidates are handled during the selection phase of the electoral process. If women are selected to party lists to broaden the party's appeal, but placed toward the bottom of the list so their chances of assuming office are low, women's prospects for political office remain grim. In this scenario, the PR system puts women in a better position with regard to selection, but the outcome of few women legislators remains the same after election. However, if women are selected to party lists and placed towards the top, then their election is virtually guaranteed so long as the party wins a share of votes above a certain threshold.

Multimember districts are not necessarily associated with proportional representation; many state legislatures in the United States have several members per district without a PR system. The multimember district proves more favorable to women for two reasons: first, more positions are available and thus more opportunities to get elected; and second, member turnover is greater. A small number of members per district is associated with a low rate of member turnover, partially explaining why the change in gender balance of some governing bodies has been so slow.

Rule determined that a benchmark of five members per district was the threshold above which women could reap gains from multimember districts. While it is useful to single out the electoral system characteristics which favor women's political representation, few countries are poised to revise their electoral institutions on account of gender equality. With economic development providing no guarantees for women's representation and electoral system reform a distant possibility, other mechanisms are necessary in order to further women's political empowerment. The quota for minimum representation is one such mechanism. Though the quota is highly controversial, it is an effective means of achieving greater numbers of women in legislatures.

The high proportion of female representation in Nordic countries owes in part to the internal party quotas for women adopted by the political parties in the region. The adoption of an internal party quota by one party can have a domino effect, forcing other parties to adopt quotas as well so as not to allow the original quota-adopting party a greater advantage with regard to the electorate. Just as the ordering of female candidates on the party list is critical to women's actual political representation, the design of the party quota is also crucial. If the quota is simply for the number of candidates a party must put forth, there is no guarantee that all the female candidates will be elected.

If however, the quota calls for a number of seats in the legislature, a minimum proportion of female representation is guaranteed. Quotas are often dismissed, by both men and women, out of the concern that a stipulation for minimum representation turns into a ceiling that women cannot break through. (Recent electoral returns from Taiwan, which sets aside 10% of seats in its national legislature for women, contradict this fear by showing that a floor for women's political representation need not become a ceiling.)

Some countries are thus more comfortable setting targets for women's political representation, akin to the UN target of 30%. The lack of an enforcement mechanism on such a target, however, means that no tangible costs will be incurred if the target goes unmet. As previously mentioned, only 15 nations have currently met the UN's 30% target. Given that electoral systems are relatively fixed and proportional representation is not likely to be instituted in political systems that do not already rely on it, quotas provide the best hope for increasing women's political representation in the near future. Quotas can be adopted as temporary measures and the design of quotas is flexible.

Parties can adopt internal quotas or legislatures can set aside a certain proportion of seats. They do not interfere with the underlying institutions of the electoral process; they only improve the gender balance within the institution. Quotas, however, are not without controversy. Privileging one population group over another population group through a quota for minimum representation is often decried as undemocratic and unfair. Another serious issue with political quotas for women concerns the elevation of certain individuals to a position of power based on gender, rather than qualifications.

By examining policy debates and the influence of cultural and socio-economic characteristics particular to each case, I will build a case for quotas as a temporary measure to spur women's political representation. Methodology The question of women's political representation and their educational attainment lends itself well to case studies in Asia for several reasons. First, traditional views regarding women remain strong in Asian countries. Despite the region's diversity, common elements of gender bias can be found across cultures.

In East Asia, Confucian thought continues to influence attitudes toward women. Confucian thought in East Asia advocated for hierarchical relationships in society, placing women at the lowest levels and excluding them from education, economic activities, and political life. In South Asian countries where Hinduism continues to be influential, the legacy of caste and hierarchical social relationships also affects women's societal status. Western imperial powers and Christian missionaries even invoked the abuse of women as grounds for "educating" the indigenous peoples of Asia.

Though the historical practices of foot-binding and bride-burning are now outlawed, women and girls in Asia continue to be held back by a lack of property rights, preference for sons, and traditional views which dictate that a woman's proper place is in the home. Secondly, Asia has experienced considerable political development in the past sixty years. Most of the major countries in Asia won their independence from colonial rule following World War II and adopted new constitutions. Many of these constitutions recognized women's right to vote and hold, granting these rights to women across Asia for the first time.

After nearly sixty years since the formal recognition of women's political rights, the political landscape has had ample time to adapt to the expansion of the electorate. However, women's political representation across Asia remains low, ranging from a low of 6.8% in Mongolia to a high of 27.3% in Vietnam. Asia's political development has paralleled the rapid economic development of several of its major nations, particularly those in East Asia and more recently, the economic growth experienced in India. Economic development across Asia and the protection of women's rights have interacted to expand opportunities for women to obtain education.

omen's educational attainments in developed Asian nations are high. If one believes that women's education necessarily leads to empowerment, one might guess that developed that developed Asian nations would have achieved greater female political representation than developing Asian nations, due to the greater number of opportunities women in the developed countries have. One might also guess that women would have achieved greater representation in democratic Asian nations, due to democracy's emphasis on rights and egalitarianism.There appears to be very little relationship between women's educational attainment, overall development and women's political representation.

The literature conflicted over whether socioeconomic variables such as labor force participation and educational attainment directly influenced the proportion of female members within a given legislature. Women's educational attainment in each country and show that while both countries have roughly achieved gender parity in educational attainment, gender inequality continues to exhibit itself in the concentration of males in certain academic fields and the females in other academic fields.

The concentration of women and men in different fields influences the types of opportunities available to them in the work force, and show the persistence of traditional attitudes toward women in modern society. In the Japan case study, how these attitudes manifest in Japan's political culture and interact with the electoral system to keep women's representation in Parliament low. In the Taiwan case study, how the country has achieved a constant level of women's representation through the use of the reserved seats system for women. Because the two countries are similar across a number of dimensions, that a reserved seats system for women in Parliament could also be effective in Japan.

The third case study however, will show the political difficulty of instituting a reserved seats system. In India, a proposal to set aside one-third of the seats in Parliament has been bitterly contested and has all but stalled. A brief discussion in gender inequality in India will show that traditional attitudes with regard to gender have a profound effect on women's lives, potentially more than similar attitudes do in developed Japan and Taiwan and then outline how the debate on reserved seats for women has evolved in India, and discuss why a similar proposal which instituted reserved seats on the local level passed with no trouble.

Together, these three cases show that gender inequality continues to constrain women's opportunities and the increase of female participation in the parliaments of the countries discussed would represent a considerable achievement for women in those countries. Despite differences in the ethnic makeup of their populations, population size, development level and electoral systems, both Japan and India have experienced similar trends in women's political representation. Female representation in both of these countries has historically fallen within a narrow range and neither country has achieved 10% female representation in Parliament.

Reserved seats for women may ultimately be the best means of achieving an increase in female representation in the short term, but the political controversy of over reserved seats decreases the likelihood of adoption by either Japan or India. Underlying my analysis is the assumption that the people respond to incentives and without a realignment of those incentives, improvements in women's political representation will be slow. The political parties aim to control government and do not view female candidates as an integral part of their campaign strategies and argue that the design of the electoral system defines the incentive environment, and the inclusion of quotas would be sufficient to transform the incentive environment.

If women are directly linked to a party's victory, political parties will change their behavior and recruit more female candidates. One of the arguments supporting an increase of women's representation in legislatures invoked the potential transformative effect of women's leadership and will not address the effect of women's leadership once in office, and instead base my argument on the grounds of human rights and equality. Women's political representation is important in and of itself.

Japan When compared to its situation at the end of World War II, today's Japan is a seemingly different country altogether. Japan's economic gains since the end of the war have positioned the country as the second-largest economy in the world, second only to the United States. The United Nations places Japan 9th among 177 nations on the Human Development Index, in recognition for its economic wealth, universal literacy, educated populace and long life expectancy. Japan's development has not only occurred in the economic dimension, but in the political realm as well.

After a long period of one-party rule, Japan now functions as a parliamentary democracy with competitive elections. Despite a dramatic transformation of Japan's economic and governing institutions in the post-war era, women's status remains low in comparison to men's. Comparison of Japan's gender-related development indicator (GDI) and gender empowerment measure (GEM) to its human development indicator (HDI) reveals that gender inequality is more pronounced in politics than in the economics. Japan places in the top deciles of nations regardless of whether one is using the HDI or GDI measure. (Japan's GDI ranking is 12th out of 144 nations.) In contrast, Japan ranks 38th out of 78 nations for which the GEM is calculated.

When looking only at GEM measures for OECD countries, Japan fares far worse, with only 3 OECD nations scoring lower than Japan: Hungary, Greece, and the Republic of Korea. High rates of female education and increased economic opportunities have contributed to the economic empowerment of Japanese women, but politics remains dominated by males. The proportion of Japanese women in the House of Representatives has not yet surpassed 10% in the chamber's 58-year history. Given the disparity between overall economic development and low rates of female political representation, Japan presents a compelling argument against the claim that economic development necessarily combats gender inequality.

The women's low rates of political representation can be attributed to Japan's gender ideology and attitudes toward appropriate gender roles and examine women's education rates and argue that gender ideology continues to negatively affect women's education though the effect is less easily detected. After showing how gender ideology affects women's education, will trace women's political representation throughout Japan's democratic history and will link the historically low rates of female political representation to the different designs of Japan's electoral system, and show how attitudes toward women's appropriate societal roles currently keep the proportion of female representation low.

Gender Ideology and Education in Japan Prior to the Meiji Restoration of 1868, Japanese women received little formal schooling, in accordance with Confucian tradition. The restoration of Emperor Meiji, however, ushered in an era of industrialization and urbanization, placing a greater premium on education as a requisite for national development. The Meiji government, seeking to accelerate development by whatever means possible, decided that the education of women was necessary in order to make them "wise mothers," or *ryosai kenbo*.

Wise mothers could provide for the development of sons and relieve fathers of their care giving duties. Men would thus be free to devote themselves more fully to efforts to economic activities. The government promoted *ryosai kenbo* to justify women's education, and the idea took hold, reversing a well-established tradition which deemed schooling appropriate only for males. . Though the Meiji government made women's education acceptable, its embrace of the *ryosai kenbo* is built on strict gender roles and the public-private dichotomy. The education of women is valued only through its value to males, rather than valued in its own right.

Moreover, only a certain type of education is deemed acceptable for women: that which will prepare her for a lifetime of domesticity. Government endorsement of such thinking intensifies the harmful effect on women's status by validating women's domestic identities as their only identities on the public level. It is no surprise then, that once female education was accepted in Japan, girls were segregated in their own schools for education that was both separate and unequal. Strict gender roles were thus reinforced by the education system, as subject matters taught in girls' and boys' schools differed widely. Educational opportunities at higher levels were also barred from women: no universities admitted female students in the pre-war era.

Only the wealthy could afford to attend private women's colleges, which essentially functioned as finishing schools. Under the US occupation following the end of World War II, the Japanese education system was reorganized. The 1946

Constitution established a right to education which applied to women as equally as it applied to men. Education was made compulsory at the elementary and middle school levels for nine years; following middle school, students could go to a three-year secondary school and then to a four-year college.

Coeducation was established at all levels of schooling and universities were forced to admit female students. Despite the establishment of seemingly egalitarian institutions of education, in practice the quality and content of women's education remained inferior to men's. Though public schools now enrolled both male and female students, males and females were tracked into different subject areas at the primary and secondary levels, a practice known as gender-streaming. In 1958, junior high schools began to require that girls take home economics while boys enrolled in technical education courses.

In 1970, home economics became required for girls in secondary schools, but not for boys. High economic growth and industrialization in the 1960s and early 1970s created demand for skilled labor, to which institutions of higher education responded by restructuring their offerings to emphasize science and technology. The climate for female education during this period was thus reminiscent of the *ryosai kenbo* era but gender inequality was less overt. Gender-streaming in lower levels of schooling led to de facto inequality at the university level, as women were ill-prepared to study technical subjects. Because industry was still seen outside the appropriate sphere for women, few incentives existed for them to overcome their educational disadvantage and pursue education in related fields.

The enrollments of junior colleges in the 1960s reflect the incentives women faced in this period: student populations at these two-year institutions because overwhelmingly female. Formal gender-streaming was finally abolished in 1989. The Japanese ratification of CEDAW in 1985 provided Japanese feminists with an opportunity to attack government for its complicity in maintaining gender inequality through gender-streaming. In 1989, by Ministry of Education mandate, home economics and technical education became compulsory for all secondary level students regardless of gender. However, the beliefs central to gender-streaming continue to influence women's education.

Though gender parity has been nearly perfect at primary and secondary levels since 1965, women have historically lagged behind men in their university enrollments. Recent progress has narrowed the gap, but women's share of the university population remains below 50%. These statistics show that women are consistently underrepresented in technical colleges and overwhelmingly overrepresented in junior colleges. The share of women in universities has steadily increased since 1980, reflecting a more supportive environment for women in higher education. Examination of the subjects male and female students are studying once at university reveals, however, those women continue to be underrepresented in the sciences and technology, and overrepresented in traditionally female-dominated fields such as the humanities and nursing.

At the undergraduate level, women's under representation in science and engineering is not severely pronounced. However, the share of women who pursue graduate degrees in science and engineering experiences a profound decrease. Women continue to be overrepresented in the humanities, home economics and education, but their share of total student's declines with successively higher degrees. In the humanities, women constitute 67.5% of undergraduates but their share of total students at the masters and PhD level decreases toward parity. These statistics show that while gender ideology does not strongly affect women's educational attainment up to the university level, it continues to influence attainment at the post-secondary level.

Gender influences the type of institution women attend and what subjects they study. With few women earning advanced degrees in technical fields, the notion of men's natural superiority in these fields is unlikely to change anytime soon. Female under representation in science, technology and industry-related fields show that economic incentives have not yet aligned to encourage and support women to pursue education in these fields. Thus, despite women's gains in education, they have not been fully embraced as legitimate contributors to national development. Gender patterns evident at the academic level are also persistent once women enter the work force. Segregation in academic subjects leads to segregation in the occupational structure.

Women's employment is viewed as temporary, and their true vocation is within the home. The idea of the *ryosai kenbo* became an ideal for the modern Japanese middle class family, because to be able to sustain a family on one income was a mark of economic privilege. Thus, for many Japanese women, to be a housewife is considered a distinction of honor and an ideal to which to aspire. These statistics show that women's proportion of employment in non-agricultural industries has been increasing over time, finally arriving at 41.0% in 2003. With regard to type of occupation, women's representation among professional and technical workers in Japan has been relatively stable since 1975, falling within the 43-46% range.

Women's share of the clerical work force has only grown since 1975. Such patterns should not be surprising, given that the majority of clerical workers are graduates of junior colleges, which are overwhelmingly female. Furthermore, clerical work is the type of work that lends itself to high turnover, allowing women to work for short spans of time. Statistics show that women have also been severely underrepresented at the manager and official level, showing that women are not thought of as leaders. Their low numbers among leadership positions are a signal that leadership is thought to be the men's domain.

This has consequences for women's political representation, because many women have not had the opportunity to prove their leadership qualities and hone their skills in a business setting. Business and political circles feed into each other in Japan, and so someone who has not been tested and proven as an effective leader in business is less likely to be recruited to run for national office. If women do not hold leadership positions in business, they cannot rise to hold leadership positions in politics either. Women's Political

Representation in Japan In contrast to gender inequality in education, gender inequality in the political sphere is visibly pronounced. Women's representation is markedly low in Japan's bicameral Parliament.

The Inter-Parliamentary Union ranks Japan 98 out of 125 nations for women's political representation, behind most other developed nations. In the upper house of the Diet, known as the House of Councillors, 33 representatives out of the total 242 are female, amounting to 13.64% female representation. In the House of Representatives, 34 representatives out of the total 480 arc female, amounting to 7.08% representation (IPU 2005). The higher proportion of female members in the House of Councillors can be attributed to its earlier employment of the mixed electoral system.

The House of Councillors instituted the mixed system in 1982, with the House of Representatives following twelve years later. In keeping with the United Nations' practice of examining the lower house of a bicameral Parliament, I shall limit my analysis to Japan's House of Representatives. Throughout the majority of the chamber's history, women's political representation has hovered between 1-3%. This period is bracketed on the table to show its significance. Only 4 House sessions fall above this range: the first session in 1946 and recent sessions since 1996.

Though nearly 60 years have passed since the first election in Japan, women's political representation has not surpassed the 1946 level of 8.37%, the highest level of representation women have achieved. The proportion of women in the House of Representatives must be viewed in the context of Japan's electoral system. In fact, fluctuations in women's representations from 1946-1947 and 1996-present closely parallel reforms in the electoral system prior to the 1947 and the 1996 elections. I will discuss each of the electoral reforms and how they affected women's candidacy.

The 1946 election was the first in which women could vote and run for office. Out of 79 women candidates, 39 were elected. The high success of rate of female candidates in a country unaccustomed to women in public office can be explained by several factors. According to Ogai, traditional gender attitudes lead the public to associate female candidates with peace, particularly important to the citizenry as the war was still fresh in their minds. Another factor was the design of the electoral system with large constituency districts.

The districts, with anywhere from two to fourteen members, provided favorable electoral conditions to women. As explained in the earlier section on women's political representation, women fare better in large constituency electoral districts due to the increased number of seats and the ability to win with a plurality of votes, rather than a majority. In 1947, however, the electoral system was revised. Policymakers who feared the National Diet was too ideologically diverse redesigned electoral districts as medium-constituency districts.

With the size of districts reduced, the number of seats per district decreased to only three to five members per district. Though still a multimember district, candidates needed a greater proportion of the vote to win a seat. With less than a year of female political representation, female candidates had not had many opportunities to prove their worth as legislators. Thus, negative attitudes toward women continued to be influential in voters' preferences. The reduction of seats per district was purposeful, as the "alteration of the electoral system hindered political outsiders such as the Communist and Socialist parties, and women".

Seen in the context of rising Cold War tensions in Asia, the move to contain left-leaning political elements made strategic sense for the country but constructed a greater obstacle to women's candidacy. One might suspect that the 1947 revision of the electoral system would have exacted a one-time penalty on women candidates, and after a period of adjustment and refining of political strategy, women's representation would begin to rise.

The 1947 electoral system, however, allowed the Liberal Democratic Party to consolidate its power and establish its dominance over Japanese politics. Its majority in government lasted for 38 years. The LDP focused primarily on national development, and little attention was paid to social aims. The party did not strongly support female candidates and made few efforts to recruit female candidates. For a ten-year span, none of the female members of the chamber were affiliated with the LDP, showing the party's lack of commitment to women's political equality.

The LDP's focus on economic development likely contributed to their lack of support for women's issues, as women continued to be seen outside the economic sphere. Thus, the relatively low proportion of female representation between 1947 and 1993 can be attributed to the combination of a change in the electoral system and the lack of the ruling party's commitment to female candidates. The LDP lost its majority in 1993 after an internal rift, and the coalition government which formed in its place succeeded in passing electoral reform with the intention of preventing one-party rule from occurring again.

The 1994 reform called for a mixed system of proportional representation and single-member districts, similar to the 1982 system adopted by the House of Councillors. The House of Representatives would seat 500 members total, with 300 members elected through single-member districts. The remaining 200 members would be elected by proportional representation, in 11 regional districts with multiple representatives. A modification in February 2000 reduced the number of PR seats to 180, bringing the total membership of the House to 480 members.

Christensen predicted that the introduction of the mixed system would carry mixed results for female candidates. Single-member electoral districts are the least favorable electoral arrangement for female candidates, while proportional representation presents the most favorable environment for women's candidacy short of outright quotas. Recent returns in the 1996, 2000 and 2003 elections seemingly confirm that the 1994 electoral reform created a system more favorable to female candidates. However, women's representation has not yet returned to the 1946 level of 8.37%. Additionally, with only three elections under the revised system, it is difficult to determine whether the reform continues to have a positive impact on women's political representation.

Proportional representation does not guarantee higher proportions of female legislators in and of itself; parties must make a commitment to recruiting and supporting female candidates on the party list in order for women to realize gains from the PR system. Ogai does not rule out the potential for parties to abandon support of women on the party list if the aim of increased female representation were to come into conflict with interest group pressures. The new system may present more favorable conditions for women's candidacy, but the incentives faced by party leaders will determine whether such conditions can be harnessed to increase women's political representation.

Non-Electoral Barriers to Women in Public Office Outside of electoral design, two well-established aspects of the Japanese political culture continue to pose barriers to women's political representation: money politics, known as *nagatcho* politics, and the personal network system, known as the *koenkai* and briefly describe each aspect here and explain why electoral reform cannot singularly overcome these barriers. *Nagatcho* politics refers to the idea that money controls Japanese politics. Those who exert influence in the political realm usually arrived at their positions through their influence in finance and industry.

The mark of a successful politician is not his personal wealth, but his ability to use his influence in business circles to broker deals. Due to the Liberal Democratic Party's emphasis on development of industry, leaders of the party are closely tied to business and industry, and candidates for office have often proved their leadership in the business realm as well. Thus, women stand at a disadvantage for candidate recruitment as fewer of them have proved their mettle as business leaders. Finance and industry remain heavily male-dominated, and so the preference for political readers with influence in business causes political parties to draw candidates from an already reduced pool of women.

Women's political representation in the new electoral system could potentially plateau, as the revised system does not change party incentives to recruit candidates among business and industry circles. The importance of personal networks, or *koenkai,* in Japanese politics also poses a significant barrier to the increase of women's political representation. Personal networks rose to importance during the one-party rule of the LDP. In order for the party to retain control of government, multiple LDP candidates were often put up in the same district. Candidates thus had to focus on their personal appeal rather than party affiliation in order to win seats.

Successful candidates often had extensive personal networks through which to cultivate relations and win the votes of constituents. Professional contacts, schoolmates and relatives all form important elements of a personal network. The *koenkai* is thus related to *nagatcho* politics; leaders in business and industry have had greater opportunities to develop a loyal network of support. Women's underrepresentation in leadership positions in Japan thus limits the potential for female candidates to rely on personal networks as strong as their male counterparts. Additionally, women's traditional roles as support figures have made the public unaccustomed to seeing women as the center of a *koenkai*.

The proper role for an incumbent politician's wife is particularly critical in maintaining the personal network. The political wife cultivates her husband's network with constituents while he is away in the capital. She will go door to door and have tea with constituents, and then solicit votes for her husband during the campaign. Here the public-private dichotomy surfaces again: the political wife tends to the domestic matters of the district and fills a nurturing, care giving role while the husband is making policy in the capital. Traditional gender roles have thus become an accepted part of Japanese political culture, preventing women from seeking office in overt and covert ways. Such attitudes cannot be addressed by electoral system alone.

In order for the Japanese political elite to view more women as viable candidates, the elite must either broaden its view of successful candidacy or more women must satisfy the prerequisites for viable candidacy. In my opinion, neither of these outcomes can occur without some type of external intervention. Regardless of party ideology, party strategies to win elections are relatively conservative. Parties are reluctant to try new tactics in electing candidates when previous strategies have already proven to be successful. Thus, the political elite is unlikely to broaden its view of viable candidacy without a realignment of incentives for doing so.

Additionally, the low proportion of female leadership in business and financial circles is unlikely to change on its own as well. Development does not necessarily lead to female empowerment, and so while there may be more Japanese women engaged in wage labor, the fact that they have entered the wage labor force does not allow for the assumption that they will effortlessly rise to leadership positions. Women must battle gender stereotypes at every step of the way, from their entry into schools, to their entry into the work force, and their entry into leadership positions.

Despite Japan's economic growth in the past sixty years, attitudes toward women's societal place remain relatively fixed and will continue to pose a barrier to women's political representation in the absence of incentive realignment. Outlook for Japanese Women in Politics Japan's example shows that economic development and women's political empowerment are not necessarily connected. The low proportion of women representatives throughout Japan's democratic history has only recently begun to grow. This recent growth can be attributed to the 1994 reform of the electoral system, but whether this growth will plateau or continue remains to be seen.

Japan's electoral institutions may now be more friendly to women candidates, but social attitudes which dismiss women's potential leadership continue to pose barriers to women's political representation. Could Japan benefit from a quota of minimum female representation in the National Diet? A mandated minimum of female representation could guarantee women at least 10% representation in Parliament, an unprecedented proportion of female legislators in the House of Representatives. A quota would make a moot point of women's fitness for candidacy and force parties to recruit women in order to avoid losing seats in Parliamentary chambers.

Party incentives would thus be realigned in order to value women's contributions, rather than dismiss them. The next case study examines whether a quota can achieve greater female representation beyond the mandated minimum. Indeed, a quota loses its potential benefit if it only presents a one-time increase in women's representation. The advantage of examining the quota in Taiwan is that both countries share a number of traits, presenting fewer issues in comparing the two nations. By examining how the quota is structured in Taiwan and its efficacy in increasing women's representation, one can determine the potential benefit to women if such a quota were introduced in Japan.

TAIWAN

Taiwan has grown from a predominately agricultural economy to an industrial one in a relatively short period. In 1952, the share of the population employed in agriculture was 52% while the share of the population in industry figured only 17%. By 1990, those figures had nearly reversed themselves. The agriculture sector had shrunk to employing only 13% of the population, while the share of population employed in industry had increased to 41%. Taiwan experienced an increase in GNP per capita from US$196 to US$7,950 in the same period. In 2004, Taiwan's GNP per capita amounted to US$12,916.

Though not measured by the UN for human development, Taiwan's high literacy rates, high school enrollments, life expectancy and GNP per capita would place it in the category of high human development. Clearly, Taiwan has made great gains in development since the establishment of Nationalist rule on the island in 1949. Taiwan bears several similarities to Japan, making it a useful comparison for women's political representation. Both nations boast high levels of education and near-perfect gender parity in primary school enrollments.

The legacy of Confucian thought continues to influence attitudes toward gender in both countries, placing men at a higher social status than women. The modern Japanese and Taiwanese governments were both established after World War II, and both economies grew rapidly in the post-war era. Both countries experienced long periods of political rule by one party and revised their electoral systems in the 1990s. Similar attitudes toward gender relations, high economic development and democratic government would lead one to speculate that female political representation in Parliaments would also be similar.

However, Taiwan's 2001 session of the Legislative Yuan, the lower house of Parliament, boasted 22.2% female representation, far exceeding the 7.08% representation of women in Japan's current House of Representatives. Taiwan boasts one of the highest rates of female political representation in Asia. A on page 96 to compare Taiwan's proportion of female representation to that of other Asian governments. Taiwan's higher rate of female political representation is largely due to its system of reserved seats for females at all levels of government, mandated in their 1947 Constitution.

The long history of the quota and high levels of women's education have allowed women to win more than the specified minimum of seats, tempering criticisms of the quota as tokenism. The Legislative Yuan has even taken the rare position of taking further measures to increase the number of seats reserved for women. In 2004, the chamber passed a proposal to amend the electoral system, which included an expansion of reserved seats for women in the proportional representation system. This proposal, however, has yet to be confirmed by the upper house of Parliament, the National Assembly.

The discussion of Taiwan as a nation and government is fraught with political overtones, as Taiwan is not recognized in the international community as an independent nation. The modern government of Taiwan has its origins in the Chinese civil war of 1945-1949. When the Nationalist government of China was driven off the mainland by the Communist Party, it established itself in Taiwan. The government, which I will refer to as the Republic of China (ROC) or the Taiwanese government, was recognized as the legitimate representative of China for some time and even occupied the Chinese seat on the United Nations Security Council. Cold War tensions, however, put pressure on the United States and other nations to recognize the People's Republic of China (PRC).

As both nations would capitulate from the position that each was the true China, dual recognition of the PRC and ROC was not possible. In 1971, the UN announced its formal recognition of the PRC and replaced Taiwan's seat on the Security Council with a representative from the PRC. Since then, the majority of the international community has abided by the PRC's pronouncement of "one China, two systems," maintaining that Taiwan is not a sovereign nation.

Education and Gender Inequality Education in Taiwan is structured on a 6-3-3 system. Universal education is provided up to middle school, encompassing 6 years of elementary school and 3 years of middle school. Following the completion of middle school, students enter vocation schools or high schools and are placed based on the rigorous entrance exams.

Junior colleges, 4- year colleges and universities, and graduate schools also offer admission to students on the basis of their entrance exam scores. Taiwan's high education rates show a concerted investment in human capital, and the statistics show gender parity in enrollment rates. In some cases, women outnumber men. These statistics seemingly point to gender equality in the education sphere. However, like Japan, the effect of gender inequality in Taiwan does not affect the level of educational attainment so much as it affects the content of what students study. Taiwanese women in colleges and universities are overrepresented in the humanities and underrepresented in science and technology.

Among the 1990 graduates of four-year universities, females accounted for 66.53% of humanities majors and 22.19% of science and technology majors. In vocational schools, women are overrepresented in nursing and home economics, but underrepresented in industry. Female graduates of vocational schools accounted for 96% of nursing graduates and only 20% of graduate studying industry in 1990. One respect in which subject segregation by sex in Taiwan differs from that in Japan is that in Taiwan, women are overrepresented in the social sciences.

In 1990, females accounted for 61.09% of social science majors. Such numbers seemingly bode well for women in politics, but no studies have been found that attempt to link the high rate of women social science graduates to women's political activism in Taiwan. Hsieh argues that distribution of academic concentrations among female graduates does not occur as coincidence but as a consequence of the "interactive forces of strong state control and patriarchal values". The Taiwanese government oversees the development of curricula and textbook publication used in public education, and also administers the school entrance exams for secondary schools and higher education.

According to Hsieh, school textbooks often rely on stereotypical gender roles in their lessons, ensuring that gender ideology takes hold early on and is reinforced throughout succeeding levels of school. Furthermore, disparity in the distribution of men and women among academic subjects has implications for what fields they enter when they begin employment. Evidence presented by Hsieh suggests that women concentrate in manufacturing, service and commerce work, filling the low-skilled positions in manufacturing and performing clerical work in the service and commerce industries.

These positions reinforce the stereotype of women as auxiliary worker and dispensable labor, as the work is not particularly high skilled. Women's overall labor force participation falls behind that of men's and has hovered in the

43-45% range since 1985. Men's labor force participation in the same period, however, falls within the higher range of 67-76%.

Taiwan's Electoral System and the Reserved Seats System for Women

The Constitution of the Republic of China provides for a bicameral Parliament. The National Assembly approves changes to the Constitution while the Legislative Yuan serves as the lawmaking chamber. The Constitution, adopted in 1946, was the product of several draft constitutions developed prior to the Chinese civil war and was enacted prior to the full relocation of the Nationalist government to Taiwan in 1949.

When the Nationalist government was forced off the mainland, the governing institutions as outlined by the Constitutions were relocated as well. Some representatives, however, remained on the mainland and their presence there added legitimacy to the ROC's claim that it was the legitimate representative of China. Thus, members of Parliament who had been chosen on the mainland in 1947 and 1948 retained their seats in Parliament for quite some time though they could not participate directly in government decision-making.

As a result, elections for the legislature were not held until 1969, and then not held in full until the 1990s. The impetus for election of new representatives among those living in Taiwan arose from necessity; as mainlander representatives began to die of old age. Though the Constitution established a democratic government, Taiwan was effectively under authoritarian rule until 1986. The ruling party under Chiang Kai-shek established martial law and tolerated little political opposition. Martial law was finally lifted in 1986, allowing elections to finally become competitive.

The abolition of martial law allowed for direct elections of the full Parliament to occur and also paved the way for electoral reform. The current electoral system was instituted in 1991. The Legislative Yuan has 225 seats, 49 of which are elected through proportional representation. The remaining 168 seats are directly elected by single-nontransferable vote

(SNTV) in multimember districts. Of the 49 seats on the PR list, 8 seats are reserved for overseas Chinese while the other 41 are known as national constituency seats. Unlike the quota for overseas Chinese in the Legislative Yuan, seats are reserved for women at all levels of lawmaking bodies through Article 134 of the Constitution of the Republic of China.

Article 134 reads, "In the various kinds of election, quotas of successful candidates shall be assigned to women; methods of implementation shall be prescribed by law". In 1947, the Legislative Yuan fleshed out the provisions of the quota in the Original Statute on the Election and Recall of Members of the Legislative Yuan. Though the quota for minimum female political representation is popularly referred to as the 10% quota, the statute actually provides for a system of seat reservation in the Legislative Yuan which follows a U-curve distribution. For every ten seats in an electoral district, one seat is reserved for a female representative.

Another seat for women is added only when another 10 seats are added to the district. Thus, as the seats in a district increases to 20 seats, the percentage of reserved seats for females decreases though the absolute number of female representatives stays the same. Only when the 20th electoral seat is added does the percentage of female representative go back to 10%. The quota functions as a provision of minimum representation, ensuring that women are not excluded from government and policymaking. The system forces parties to recruit female candidates lest a seat in a district go to a woman of another party.

Though the level of minimum representation is small, the quota effectively raises women's political status by linking women to party control of government. The rationale behind the quota dictates that without such a measure, women would be underrepresented due to the influence of patriarchy and Confucian values in Chinese society. The quota makes women competitive as candidates, rather than allowing the dismissal of their candidacy on the basis of their sex. One may wonder why a culture so influenced by patriarchy would move to correct women's subordinate status in the first place. The quota for women has its origins in ROC founder Sun Yat-Sen's commitment to women's equality.

Sun, who led the Chinese revolution against dynastic rule in 1911, is also claimed by the Nationalist party as its founder. Though the Nationalist leadership at the time of the 1946 Constitution was more conservative than Sun, Nationalist leaders continued to rely heavily on Sun's political vision for a new China. This vision called for increased equality for women, and so the Nationalist government's decision to include the quota for women must be seen in the context of Sun's legacy. Though Sun was claimed by the Nationalists, the Chinese Communist Party (CCP) also revered him and the issue of women's equality was a tenet of the CCP's platform. Thus, CCP members who participated in the drafting of the Constitution could support the provision for reserved seats without an ideological conflict.

An additional factor which allowed for the inclusion of the quota is that because the Constitution was establishing a new government, the political costs of reserving seats for women were low. Those who ratified the Constitution were not directly threatened because no elections had yet been held. Thus, no one was in jeopardy of forfeiting a seat in the legislature for supporting the provision. The respected figure of Sun and the correct incentive climate thus aligned to allow for the provision's inclusion. Effectiveness of the Reserved Seats System in Taiwan Determining the exact effect of the quota on women's political representation is difficult, as no elections in Taiwan have been conducted without it.

However, because Taiwan's current electoral system combines elements of Japan's electoral systems before and after the 1994 reform, Japan can be used as baseline case for women's political representation in an Asian democracy. Other similarities between the two countries, such as cultural attitudes, level of development and high levels of education, facilitate the comparison. As mentioned before, Taiwan employs a mixed electoral system of proportional representation and single nontransferable vote (SNTV) for non-PR seats.

Prior to Japan's electoral reform in 1994, Japan used the SNTV method in multimember districts for the House of Representatives. After the 1994 electoral reform, Japan also went to a mixed electoral system, replacing SNTV with single-member districts. It is unclear whether SNTV in multi-member districts constitutes a greater electoral advantage to women than single-member district elections, as party was an influential factor in keeping women's representation low in Japan. On the one hand, multimember districts favor women by making more opportunities available and eliminating the necessity of winning a majority of votes in the district.

However, in SNTV systems, parties may have to run several candidates in one district in order to make a bid for as many seats as possible. This political strategy places more emphasis on the individual candidate rather than party identification, thus rendering it similar to single-member district elections and the focus on the candidate. Because the SNTV system has the potential to invoke the barriers women confront in single-member district elections.

Japan's SNTV system was used in 17 elections, from 1947 to 1993. Female political representation over this period peaked at 3.22%. In Japan's post-reform mixed system, female representation has peaked so far at 7.29%. One can thus conjecture that without the quota, under the best conditions, female political representation in Taiwan would fall within a similar range as Japan, from 3% - 8%. Though an exact forecast is not possible, this approximation is nonetheless useful as a basis of comparison actual levels of women members of Taiwan's Legislative Yuan.

The 1969 election in Taiwan yielded a higher share of female representation in Parliament than Japan has had over its democratic lifetime. Additionally, the table shows that women's representation has largely hovered around 10% between 1969-1992 before the start of an increase with the 1995 election. The fact that women's political representation hovered near the 10% range shows its efficacy in maintaining a constant, even if small, proportion of female representation. The comparison of Taiwan's electoral statistics to the range of Japanese women's political representation thus allows us to determine that the political quota in Taiwan has been effective in increasing women's share of legislature.

Taiwan's recent gains in representation share for women following the introduction of the mixed electoral system somewhat mirror the gains Japan has experienced following the introduction of the mixed electoral system, though gains in Taiwan are more pronounced. This suggests that while the mixed electoral system is instrumental in promoting female political representation, the overall level of female representation can be increased with the use of a quota for minimum female representation.

Quota Criticism and Taiwan's Experience

Though effective in promoting women's political representation, quotas are controversial in their adoption and implementation. The main arguments against quotas, largely concern tokenism of female political representatives and the functioning of the quota as a ceiling rather than a floor. Taiwan's experience contradicts the argument that quotas necessarily function as ceilings rather than floors. Electoral returns in 1995, 1998 and 2001 show women winning more than the legislated minimum of 10%.

Coincidentally, these elections came after the 1991 electoral reform and hint at an interaction between the revised electoral system and the quota to result in a greater share of women's political representation. The quota, then, does not need to be set very high in order to guarantee representation so long as supportive electoral institutions like the PR system are present. Taiwan already ranks high in comparison to other nations with regard to women's political representation.

Using the 2001 figure of 22.2% female representation, Taiwan would rank 30 among the 125 nations surveyed by the Inter-Parliamentary Union, falling within the top quartile of countries. More research would be necessary in order to determine whether female members of the Legislative Yuan are treated as tokens rather than important political players. One would have to survey the committees on which these members served in order to evaluate whether women are marginalized in certain committees and turned down for committee leadership. One would also need to examine the party structure and determine whether women were marginalized within the party and excluded from party leadership positions.

These issues show that gender inequality in political representation, as in education, is not merely about the magnitude of female representation. However, it is not clear to me that the potential for tokenism outweighs the need for women to be represented in legislative bodies. For reasons discussed in earlier chapters, women's lack of representation among the legislatures of the world signals continued inequality and injustice against women. Until women can have the same kind of opportunity to participate in government as men do, rather than just possess the same right to do so, women cannot hope for increased gains in their societal status.

Taiwan's Lessons for Japan

Taiwan shows that a nation with well-established patriarchal traditions and attitudes can support women's formal political representation. The recent proposal to increase reserved seats for women, though not yet confirmed by the National Assembly, shows that the political will can and does exist to support women's candidacy. Given that Japan and Taiwan are similar across a number of dimensions, Japan would do well to adopt a quota of at least 10% minimum representation. Such a measure would at least secure 10% female representation in Japan's House of Representation, a level of representation not yet experienced.

It is particularly noteworthy that while Japan's "natural" level of female representation hovered between 1-3% for a number of years, Taiwan's level of female representation has hovered around the 10% level with the exception of recent elections. Japanese women's political representation during the medium-sized electoral years operated under a ceiling though an actual ceiling was not in place. The adoption of a quota, then, could at least help Japanese women attain a higher level of political representation, even if it held constant for a number of years.

Though Japanese women could gain a great deal from a reserved seats system similar to Taiwan's, politics is not only about potential benefits. Consideration of costs and benefits, and to whom those costs and benefits accrue, is central to political decision-making. Taiwan's case is unique in that the Constitution contains a provision for reserved seats. Lacking a similar Constitutional mandate, Japan would have to pass new legislation in order to institute a reserved seats system. In doing so, however, current members of the House of Representatives leave themselves vulnerable to losing their seats.

The political costs and benefits of passing such a measure do not necessarily align in order to compel the institution of a reserved seats system in Japan anytime soon. The final case study shows the political difficulty of passing quotas, even when other provisions for reserved seats have been made. While Taiwan's example shows that countries could benefit from a reserved seats system for women, India's example illustrates the near-impossibility of introducing such a quota on the national level. If the quota is effective but politically impossible, its worth as a measure to increase female political representation comes into question. Women's political representation in India is similar to that of Japan's.

The proportion of female legislators has historically fell within a narrow range and has not yet reached 10%. In other respects, however, India could not be more different from Japan. India's population size, socioeconomic stratification, and religious and ethnic diversity frame issues of gender much differently from issues faced by Japanese women. Furthermore, while Japan is well-developed, India is still considered a developing nation. Gender inequality is thus compounded with issues of access and resource availability as the Indian population faces more strict economic constraints than the Japanese.

Though measures have been taken to increase women's political representation in local government, a similar measure to increase women's representation at the Parliamentary level has stalled. India thus provides an instructive case study for how gender inequality interacts with political incentives in order to prevent further gains in women's political empowerment. The majority of my discussion will focus on the issue of reserved seats for women in government. I will compare the proposals to implement reserved seats for women at the local and national levels to determine why the proposal affecting local governments won passage while the national level proposal has stalled.

Gender Inequality in India

In the Japan and Taiwan case studies, gender inequality was not easily discernible through school enrollment data. In India's case, however, women's low status can be easily observed through several development indicators, school enrollment data included. Pronounced disparity in these indicators not only reflects women's disadvantage in relation to men, but women's absolute disadvantage in society. The severity of gender inequality in India is perhaps best represented by the notion of "missing women," a term coined by Nobel laureate Amartya Sen.

Though population sex ratios across history and countries have long shown more women than men to be present in a given population, the opposite is true for several countries in the developing world, particularly in Asia. The sex ratio in India has not even reached unity between males and females since measurements began in the early 20th century. Using the sex ratio of Sub-Saharan Africa of 1.022 women to men, Sen calculated the population of women who should be alive and compared his estimated figures to the actual population of women in certain countries.

In India, 37 million women were "missing" from the population in 1992; using figures from 2001, Klasen revised Sen's estimate and calculated that 39.1 million women were missing from India. Literacy provides another indicator which clearly reflects gender inequality. In Japan and Taiwan, universal literacy was achieved early through universal schooling and high rates of female enrollments in schools. Though India also mandates primary education for school-age children, access to schools is uneven across the country and so the opportunity to obtain education is not assured. Thus, despite similar mandates regarding compulsory education in Japan, Taiwan, and India, India has not yet achieved universal literacy.

The average rate of literacy for the population 15 years of age and older is only 61.3%. When this figure is disaggregated by gender, it shows that 69.0% of males are literate, in comparison to 46.4% of females. This development hurdle shows that many grown women are illiterate and uneducated, factors which limit them to the domestic sphere and constrain their potential for political activity. One significant contributor to imbalanced sex ratios and low female literacy is son preference, a pattern of thinking and associated behaviors which values the son more than the daughter. Though son preference has been linked to sex-selective abortion and infanticide, the most probable and widespread manifestation of son preference is the systematic deprivation of girls during childhood.

The comparative neglect of girls during their formative development years explains both the imbalanced sex ratios as well as women's lower rates of literacy. In a developing country like India, families under strict resource constraints allocate more to sons and less to daughters, who constitute a seemingly lost investment. Thus while sons are sent to school, daughters stay home for "domestic education." While son preference is often explained in economic terms, a cross-country study by Das Gupta et al finds that it is not limited to countries where the population is relatively poor.

The practice is also strong in South Korea, where the standard of living is relatively high, particularly in comparison to that of India's. Son preference requires a rigidly patrilineal kinship system which shapes incentives for preferring sons to daughters. Economic conditions exaggerates the effect of son preference, but rules regarding inheritance, property ownership, and family identity form the primary cause for focusing resources on sons. Das Gupta et al find that son preference is particularly pronounced in northern India, where the rules of kinship are more strict than in southern India. While it is rare for a daughter to inherit land and property in northern India, there is more flexibility for women's property ownership in the southern region of the country.

If the kinship system dictates that men hold sole inheritance and ownership rights, their position in the family is fixed while women are mobile, and even dispensable. A woman's worth to the family centers on her ability to bear a son and continue the family line, narrowing her identity to her reproductive capacity. Furthermore, the kinship system dictates that sons provide for parents when the parents are elderly. Son preference therefore implies some degree of self interest on the part of parents, as sons provide future security. Women in India are thus closely tied to the private sphere. Their narrow identity as reproductive vessels and their relative lack of education limits their opportunities for self-empowerment and assertion of their individuality in the public sphere, as their identities have already been compromised for them. Such factors thus bode ill for women's assertion of their interests and individuality in the public sphere.

Women's Political Representation in the Lok Sabha

After India won its independence from Great Britain in 1947, the Republic of India was established, a federal republic of 28 states and 7 union territories. The Constitution created a bicameral Parliament, with the direct election of representatives to the lower house and the indirect election of representatives of the upper house. The lower house, the Lok Sabha, or the House of the People, currently seats 545 members. 543 members were elected to office while the remaining 2 were appointed by the President.

The Constitution stipulates that the chamber can seat up to 552 members, and the President may appoint 2 members of the Anglo-Indian community if it is underrepresented. The Constitution also provides for the representation of other minority groups and members of the other backward classes and stipulates reserved seats for members of these groups. Women in India have benefited from institutional protection of their rights and support for women's equality from influential political leaders. The 1950 Constitution established women's right to vote and hold office, and also contained provisions protecting individual quality and outlawing discrimination on the basis of sex. Women had played an important role in the resistance movement, and both Gandhi and Nehru publicly supported women's equality.

Like Japan, however, women's representation in the lower house of the Indian Parliament has been low throughout the chamber's history, despite the establishment of democratic institutions and provisions for women's rights. The Inter-Parliamentary Union ranks India 93 rd out of 125 nations for women's political representation, just a few places ahead of Japan. The statistics show that women's representation has been relatively stable throughout India's democratic history, falling between 4-8% over the past fifty years. The low proportion of women in the House of the People can be attributed to its electoral system. India uses the single-member district system, the electoral design least favorable to female candidates, as parties have only one chance to win the district.

In order to gain control of government, parties must win as many districts as possible. In comparison, the multimember district allows parties to run multiple candidates in a district and thus parties have the flexibility of trying to gain control by winning as many districts as possible or else winning as many seats as possible within districts of party-friendly constituencies. The presence of multiple political parties on the national level in India increases the competitiveness of single-member races. The candidate who earns the most number of votes within the district wins the seat, but with multiple opponents, candidates must strategize carefully in order to maximize their number of votes. Due to women's comparatively low status in society and the conceptualization of women outside of the political sphere, the demands placed on female candidates for national office are set at a high bar.

Hoskyns and Rai surveyed the women members of the 1991 Parliament and found that their profile did not match that of the general female population of India. 80% of the female members held graduate or postgraduate degrees, a startling proportion considering that between 1950 and 1990, the average number of girls enrolled per hundred boys in secondary school was only 33.6. With the exception of those women who earned their seats through the quota for members of scheduled castes, most female representatives came from wealthy families and/or families belonging to the political elite. Class and family connections thus eased their paths into office, allaying concerns about their candidacy.

The lack of women's representation in the House of the People, then, implicates the gender bias of political party leadership more than it implicates the bias of the electorate. Female candidates for public office are vastly outnumbered by male candidates. In the 2004 parliamentary elections, out of 5436 candidates for seats in the Lok Sabha, only 355 were women, amounting to 6.5% of the candidate pool. As the Hoskyns and Rai profile argues, the lack of female candidates may be because few women can meet the high standards set for female candidacy. Of the women running for office in 2004, 45 were elected, amounting to a 12.7% success rate.

Though the success rate of male candidates was in fact lower, at 9.2%, men's gender is not considered a factor in their elections as men have always dominated Indian politics. The higher success rate of women candidates is virtually negligible as their proportion within the House of the People is so small. Due to the competitive nature of Indian elections, parties have few incentives to confront their biases against women candidates and "risk" a district election by running a female candidate. The Japan case shows that though development may raise women's educational attainment and participation in the labor force, increased political representation for women do not naturally extend from those two trends. Thus, in order for women's representation to increase, a realignment of the incentives facing political parties would be necessary.

As India's electoral system has not undergone a revision in the same vein as Taiwan or Japan, wholesale electoral reform is unlikely. Thus, the policy intervention to increase women's representation that seems most fitting for India is the quota. India has a history of quota use, having first instituted caste-based quotas in 1950. The recent passage of the 73rd and 74th Constitutional amendments instituted a reserved seats system for women in local government, paving the way for a quota for women on the national level. Indeed, such a proposal was offered in 1996, but has since stalled.

Consensus on the Local level, Contention on the National level

The debate over reserved seats for women legislators in India originated in the 1920s, when several newly formed women's organizations began to advocate for women's political rights. The question of reserved seats did not resurface again until the 1974 report from the Committee on the Status of Women was released. With the exception of two committee members who dissented, the Committee voted in the majority to reject the reservation of seats across all legislative bodies, citing concerns that such a measure would promote the separatism of women.

The Committee did agree, however, that quotas for women should be implemented in village and municipal councils in order to protect the interests of poor and rural women. The Committee also encouraged political parties to set internal quotas for women candidates and supported the establishment of all-women councils on the local level. Nearly a decade passed before any action was taken to implement the recommendations of the Committee. Individual states moved first to adopt reserved seats for women on local councils.

The southern state of Karnataka was the first to institute such a quota, mandating that 25% of seats in local councils be filled by women. More states followed Karnataka's example in the following years. When the Congress party took control of government in 1991, amendments to institute the 30% quota across all local and municipal councils were offered in Parliament. The 73rd and 74th amendments, which provided for one- third reservation of seats for women in local and municipal councils, passed in December 1992 and won ratification by all state governments by April 1993. The amendments not only provided for one-third representation of women, but also set aside one-third of the leadership positions in local and municipal councils for women. The measures were endorsed by the major political parties of India, signaling widespread consensus of their adoption.

A Constitutional amendment to institute a reserved seats system for women in Parliament soon followed, proposed by the United Front party in 1996 and supported broadly by women's groups in India. The 81st Constitution Amendment Bill proposed one-third reservation of seats in both chambers of Parliament, but the bill met stiff opposition from other political parties as well as from members within the United Front party. The bill posed a significant threat to the male-dominated Parliament, as many representatives stood to lose their seats if the 81st amendment was adopted.

Yet members of Parliament were placed in a difficult situation: supporting the bill would be equivalent to political suicide while blatant opposition to the bill would be politically incorrect. Thus, much of the dissension regarding the 81st amendment occurred within party ranks and riders were attached to the bill with the intention of stalling it in Parliament. One particularly contentious issue regarding the 81st amendment was the call for a provision to reserve a separate quota for minority and other backward classes (OBC) within the one-third reservation for women.

Members who represented the lower castes viewed the measure as an attempt for the wealthy Indian political elite to seize more seats in Parliament, assuming that most of the women who would secure office after the amendment was instituted would be well-educated, socially privileged and wealthy. Women's organizations accused parties which supported the demand for the quota within the quota as engaging in obstructionist tactics to stall the bill and ultimately kill it. Advocates of the 81st amendment argued that while minority and OBC representatives did not want to relinquish power to elite women, the same members would also be reluctant to relinquish power to OBC women.

Women's organizations have since refused to compromise on any aspects of the bill, maintaining that they would not accept dilution of the language even if the bill was ultimately defeated. Currently, the bill remains in legislative limbo; it is unlikely it will be passed in the near future.

Lessons from India's Experience

The example of the 81st amendment demonstrates that even when previous commitments to gender equality have been made by the political leadership, other factors may inevitably trump good intentions. Competing social aims and the preservation of power converged to derail the 81st amendment. While the diversity of India's population focused the dispute on class and representation, any country debating a proposal to reserve legislative seats for women will encounter difficulties, as those who would pass the legislation would leave themselves vulnerable to electoral defeat. The incentives for passage do not align.

The controversy regarding the allocation of minority and OBC seats within the one-third quota for women raises the question of who can legitimately represent women, particularly in a population as diverse as India's. The implicit assumption of the 81st amendment is that men cannot represent women, so measures must be taken in order to ensure that women's interests are not ignored. However, critics of the 81st amendment also argue that the implicit assumption that women can represent women also does not hold. Hoskyns and Rai's case study of the female members of the 1991 Parliament seemingly confirms this argument.

However, because women have never before held 30% representation in the Indian Parliament, it is impossible to predict what their composition will be and whose issues they will represent. The institution of a reserved seats quota could potentially create a powerful women's caucus-likely the hope of the amendment's supporters and the fear of its opponents. Borque and Warren write, "After actively discriminatory policies have set inequalities in motion, sex-neutral policies are sufficient to maintain established patterns." The issue of women's political equality falls within the purview of Borque and Warren's argument. The long history of female disenfranchisement established men's dominance over politics and its legacy continues today.

While the conferral of women's political rights constituted a major achievement in and of itself, recognition of women's rights is insufficient in and of itself to attain true gender equality in the political sphere. I have argued that exogenous change in the form of reserved seats for women is necessary to overcome gender inequality in political representation. The adoption of reserved seats for women, though controversial, would realign party incentives to recruit female candidates by tying female candidacy to party victory. Women would thus move farther away from the political periphery and towards greater acceptance in politics.

Taiwan's achievement of higher levels of female political representation could be attributed to their use of the reserved seats system, showing its efficacy in maintaining female representation at a certain level in a country with strong bias against women. One common argument against the adoption of political quotas for women is that such quotas inevitably turn into ceilings rather than floor. The Japan and India case studies show that a ceiling for women's political representation has already existed in both countries, despite the lack of a formal quota.

The adoption of a quota in either of these nations could at least serve to move the ceiling to a higher level in order to afford women greater representation. Additionally, recent electoral returns from Taiwan show that the reserved seats system need not be a ceiling, as Taiwanese women have been winning in excess of the reserved seats. Though gender ideology is certainly influential in keeping the level of women's representation low, women's relative lack of representation is largely shaped by institutional factors and thus its redress is best found in institutional modification.

The endogenous approach to gender equality carries little, if any effect in the political realm. The address of gender inequality in the politics necessitates exogenous change. Exogenous change in the form of institutional modification is effective in promoting women's political representation because it restructures the incentives of the political machinery to recruit female candidates. The incentives to implement such change, however, are few, as those who would vote to institute such changes would jeopardize their own political power. However, hope is not all lost. The recent proposal by the Taiwanese government to increase reserved seats for women shows that when the political will exists, reform can occur.

3

Women, Citizenship and the Politics in Philippines

Politics is an arena that the majority of women in the Philippines do not want to get involved in because of its history of violence, corruption and conflict. The National Commission on the Role of Filipino Women noted that the few women candidates who have run for public office have succeeded in securing public posts. But despite their high success rate in elections, Filipino women still have dismal participation as decision-makers in the public sector. A gender analysis gives a better picture of why the majority of women are not involved in politics.

There are three roles that women and men typically perform in the Philippines: the reproductive, the productive and the community management roles. Women are so tied up with the reproductive and productive roles that they do not have time to spare for participation in community management. A woman with two to four children usually wakes up at 4 or 5 a.m. and ends her day at 10 p.m. This amounts to nearly 18 hours of work, leaving her 6 hours to rest and sleep. Meanwhile most men, who are not occupied in this role, have more time to get involved in community affairs, like politics and governance.

The smallest unit in the Philippine political structure is the *barangay* where people know one another. Yet women are hesitant to run in the elections because they have not developed people-skills after years of being isolated in their homes. These women have not learned how to relate well to people and how to articulate their thoughts and feelings; they have not developed the self- confidence needed to become a leader in the community. Being poor is also a big "disadvantage given" the existing arrangement in politics where money for campaign expenses is a major requirement. As of 2008, the Philippines had two women presidents, Corazon Aquino and Gloria Arroyo.

Non- profit organizations in the Philippines played a key role in the nonviolent revolutions known as "People Power" that helped these women ascend to the presidency. But these two women were known by the people because they were related to famous men. We still have an elitist democracy and women who are not members of the rich ruling class have an uphill struggle. Organized poor women do not expect the elite women to represent them; they know they will not stand for their voices because they have their own class interests. There are, however, political organizations set up by progressive women and two such organizations recently secured party-list representation in Congress.

The women party list representatives successfully used the funds allotted them to organize marginalized women, which strengthened their programs and allowed them to pass pro-women legislation. So far there are five pro- women pieces of legislation in Congress, all products of the concerted effort between women's organizations and pro-women legislators. There is still hope after all. If more women are conscientious, organized and involved in politics, their voices will not only be heard, but their needs will be addressed because they are part of the decision-making structures that decide the priorities of the government, as well as the budget that goes with it.

Gradually men will recognize that the women are their equal partners. The task at hand is to help women realize that they can make a difference and should play an active part in politics and governance. More power to the women The Philippines is on the threshold of yet another critical political upheaval. Waging a desperate battle to salvage what is left of his political and moral authority to govern is President Joseph

Estrada on the one hand, and various civil society groups and breakaway politicos calling for his ouster on the other hand. Besides the President's attention is now focused on the Vice-President, who recently broke rank with the administration by resigning from the cabinet as Secretary of the Department of Social Welfare and Development.

What is significant about this is that the Vice- President, the person most to gain once the President is unseated, is Gloria Macapagal-Arroyo, a woman. But is it really significant? Another political figure playing a major role in the unfolding drama of Philippine politics is former President Corazon Aquino, the first female to occupy the highest office of the land after a popular uprising toppled the dictatorship of Ferdinand Marcos. But then again how significant is the role of these women in the current political equation of the country? Are they indicative of the status of women in Philippine politics?

A breakthrough in the recognition of the contribution of women can be found in Section 14, Article II of the Constitution, which provides that "The State recognizes the role of women in nation- building, and shall ensure the fundamental equality before the law of women and men." This provision is cognizant of the contribution of women in the overall life of the country, and thus is supposed to signify the State's support in pursuing the general development of its female constituents. From the time Filipino women were granted their right to suffrage in 1937, it has been consistently noted that female voter turnout proved to be higher that male turnout.

Without basic reforms to our political structures and systems we cannot hope to achieve great improvement in the lives of women and other marginalized peoples. Electoral reforms are in order. The party-list system, introduced into Philippines elections only three years ago as a system of proportional representation, must be expanded and further democratized. A system of representation in the various decision-making bodies of the local government units must be established. Local sector representation must be incorporated into the local government councils to ensure representation of marginalized sectors and groups.

The women's movement has done a great deal in working for the empowerment of women and gender equality. They have developed social support structures to increase gender awareness amongst women and men. But the women's movement cannot do it all alone. There must be a consolidated effort between governmental and non-governmental groups to put flesh into the rhetoric of women's empowerment, with the eventual goal of making women into a genuine political force. Government agencies such as the National Commission on the Role of Filipino Women are developing, implementing and overseeing various programs on women. A gender desk can be found in other government line offices. The National Anti-Poverty Commission has included women as a disadvantaged group.

Quite a number of gender-related bills are pending in Congress. However they are likely to languish considering that our representatives are preoccupied with other concerns. In the end, a law is only as good as its implementation. And its implementation will heavily depend on the political will of those in power, the resources they allocate, the efforts of various women's groups and the Filipino women who stand to benefit from it. The political party Akbayan is so far the only political group that has a constitutionally-mandated quota of thirty per cent for women in its leadership in all of its party units. Akbayan believes that women should be encouraged and challenged to take on more leadership roles, not only within the party, but also on the level of public governance.

PROSPECTS OF WOMEN IN PHILIPPINE POLITICS

While women have made inroads into such a male-dominated field as politics is, the challenges still remain great. The male-centered culture is still very ingrained in the consciousness of Filipinos, aided and abetted by deeply entrenched political structures. The politics of patronage and personality still command the Philippines political landscape. It isn't likely to disappear anytime soon. But if we want our women to break free from the bondage of marginalization, gender stereotyping, subordination, multiple burdens and violence, we must somehow work to achieve significant political reforms.

The income many women earn is not even enough to supplement the needs of the household, making them dependent on their spouses. Because the productive sphere is given more societal importance, and women are viewed as the "weaker sex", women are generally ambivalent and unenlightened about their role in politics and governance, thus making them less confident compared to men in such engagements. Women are associated primarily with their reproductive functions, although they perform a host of other activities that would be considered strictly within the productive domain.

This is particularly true again in lower-income families where they can't afford to employ household help. In general, women's personal views on power, governance and politics are largely associated with male characteristics, and given that, they do not enjoy the same level of confidence compared with men. Women would rather avoid conflict rather than engage in it, thus leaving the field freely open to the opposite sex.

There has been some advancement in terms of policy advocacy for women. In 1995, former President Fidel Ramos signed into law Executive Order No. 273, also known as the Philippine Plan for Gender-Responsive Development 1995-2025 (PPGD). This law takes off where the Philippine Development Plan for Women (PDPW) left off after its four-year mandate expired in 1992. It is the government's 30-year framework for pursuing gender equality and development. A voluminous document, incorporated into its development framework is the vision of its contribution to the human, economic and industrial development sectors.

The law names seven special concern sectors, namely: Women and Migration, Prostitution, Violence Against Women, Women and Family, Indigenous Cultural Communities and Ancestral Domain, Peace, and Politics and Governance. Owing to the deeply entrenched legacy of structure and perceptions that engender a culture of inequality, being a woman does not automatically guarantee a female will have a political consciousness. A bill on women in Congress does not get the automatic support of the female members of the House. Some may even be hesitant to support it.

Women cabinet members have also been relegated to traditional positions such as heading the Department of Tourism, the Department of Social Work and the Department of Health. A female Secretary of National Defense is not in the offing at any time in the near future. There might be exceptions, such as having a woman for a Director of the Bureau of Treasury. But still, they are exceptions. Age does not seem to be a significant factor in gauging a female politician's approach toward politics. The strongest influence on her approach and position on issues would still be her family and other class considerations. Age would only be significant if we assume that younger women are more open to change and more likely to use reason than the older generations.

OBSTACLES AND CHALLENGES

While there has been a significant increase in women's involvement in politics and governance, many women are still hindered from exercising their right to participation. This is particularly true for lower income women and those from low-income families. As economic power is a good indicator for a woman's access to political participation and power, the have-nots face numerous obstacles. In workshops conducted through the Women in Governance project, which Akbayan is a part, dependence on husbands is one obstacle frequently identified by married women coming from low-income families. A number of them may hold odd jobs, but there were more registered male voters. Women in political posts have markedly increased over the years.

The country's Vice-President is female. Of the 217 members of the current House of Representatives, 27 are women. One of them, Loretta Ann Rosales, is Akbayan's representative. In the Senate, four of 24 members are women. Elected positions held by women at the local government level are steadily on the rise. Statistics show that in the 1997 elections female-headed *barangays*, or village level local government units were at 11.85%, while the total women *barangay* officials were slightly higher at 20.46%. Percentages of local chief executives who were women from the municipal, city and provincial levels were within more or less the same range. A sizeable number of the bureaucracy is female. In fact, they were 54.32% of a total 1.32 million government personnel in 1996.

Over the past decade, the diplomatic corps has doubled its female ambassadors. While as far as the judicial branch is concerned, there is only one woman in the Supreme Court, the number of female judges in the lower courts has doubled in less than five years. What these statistics do not show is the quality of women's participation in politics and governance. While there may be more women in the government bureaucracy, they tend to occupy second-level positions, meaning men still hold key managerial and executive posts. Even the salary scales for women, which are pegged to positions and ranks, are lower than men's. A study by the Department of Labor-Institute of Labor Studies found out that access to opportunities was greater for men than for women (e.g. promotions, access to training, etc.)

In the legislative arena, of the 24 bills on women filed by a mix of both female and male members of the House of Representatives, not one has been passed thus far. In a few months, the country shall be facing another round of elections for representatives. At this early juncture, our members of Congress are already gearing up for that election. This has added to the present turmoil that the impeachment proceedings filed against President Estrada is causing. With this kind of scenario, chances are bleak for any of the women-related bills in this Congress, as they are not considered priority legislation. The numbers illustrate that women are making some progress in the field of politics and governance, but what is still disturbing is the quality of their participation, which still has a long, long way to go.

WOMEN IN PHILIPPINE POLITICS

Politics is mainly about power. And within the context of Philippine politics, as well as for a large of the world, women have not traditionally been the holders of power. Some countries are clearly more advanced than others in rectifying this historical error. In the Philippines, steps are also being taken towards this direction. How far this process goes depends on the political will of those in power, the support of the people and the conscious efforts of the Filipino women in general in working toward political, economic and social equality. Politics, as in many spheres of life in the Philippines, is still very much a male enclave. From the smallest government unit to the national level, men dominate over men. Gender relations remain traditional and male-centered.

The small numbers of women who are in power unfortunately are still devoid of genuinely enlightened consciousness on the subject of gender. A number of women legislators for example, had very little reluctance to admit that they have been voted into position largely because their families wield either political or economic power, or both, and because they have been chosen to carry on the role of their male kin. Many of the female members of the Senate and House of Representatives are members of a political family or closely related to a male politician. They are the wives, daughters, or sisters of political figures.

REMNANTS OF COLONIALISM

"Filipinos spent 400 years in the convent and 50 years in Hollywood. That's how best to describe our colonization by Spain and America," said Tapales, referring to Spanish Catholicism and U.S.-imported mass media. Before the Spanish arrived, Filipino women could own property and achieve status as medicine women and astrologers. "But with the coming of the Spaniards and Catholicism, the Filipino women's role was relegated to that of church and home." The spirit of the native Filipina woman was changed, Tapales said. At the time of the Spanish-American War in 1898, the Philippines declared independence from Spain.

Spain lost the war and ceded its colonies, including the Philippines, Puerto Rico, and Guam, to America. America introduced the public education system, a very important step for women. Americans also brought elections and political parties. "The women for 400 years, within the convent walls metaphorically speaking, have remained in the private domain," said Tapales. Even as women entered the American-inherited school system and became professionals, they still shied away from the political process because it was in the public realm. Politics were seen as dirty, and, more importantly, women could not take positions higher than their husbands'.

With this cultural history in mind, Tapales in her PhD dissertation at Northern Illinois University looked at covert politics, or politics beyond the electoral process. The approach showed that women "are powerful even if they are not in the electoral process." Women have had success implementing policy by being on executive staffs, advising politicians, and advocating from within non-governmental organizations (NGOs).

UN GOALS NOT MET

The Beijing Declaration in 1995 at the United Nation's Fourth World Conference on Women encouraged greater female participation in politics. In February 2005, the UN reviewed women's progress. Tapales participated in this review and reported that, in the Philippines, despite an increase in the quality of female politicians, there was not a great enough increase in quantity. The UN's global target was a 30 per cent rate of participation by women in government. There have been two female presidents in the Philippines: Gloria Macapagal-Arroyo, serving currently, and Corazón Aquino, who came to power in 1986. Both were beneficiaries of unorthodox "People Power" revolutions in which a male president was deposed.

Aquino's claim to having been elected in 1986 sparked the first People Power upsurge. The Philippine Congress has had as many as 17 per cent women delegates. In her study, Tapales collected data from local elections every three years from 1992 to 2001.

The numbers show that there was an increase in the proportion of women elected as local chief executives—mayors, governors, and captains of villages called *barangays*. For governors, the percentage of women elected steadily increased from 6.6 per cent in 1992 to 19 per cent in 2001. Municipal mayors saw a similar increase, with women's share increasing dramatically from 2.9 per cent in 1992 to 13.5 per cent in 2001. While these trends reflect an increased political role for women, Tapales pointed out that the Philippines has not yet reached the 30 per cent U.N. target. To reach this target, other countries, such as India and Pakistan, have adopted programs that set aside congressional or other leadership seats specifically for women.

WOMEN WHO WIN

As part of her study, Tapales sent out questionnaires for female politicians. She learned that most successful female candidates had certain characteristics in common. They were often married and between 60 and 65 years of age, which means they had completed the task of raising their children. They had spent about five years in lesser elected posts. A few had been village heads, or *barangay* captains. Most were politically active before being elected as political campaigners or members of the media or NGOs.

Most came from political families, their husbands or fathers also elected politicians. The women considered several factors important in their elections: family support, a well-recognized family name, their personalities, and the support of parties or organizations. Tapales said that the strength of such "kinship politics" does not indicate that these women are ill-prepared or unqualified to be successful. Kinship moves women into power, said Tapales, but the women she interviewed—their husbands often echoing this sentiment—said that they should be judged by what they accomplish in office. "The women who are in overt politics are really in the dynasties," Tapales says. "However, these women do things based on their own perceptions."

Tapales discovered that the increase in the number of women winning local elections was also a phenomenon related to term limits. Governors and mayors can serve three terms or nine years, after which they must step down for at least three years. Not infrequently a woman fills her husband's position on a temporary basis, between his nine-year stints. These women, known as "breakers," step down when required, even though some would prefer not to. Some of the women Tapales interviewed said they would rather step down than cause trouble in the family.

Breakers, Tapales said, account for much of the increase in percentages of women elected to local leadership positions in 1998 and 2001. Female politicians who carry on the work of their husbands are also partly responsible for the increases. President Aquino, for example, carried on the legacy of her assassinated husband Benigno Aquino, Jr. Marides Fernando, mayor of Marikina City, took her leadership role after her husband, Bayani Fernando, reached his term limit; she has stayed in the position since 2001.

Grace Padaca, governor of Isabela since 2004, is one counterexample to the general profile of female local chief executives. Padaca, who walks on crutches because of childhood polio, won her seat without family connections.

FEMALE AGENDA

These female leaders, said Tapales, do not initially appear to have priorities specifically geared toward the well-being of Filipino women. They focus instead on what they see as the needs of their constituents in general, issues such as agriculture and employment. Tapales found that local chief executives expressed concern for women and families, particularly in creating child-friendly communities with adequate daycare facilities and nutrition. They established provincial offices for women and found funding for these types of projects.

On a national level, women made changes that benefited their female constituents. President Aquino issued the 1987 executive order called the Family Code, which eliminated gender bias in adultery cases and introduced annulment into a country that did not allow for civil divorces. A 1991 code created sectoral representation in local councils; special seats were to be created for a women's representative, workers' representative and other groups' representative. This code, said Tapales, was never implemented because Congress did not pass a law to fund such elections, nor did it provide for a date to hold the elections.

In 1992 a bill was passed allowing women into the military academy and other male-dominated organizations. It also provided for women to establish credit and own land without the consent of a father or husband. Quantity Is Important With all of these accomplishments in the so-called female agenda, Tapales said that the general thought is that Filipina women are strong enough to move their agendas forward. They do not need affirmative action, many politicians-even female politicians-say. The quality of women's political participation is important, says Tapales, but so is the quantity.

Many people pushing for a female agenda are more effective than just a few. Tapales believes in affirmative action programs, quotas for elected politicians. She says that there is a need for better mechanisms than family connections for women to enter the political realm. While her PhD project showed her the power of covert politics, Tapales says that it is time for women to take more elected positions. "Let's put more women in overt politics," she says, "because in overt politics you really can do more than be influential behind the scenes or be an advocate of NGOs."

This should be considered as a work in progress which the author aims to further develop as a comprehensive situation paper that can both provide the reader a consolidated picture of the gender equality challenge in the country and motivate them on the need to contribute in changing the so-called "divides and mirages" in Philippine sexual politics. According to the latest gender disaggregated data, women constitute 37.9-million (49.6%) of the 76.5 million Filipinos as of May 2000. Almost 15.5-million are between ages 15 to 40 reflecting a young female population. However, while women constitute nearly half of the population, its status in the Philippine society is still characterized by sharp contradictions of obvious gains, on one hand, and glaring inequalities on the other.

One can find both major advancements for women's role and graphic gender inequality in specific areas of the society. The Human Development Report 2002 (UNDP) revealed that 35% of Filipino administrators and managers are women which is one of the highest in the world. Additionally, approximately 17.2% of all the legislative seats are occupied by women and 2/3 of professionals and technical workers are women. This puts the country's Gender Empowerment Measure (GEM) of 0.523 as the highest in East Asia. But a dark side of these gains exists. Thousands of women are discriminated in employment by virtue of marriage and parenthood.

Many more are contracted for 5 months to avoid regularization of employment while a glass ceiling for women pervades in many sectors of the society-especially in the fields of politics and the economy. Although the Philippines appears to be ahead of its neighboring countries by having 2 women presidents already, major hurdles are still in place for women to gain a firmer foothold in politics. It is still basically an elite-male dominated political landscape. While there is a perceptible increase in the number of women elected into government posts, assumption to institutional leadership does not necessarily translate into the expected degree of political clout. The question of resources also affects women's access to decision-making positions since women and men dc not enjoy the same access to resources that yields power.

The lack of economic power, similarly, deprives women of their rights and opportunities. Even the framework for sectoral political representation has evolved into missed opportunity. The party-list system, which provides for a focused women representation in the House of Representatives, is not useful nowadays due to the failure of any women-based party to get any seat in the 2001 elections. Fortunately, this is compensated by incremental increases in women politicians and bureaucrats at the national and local level. Additionally, the presence of a broad and active women's movement keeps the gender discourse alive with issues like reproductive rights, anti- abuse of women in intimate relationship (AWIR), domestic violence, anti-prostitution and trafficking, anti-rape and incest, equal employment laws, creation of Commission on Equality of Employment of Women, amendment of the anti-sexual harassment law and even the effective use of gender and development budget.

However, it must be noted that the Philippines is known for being a "motion is substance democracy". The consultative nature of government processes and the vocal posture of the women's movement can be seen as one of the successes of gender discourse. But the slow legislative mill and half-hearted policy reforms makes the discourse somewhat hollow in terms of final outcomes. While the Church has been promoting greater involvement of women, its stance on reproductive health brings it to the opposite side of the women advocacies. Thus, the struggle of the women's movement for more genuine gender equality and mainstreaming continues.

GENDER MAINSTREAMING IN LAW

The Philippines is known for its very liberal and progressive Constitution that was formulated during the euphoria of People Power Revolution in 1986. Gender equality is a key element of this Charter and as enshrined in Article II Section 14 of the 1987 Constitution, "the State recognizes the role of women in nation-building and shall ensure the fundamental equality before the law of women and men." Considering the unequal gender relations in the country, the Constitution further provided for women representation (as one of the 9 marginalized sectors) in the legislature through the party-list system (which should cover 20% of the lower house).

Finally, Article 13 Section 14 specifically mentioned that the "State shall protect working women by providing safe and healthful working conditions, taking into account their maternal functions, and such facilities and opportunities that will enhance their welfare and enable them to realize their full potential in the service of the nation". This legal framework promoting gender equality is in turn elaborated in various legislations and these include the following:

- Local Government Code of 1991

  Provides for the election of sectoral representation, including women, in local legislative councils.
- Party List Law

  Provides for the creation of women-oriented or women-based parties to compete under the party-list system. Women is one of the 9 sector identified in the law.
- Labor Code (1989)

  Covers issues such as night work prohibition, specifies that employers must provide special facilities for women, prohibition of discrimination against women in respect to terms and conditions of employment, prohibition of discrimination by reason of marriage of a woman worker.

WOMEN IN NATION BUILDING LAW

Republic Act 7192 (1991) is an act promoting the integration of women as full and equal partners of men in development and nation building. The law provides that a substantial portion of government resources be utilized to support programs and activities for women. The law also encourages the full participation and involvement of women in the development process and to remove gender bias in all government regulations and procedures. In relation to gender budgeting, the law specifically mandated all agencies to allocate a minimum of 5%, increasing to 30%, of all official development funds in mainstreaming gender concerns. Through executive directives however, this 5% allocation is further expanded to cover the total budget appropriations, not only development funds, of all government agencies and local government units in the country. This is known as the Gender and Development Budget or GAD.

- 1988 Comprehensive Agrarian Reform Law

  Gave Filipino women the right to own land that previously reverted to sons and other male family members.

- Republic Act 7688 (1994)

  An act giving representation to women in social security commission.

- 1990 Day care Law (RA 6972) and 1996 Paternity Leave Act

  Both of which acknowledge that children is both a parental and state responsibility.

- Anti-Sexual Harassment Law

  RA 7877 (1995) an act declaring sexual harassment unlawful in the employment, education or training environment.

- Republic Act 7822 (1995)

  An act providing assistance to women engaging in micro and cottage business enterprises.

- Republic Act 8353 (1997)

  An act expanding the definition of the crime of rape reclassifying the same as a crime against persons.

While the constitutional and legal framework acknowledges the need for gender mainstreaming, gender equality is indeed still a work in progress. Thus, one can find a myriad of projects, initiatives, and processes on the gender challenge that are corollary to gender-oriented legislations.

This includes:

- Philippine Plan for Gender Responsive Development (1995-2025). The National Plan for Women that consolidates the action commitments of the Philippines during the Beijing World Conference on Women. This is the over-all frame that is also the point of reference for the discussions and monitoring of gender mainstreaming.
- Gender and Development Budget (GAD). Integral to the national plan, it is aimed at "institutionalizing gender

concerns in the mainstream development process and agenda and not just peripheral programs and projects of the government". Concretely, it prescribes for the allocation of 5% of the government agency's/local government unit's budget on gender-responsive activities and projects. As a result, implementation of the development programs and policies of government also 1means women partaking a role in governance. As primarily stakeholders in the development process, women have the right to maximize their involvement in governance, be it at the local or national level.

- Framework Plan for Women (FPW). This is part of the Philippine Plan for Women which the current administration developed to focus on three thrust namely: promoting women's economic empowerment; advance and protect women human rights; and promote gender responsive governance. This plan identifies the concrete gender issues that will be addressed, pinpoint targets and indicators, name programs, formulates the implementation plan, and set-up tools for monitoring and evaluation.

It is obvious that the Philippines has a well-developed legal framework for gender equality. This is even reinforced by the ratification of international instruments on women (e.g. Convention on the Elimination of all Forms of Discrimination against Women or CEDAW) and clear commitments to the outputs of the UN Women Conferences. This is already a good handle for gender equality but their implementation and the "real politics" surrounding these legal norms leave so much to be desired.

THE POLITICAL-ELECTORAL SYSTEM

The 1987 Constitution describes the Philippines as a "republican and democratic State". Presidential form of government and a multi-party system with regular elections held once every 3 years. There are 3 branches of government: Executive, Legislative and Judiciary. Both the president and the vice-president have 6-year terms. The President presides over a bureaucracy of 27 Departments (Ministry). The single-term President and the Vice-President as well as the Senators and Party-List Groups are elected nationally. On the other hand, their respective constituencies elect District Representatives and municipal/city officials. The Congress is composed of two houses: House of Representatives (Lower House) and Senate (Upper House).

The House of Representatives are composed of district representatives and party-list representatives. There are currently 211 District and 12 Party-List Representatives. Party List Representatives are supposed to make up 20% of the Lower House but current problems in interpretation as well as implementation of the Party List Law remains problematic. Thus, only 5% of House is filled-up by party-list representatives. Each Representative has a term of 3 years. The Senate has 24 seats, half of which are up for elections once every 3 years. Each Senator has a term of 6 years. The Judiciary system is made up of the Supreme Court and the Lower Courts. The Supreme Court is composed of a Chief Justice and 14 Associate Justices.

There is an appeals court as well as regional and municipal trial courts. A Sharia court also exists for the Muslim population. The electoral system in the Philippines can be described in many ways. Its main character however is the plurality system in which all elective officials (except those under the party-list) are elected by direct vote of the people. This means that a citizen basically vote individuals-from the President to the village chief and councilors. Elections are held every 6 years for the President, the Vice-President, and for the Senators and every 3 years for the Representatives and the Local Government officials. In sum, it is a mixed system of party-list and direct vote on individual candidates. But beyond this Philippine electoral politics is still beholden to patronage and the 3Gs-guns, gold and goons. Patronage politics and personality politics are still the norms rather than the exception.

The multi-party system that emerged out of the post-Marcos democratization has not dislodged the traditional politics and elitist democracy that governed the country for many years. Thus, there is a multitude of political parties that exist. Firstly, the main political parties are not ideological or programmatic. They are primarily "personality- oriented" that revolves around a presidential candidate or a political family. This makes the measurement of women membership almost impossible since these parties have "revolving door membership" as individual or organizational alliances constantly shift in every election-with the winning president's party taking a windfall in membership at the start of his/her term.

Pura Villanueva Kalaw and Paz Mendoza Guazon, Pilar Hidalgo Lim, President of the National Federation of Women's Clubs and Josefa Llanes Escoda, president of the Girl Scouts of the Philippines". The General Council of Women was then established in Manila to direct the plebiscite campaign. Its aim was to draw the support of the broadest number of women. As it turned out, 447,725 women voted yes in the 1937 plebiscite. Interestingly, 44,307 women voted against the provision. What followed was a colorful history of women's foray into the various levels of electoral victories but generally pushed by familial affiliation and elite association. The year 2001 was a watershed in the era of "women in politics".

The women sector lost their representation with the failure of any women party to reach the 2% threshold of the party-list elections. The two competing parties garnered less than 200,000 votes amounting to 1% of the party-list vote. In a study commissioned by the Ateneo School of Government and the Friedrich-Ebert-Stiftung, the amorphous sectoral association did not spare the women's sector that is supposed to be the most cohesive as it deal with a group defined biologically. The study concluded that obviously "...there exists no sectoral vote. Groups representing sectors cannot rely on their sectoral constituencies to win them seats.

Certainly, the sectors have the numbers. Millions of peasants and workers can elect many representatives in the House. However, none of the sectors seem united enough or are aware of themselves as a sector with special interests and a point of unity in the electoral arena. Perhaps their votes are more oriented toward causes, personalities or parties." This observation is bolstered by the fact that in the 1998 party-list elections the women sector garnered 520,565 votes or 5.7% of the total votes cast. Six (6) women parties competed but only 1 party gained a seat only to lose it almost two years ago with mere 135,211 votes of 0.89%. The other competing party – Women Power Party-lost terribly by getting only 25.9% of the women's vote or a mere 46,831 or 0.3% of the total votes.

This "sectoral defeat" is aggravated by the fact there are more women registered voters than men (17.2-million to 16.9-million). The 2001 elections even showed a female turnout of 76.7% while the males are pegged at 75.9%. It must be noted that female participation declined from 87.1% in 1998. While this may be explained due to the fact that 1998 was a presidential election-when turnout is normally higher-it still underscores the absence of a "women vote" in the country. Nevertheless, this system is still an important venue for political involvement in the context of 3Gs elections. There are numerous obstacles for women to partake a bigger role and impact in politics. Leadership is still conceptualized in terms of male strength.

Social definitions of role still pervade the society with women are pictured as supportive of the "leader- husband" and whose main tasks are to entertain constituents (socialization and diplomacy) and provide charity work (social welfare or even dole-outs). The double- burden challenge also contributes to the "glass ceiling "in politics. Wives are supposed to take care of the next generations of the political family. The "old boys" nature of political relations and transactions also put the role of women in the margins. This reduces the access to resources and decision-making thus diminishes their political clout. However, we can find consolation of the incremental increase of women in various fields of public service.

While comparative figures are not available, the conventional wisdom and general observation is that women have become more present in the many fields of governance.

These presences are sometimes consolidated into ad hoc groupings of women. Women judges have a formal national organization while a network of local women officials are grouped under the so-called "4-L" which stand for League of Local Lady Legislators. We have to count also under this category the existing women's party as an interface of politicians and civil society activists. However, the most prominent "semi-politician's" group (or some would say future politicians) is the Congressional Spouses Association Inc. which gathers the husbands and wives of the Representatives.

For all intents and purposes, this is a women's group that has made some impact on women's issues like in the creation of women crisis centers around the country. Another significant venue for women in politics is the local government unit (LGU). Women have utilized many ways of participating in local decision-making. Since women organizations are spread-out all over the country (either as non-governmental organizations or people's organization), they are constantly included in normal consultations on local issues and concerns. As NGOs and POs, they can participate in the local development council if they are accredited.

Some cities even have a Women's Code or Charter that governs the promotion of women participation and the development of programs and services. To further elaborate the women's presence in the local level, the Department of Interior and Local Government has recently consolidated the women dimension of the local governance. Recent data showed that so far some 90,714 or 25% of the 354,387 total positions in local government units, from governors to Sangguniang Kabataan chairpersons are occupied by women. Specifically, out of the 354,387 total elective positions, 90,714 positions are occupied by women which includes 16 governors (out of 79), eight vice governors (out of 79), 97 board members, 16 city mayors (out of 114), nine city vice mayors (out of 114), 182 city councilors, 225 municipal mayors (out of 1,493), 144 municipal vice mayors and 1,731 councilors, 5,350 punong *barangays* (out of 41,917), 64,142 sanggunian *barangays*, and 18,794 sanggunian kabataan chairpersons.

Records also showed that a greater number of women are serving in appointive positions as *barangay* secretaries and treasurers than men. The DILG chief said a total of 49, 173 women occupy appointive positions wherein 23,983 serve as *barangay* secretaries as against 15,988 male, while there are 25,190 female *barangay* treasurers compared to 14,794 male. While these improvements in women's involvement in national and local governance are laudable gains, there are some variables that have to be considered. One is the "push factor" that leads these women to politics. A study made by Dr. Socorro Reyes of the Center for Legislative Development in 1992 revealed that 14 women members of the Congress believe that their blood relationship with a male politician helped them win their electoral seats through the use of the latter's political machinery.

Their knowledge of campaign tactics and strategies and the family's political name contributed in their winning. Our 2 women presidents are actually illustrative of this phenomenon. Corazon Aquino is the widow of the assassinated opposition leader and Gloria Macapagal-Arroyo is the daughter of a former president-both coming from the political and economic elite of the country. According to the Philippine country report on the State of Women in Urban Local Government, family connection is a major factor in political involvement. The study revealed that of their 17 women respondents "...15 had close relatives in either politics or government. Of the elected officials 8 had been encouraged by close family members to stand for election". Furthermore, "family political experience seems to be the main factor which makes Filipino women who, while aware of their own influence from the sidelines, transcend the covert area of politics...to the overt political domain of elections".

Another phenomenon is the so called "women benchwarmers". Due to term limits, wives and daughters have taken over the positions left by the husbands or fathers for one term and then the man makes a comeback. This has happened in Makati City and in some other localities. Even the wife of the ousted President Estrada's became a Senator due to votes of sympathy and of the loyalist hold-outs who are expecting his political comeback. While this simply reaffirms that the men, to a large extent, still control the political careers of women; there are some instances also where women have carved their own niche and in some cases, have outshone men as leaders of this country. One example is in the continuum of civil society activism and public administration.

Two women who now occupy Cabinet positions in the government held consecutively the presidency of the Caucus of Development NGO Networks (CODE- NGO)-the biggest NGO network in the country. Another woman Cabinet member was the former Secretary General of the peace advocates network. This demonstrates not only the strong role of women in civil society but also value of the women's movement as a 'political capital". Women's expressions of involvement in civil society could be through organizing along gender-specific issues and formation of all-women groups within broad coalitions as power-enhancing mechanisms. Groups such as the PILIPINA feminist movement, the militant GABRIELA women's group, the Ugnayan ng Kababaihan sa Pulitika (UKP- Network of Women in Politics), the KILOS KABARO (Act Sisters Coalition), and SIBOL Legislative Network have trail blazed women advocacies both in policies and in legislations.

There also exist a so-called "Philippine NGO Beijing Score Board" which evolved from the National Steering Committee (NSC) of NGOs for the United Nations Fourth World Conference on Women and this lead in the national monitoring of the government's implementation of the Beijing Platform for Action. Along with other women groups and gender-oriented institutions, they have succeeded in raising gender-specific issues such as domestic violence, prostitution, reproductive health, sexual harassment and rape. Intense lobbying efforts by the women's groups resulted in the passage of several landmark laws, among them the anti-sexual harassment law in 1995 and the anti-rape act in 1997.

The gains of the women's movement are basically achieved through various partnerships with the rest of the civil society. Women's agenda are also integrated in party platforms and even in legislative hearing and consultation. This gives a semblance of integration of gender issues in formal politics. The National Commission on the Role of Filipino Women works on the national policy of gender mainstreaming. Both houses of Congress have committee on women that investigates women issues to aid legislative actions.

Gender Budgeting (GAD) also has been used widely for gender sensitivity training and on women projects like day care centers and women shelters but some initial assessment also showed that they are sometimes used as "campaign kitty" of the politician's wife, diverted to social activities like ballroom dancing and even to cover for salaries. In sum, all these efforts are still on the level of uplifting the status of women rather than a sophisticated gender-balanced approach. There is not much differentiation on gender perspective and women's agenda. For many it is one and the same.

REASONABLE ACCESS TO EDUCATION

The Philippine educational system is a combination of public and private institutions with the State providing free education for elementary and secondary levels. The Constitution provides that without "...limiting the natural rights of parents to rear their children, elementary education is compulsory for all children of school age... (Article VIX, Section 2). There is no general discrimination of girls in education thus there is no marked differences exist in the educational status of Filipino women and men. Wide disparities exist, however, between urban and rural areas where government schools are few and far between and the peace and order situation often disrupt children's schooling. In terms of general enrolment, recent data indicated that there are slightly more boys than girls in elementary schools though in the 1997 the completion rate of girls was higher by 10%.

These proportions were reversed in favor of women in secondary or high school during the same school year.

Secondary enrolment rate as well as the completion rate for girls is higher by 10% over the boys. At tertiary and higher education level, women constitute 55.46% of the students. Another issue is the gender stereotyping of fields of study and specialization and its onward translation into the world of work where men generally occupy the highest occupational ranks and the highest paying positions. Women's larger responsibility for housework and for the family impedes their ability to use their educational training and skills for remunerative work.

One can also cite the issue of child labor. Though there are more male working children, the 1.5-million female working children are mainly sidelined from school due to demands of housework or assistance in family business. The 2001 Philippine Survey on Children revealed that among child laborers more males (59.6% against 40.4% to female) attended school during the school year 2000-2001. The following further exemplify the extent of women's share in the educational system:

- Literacy- Nationally, the literacy rate of females (94%) stood higher than the male's literacy rate (93.7%) in 1994. Employing a stricter definition of literacy (by including the ability to perform basic computational procedures), the Functional Literacy and Education and Mass Media Survey (1989) yielded considerably lower national functional literacy rates than those indicated by the censuses than men who were enrolled during the School Year 1997-1998 with 53.2% while only 46.8% for men. Specifically, women outnumbered men in Home economics courses (90.1 %), service trades (77.2%) and in Education and teacher training (69.2%). But they were a minority in Engineering (20.6%), Architectural and Town Planning (25.1%) and in Law and Jurisprudence (42.1%).
- Academic Degree Holders- During the SY 1996-1997, female graduates outnumbered the males in Trade, Craft and Industrial courses (98.6%), home economics courses (93.6%) and service trade courses (84.1%) but were a minority in Engineering courses (19.9%) and in architectural and town planning courses (29.3%).

- Skills Training- There were more men than women who are enrolled in Formal Technical Vocational Education and Training (TVET) courses during the school year 1995-1996 with women comprising only 39.4% Likewise, there were also more men who graduated during the same school year in formal TVET courses with 61.8%, leaving women with only 38.2%. However, in the non-formal training programs offered by the Technical Education and Skills Development Authority (TESDA) during the calendar year 1995, there were more female graduates with 54.4%.
- Education Institutions Officials- As of February 2000, 9 out of the total 16 regional directors of the Department of Education were women, or a total of 56.25%.
- Educational Workforce- The country's educational workforce is heavily female. In February 2002, three out of 5 (61.48%) school superintendents were women, while 38.52% were men. In the higher education institutions, there are slightly more male than female faculty members, with females covering 46.9%. The above figures indicate the reasonable access and success of women in the educational system. But at this stage stereotyping and pre-determined career path can already be discerned.

FEMINIZATION OF THE LABOR MARKET

The feminization of the Philippine labor market is one of the main manifestations of the country's integration into the global market. The international division of labor and the subsequent globalization as we see it now have transformed the role of women in society. In 1996, the labor force participation of women (LFR) was pegged at 49% but by October 2001 working women has reached 52.8% only to decline to 50.9% in January this year (vis-à-vis 80.6% for men). As of January 2003, women constitute 13-million of the 33.6 million labor force. Around 1.3-million are without work as compared to the 2.1-million unemployed men though historically women have had higher unemployment rates.

The latest available sex-disaggregated figures demonstrate further the role of women in the economy. Primarily, women have established their presence as labor and unskilled workers therefore reaffirming the graphical representation of women as workers in labor-intensive routine assembly line work. In terms of industry, the social skills of women are of course demanded in wholesale and retail trade where thousands of women are employed as "perpetual contractual" with 5-month cycle.

On another aspect, the total employed females are predominantly classified as wage and salary workers (5.6-million or 38.2%) and own-account workers (4-million or 35.2%). A total of 2.1-million or 52.2% of the employed women are unpaid family workers indicating a big segment of informal employment. Additionally, out of the total 11.9-million employed female, 2.5-million or 21.4% are high school graduates; 2.3- million or 19.4% are elementary graduates and 2.3-million or 19.1% are college graduates including those who have attained higher education. Women comprise 1.5- million or 39.6% of the total unemployed of 3.8-million. This rate has remained as of January 2003.

Even the National Commission on the Role of Filipino Women (NCRFW) declares that gender stereotyping by occupation persist. It revealed that "...there were more women than men in October 2001 among the professionals (68.5%), clerks (66.7%), officials of government and special-interest organizations, corporate executives, managers, managing proprietors and supervisors (58.1%), and service workers and shop and market sales workers (54.3%). Men, on the other hand, were mostly plant and machine operators and assemblers (92.0%), in farming, forestry and fishing occupations (83.4%) and in trades (71.7%)".

However, while the UNDP data on managers and administrators showed a 35% presence of women it is also instructive to have a look at the disaggregated data on several industries and qualify the extent of decision-making role of women in the labor market. It is the same reality in the government service. As of August 2002, the cabinet included 4 women (18.2%) heading the budget and management, labor and employment, science and technology and the social welfare and development departments. Likewise, the Commission on Higher Education, Civil Service Commission and the National Anti-Poverty Commission are also headed by women. Again, it is must reiterated here that almost 35% of the managerial and supervisory positions in government are occupied by women.

The media sector is not spared from this unfortunate reality. The paper "The State of Women and Media in Asia: An Overview" asserted that even though"...the number of women entering media is increasing, women have not gained much parity with men in terms of participation and decision-making in media. Top management is still largely male-dominated and patriarchal even as a few women hold senior positions in media organizations". None of the 6 major broadcast networks are headed by a woman and the top 4 newspapers have male chief editors. Women are basically in the high echelon by occupying positions on corporate communications and talent management. While some newspapers have women section editors, only the Newsbreak magazine has the top 3 editorial positions occupied by women.

It must be noted also that the top 3 media NGOs (Philippine Center for Investigative Journalism, Center for Media Freedom and Responsibility, and the Asian Institute of Journalism) are headed by women. Nevertheless, the paper also cited that even if "...women have become more visible particularly in radio and television as presenters, announcers and reporters, the gender division of labour is highly pronounced in production, creative and technical departments which are male-dominated. Women are usually announcers and newscasters whose youth and looks are given premium based on socially-defined standards" (ibid). And this "mirage of gender advancement" is also visible in the share of income.

According to the National Women Plan, as of 1993 for every 1 peso earned by a male, a female gets 0.358 in agriculture, 0.371 in wholesale and retail, 0.394 in manufacturing, 0.461 in finance, insurance and business service, and 0.433 in community, social and personal services. In terms of occupation, sales workers get only 0.355 pesos, production workers have 0.406 pesos, and for professional and technical workers a measly 0.461 pesos. This clearly indicates a violation of the "equal work for equal pay" principle and is bolstered by the fact that 54% of those engaged in unpaid work are women. Below are illustrations of how women are finally catching-up in the income divide in terms of nominal daily wage and average real wage.

QUO VADIS

The last three decades which saw the rise of the women's movement in the Philippines have resulted to mixed impact-with positive ratings in political participation and law reform but minus points in economic empowerment and sexual and domestic violence. The challenge of gender divide still pervades the Philippine society and the institutions and traditions that sustain it are continuously being buffeted by forces of change. However, the national efforts have to be scaled-up to regional and international level.

This is where the following groups have contributed in the gains of women empowerment and gender fairness:

- Center for Asia-Pacific Women in Politics (CAPWIP)- A non-partisan, non- profit and non-governmental regional organization (NGO) dedicated to promoting equal participation of women in politics and decision-making. It was established in 1992 by a group of women from the Asia-Pacific region who share a vision of governance that affirms gender equality, integrity and accountability, excellence, sustainable development and peace. They advocate transformative politics which is the use of power to create change towards economic, social and political equity between sexes and among sectors within the context of shaping a society that is just, humane and promotes a sustainable way of life. Their goals include: a) to create a critical mass of competent, committed and effective women politicians in elective and appointed positions in government; b) to develop a responsible female citizenry; and c) to influence female politicians and electorate to work together to transform politics and governance for the common good.

- 50/50 Asia Pacific Campaign- This is part of the Global Campaign led by the New York-based Women's Environment and Development Organization (WEDO). The campaign challenges governments all over the world to work for "a provisional minimum target of 30% representation of women in cabinet ministries and legislatures as well as local authorities by 2003 and equal representation by 2005". The campaign aims to improve the status of women worldwide as they are grossly under-represented in the higher echelons of decision making at virtually every political level.
- Asian Women's Resource Exchange (AWORC)- An Internet-based woman's information service and network in Asia. It is an initiative geared towards developing cooperative approaches and partnerships in increasing access and exploring applications of new information and communication technologies for women's empowerment. AWORC aims to help expand existing regional networks in the women's movement, promote electronic resource sharing and build a regional information service that will support various women's advocacies specifically those that are very critical for the women in our region. AWORC aspires to contribute to global efforts to address gender disparity on the Internet. It is geared towards building sustainable, as well as promoting Net literacy and enhancing social activism among individual women and women's organizations.
- Coalition Against Trafficking in Women-Asia Pacific (CATW-AP)- This is an international network of feminist groups, organizations and individuals fighting the sexual exploitation of women globally. Sexual exploitation - especially prostitution and trafficking - violates women's human rights and is a severe form of discrimination. CATW brings international attention to trafficking in women and girls, prostitution, pornography, sex tourism and bride selling.
- Asian Pacific Women's Watch is another example of different Asia Pacific partners coming together in coalition to work jointly on regional issues. After the Beijing conference, 1995, the efforts of Asia Pacific NGO Working Group were directed towards the monitoring of the Beijing Platform For

Action (BPFA). The existence of these networks is a manifestation of the growing women's movement in the various countries of the region. While most of these groupings are lead by Filipino women, it is evident that common issues are now confronted by women collectively. It is widely said that the Philippines lead in gender equality in East Asia but one cannot ignore the developments in the other countries. In the end, any gain is good news and any advancement is a victory for women and gender equality.

The Philippines is an archipelagic country with a Republican form of government, Manila being its capital. The country has around 7,100 islands, including three major ones, namely Luzon, Mindanao and Palawan. These three islands and also several other smaller ones are prone to earthquakes. The Philippines has 73 provinces with a population of approximately 82,841,518 (estimation of July 2001) comprising of Christian Malays 91.5%, Moslems 4%, Chinese 1.5%, and others 3%. The religions are Roman Catholic 83%, Protestant 9%, Islam 5%, Buddhism and others 3%. The literacy rate for the age of 15 years and older reaches 94.6%.

The means of livelihood of the population is comprised of various sectors: agriculture, industry and services. Under the 1987 Constitution, the government of the Philippines consists of three branches, namely, the legislative, the executive and the judiciary. The legislative is divided into two, namely, the Senate having 24 members and the House of Representatives having a maximum of 250 members. Quantitatively, women's political participation in the Philippines is higher than in Indonesia. In the Philippines, among the 24 Senators, three are women, whereas among the 212 members of the House of Representatives, 38 are women.

Among the 727 members of the Provincial Assemblies, 120 are women. In the executive branch, among the 24 members of the cabinet, five are women, among 74 governors, 14 are women; and among 1,635 mayors, 132 are women. The high number of women holding strategic positions in the Philippines is supported by several factors, among others: political education and awareness, and the women's own motivation to be involved in politics. The history of their struggle and the challenges they faced to reach those significant positions varies.

Those coming from families with political backgrounds or from rich and famous families, such as most female members of the House of Representatives who are either wives of Senators or relatives of officials in the executive branch, do not experience any significant obstacles. However, those starting their career from the bottom of the ladder experience huge challenges from various parties. The obstacles and challenges faced by female politicians in the Philippines in improving and strengthening women's positions in the politics are generally as follows:

a. *The system:* The direct general election system requires a large amount of funds, popular candidates and political support from various parties. Female politicians often not have sufficient funds or support. Funds are required for a campaign, done mainly through printed and electronic media as well as direct campaign and by conducting training for prospective voters. In this case, female politicians often do not have sufficient funds.
b. *Culture:* The gender stereotype of women as housewives who supposedly have a lack of managerial skills and leadership qualities is the most common means to attack female candidates. Further, there is a lack of work support for women who are actively involved in politics.

The direct election of members of the Congress and other political positions in the executive branch, does not provide sufficient opportunities for women to compete, because in the end, women holding significant positions are mostly rich or popular women coming from families with political backgrounds. For that reason, female activists and parties who are aware of women's issues such as *Akbayan*, a party established in 1998 concerned with women's issues, proposed to introduce a quota system for women. The fact that famous women are elected certainly has an impact on the quality of women's political participation in the Philippines, because they do not really have any sense of crisis.

The female members of the House of Representatives coming from families with political backgrounds, for example, stated that they do not face any problem in being female politicians. However, those starting their career from the bottom of the ladder such as Vicki Vega (Councilor in Angeles City), who started her career through a long struggle, experienced structural and cultural obstacles in being female politicians. To become a politician, Vega performed her political campaign using posters, she visited the voters one by one, she went to community centers, and she was fair and realistic in giving her political promises.

Ever since she was elected, she has been actively striving for women's rights by means of training and advocacy for female candidates in her region. The Governor of Bulacan, Josephine de la Cruz, clearly explained the obstacles faced by female politicians, among others: the political structure that is dominated by men, discrimination in terms of cooperation, lack of support from political parties, limited access to leadership process and managerial skills, as well as lack of support from the men and fellow women, limited funds and lack of popularity.

Therefore, in order to become leaders, it appears that women need to work twice as hard to prove their capability as key officials either in the parliament or in the executive branch. In the context of improving women's participation in politics, Governor de la Cruz also identified women's strategic needs, such as constantly monitoring the enforcement of law and providing advocacy so that there are certain positions for women in the local government. In order to support women's empowerment activities, Governor de la Cruz also established the Women's Empowerment Commission led by her at the provincial level.

It has among its duties the task of giving input to the government regarding women's empowerment programs, monitoring the implementation of women's empowerment activities in each department and cooperating with NGOs in promoting women's issues to be included as an agenda. In order to provide more opportunities for women to participate in politics, *Akbayan*, together with the Center for Legislative Development (CLD), are of the opinion that the general election law should be amended. *Akbayan* and CLD propose a quota of 30 per cent or more for women. Direct elections mostly rely on popularity and lacks mechanisms to test the candidates' capabilities.

This disadvantages not only female candidates, but all other candidates, due to the neglected factor of capacity in leadership, as stated by Prof. Emmanuel A. Loyco from CLD. In implementing activities to improve women's participation in politics, cooperation with NGOs is quite an important thing to be conducted by female members of the House of Representatives and also by women's empowerment bureaus in the Philippines. They are cooperating in:

1. Identifying women's needs.
2. Determining priority issues to be included as part of the agenda of the legislative and the executive branches in formulating policies.

The support for strategies to strengthen women's political participation also comes from civil society groups in the form of:

1. Civic education.
2. Training for candidate female members of the legislative/ executive or female political cadres on gender and gender perspectives in the policy-making process as well as campaigning skills such as through the media, how to act and organize a campaign using one's own funds.
3. Support for female legislators in identifying issues to be included in the agenda of legislative sessions through research.

According to Prof. Emmanuel A. Leyco, the candidates must bear in mind that it would be more effective if the campaign raises issues about the community's practical needs, such as the economy, job opportunities, etc., rather than women-specific issues such as rape. It would gain the sympathy of various actors including men, because the economy is everyone's concern. Integrated activities of practical (economic) needs and strategic (advocacy) needs of women in order to strengthen women's position in the community are also conducted by the Democratic Socialist Women of the Philippines (DSWP), an NGO having more than 100 branch offices throughout the Philippines.

In strengthening women's position in politics, both in the legislative as well as executive branches, the central government of the Philippines has allocated 5% of its budget for women's empowerment in all ministries. In addition, in order to provide input to the government and to monitor women's empowerment program in all departments using the government's budget, in 1975 the central government formed the National Commission for Women's Role. This commission only exists at the central level. However, in the Philippines, it seems that women's issues would get more attention if the leaders/policy-makers is women.

This is shown in the case of the Governor of Bulacan Josefina de la Cruz. She also has the responsibility of chairing the Central Commission for Women's Empowerment at the provincial level, which has the duties of identifying women's issues, monitoring women's empowerment in all departments in her province and cooperating with NGOs in strengthening women's participation in politics through training, dialogue and research. How about in Indonesia? Politics in a narrow sense is the media/instrument/facility for expressing the demands and interests of women, namely equality and fairness; for obtaining equal protection and treatment before the law.

For this purpose, women's political movement is not only about striving for the number of female members in the parliament, but more importantly about striving for their interests to be expressed. In Indonesia, women's political participation is very low compared to the Philippines. The indirect general election system gives a strong role to political parties dominated by men as the centre of political power to express the community's interests, including that of women's. A process is required to enable the sharing of the same or similar perceptions on women's issues, women's interests related to gender unfairness faced by women and also the same commitment to settle such problems as a part of the democratization process.

On the other hand, women's traditional role/stereotype, the structure of political parties dominated by men and women's limited access to information regarding their political rights as citizens have made women isolated from their public role, specifically their political role. Therefore, a process is required for the empowerment of women with respect to their political participation, the empowerment of political parties so as to give ample room for the women in parties through amendments of laws regarding the general election, the empowerment of women's role bureaus at the provincial and regional levels in order to better identify women's strategic needs in politics by cooperating with NGOs concerned about women's issues, and also the empowerment of female legislators to enable them to be more vocal in expressing women's interests in the legislature.

1. The empowerment of women in politics can be conducted through the following steps:
   - Identifying female cadres concerned about gender and political issues.
   - Organizing and improving their capabilities with respect to women's political rights by using gender as the instrument of analysis.
   - Forming a group comprised of trained participants and making it as the center for women's political empowerment.
   - Cooperating with NGOs in sustainable empowerment for those having many activities including economic empowerment as an effort to meet their practical needs.
2. The empowerment of political parties through the following steps:
   - Workshops with the aim to synchronise perceptions on women's interests in politics.

- Advocacy on amendments to the general election laws so that a quota for women in the parties may be established.
- Empowerment of male and female candidates of political parties so as to have gender sensitivity.

3. The empowerment of the executive branch
   - Assistance to women's empowerment bureaus at the regional and provincial levels under the local Social Bureau so as to be more sensitive with respect to women's strategic interests specifically in politics.
   - Conducting advocacy so that there be more women holding strategic positions through regional regulations.

DEVELOPING GOVERNMENT'S RESPONSIBILITIES THROUGH THE EMPOWERMENT OF CIVIL SOCIETY

Like Indonesia, the Republic of the Philippines is also an archipelagic country consisting of about 7,100 islands, with a population of approximately 82 million people, according to the estimate in July 2001. Its social life is also varied, a result of the different ethnic cultures in the society. In terms of religious composition, Christians predominate by far at 91.5% of the population, while Muslims make up 4%, Chinese 1.5% and others make up 3% of the total. The Philippines also boasts a high literacy rate, with 94.6% literacy for the whole population (15 years upward), with 94.3% literacy for women and 95% for men.

The large percentage of the literate female population, which almost equals that of men, significantly affects women's role in Philippine regional and national politics. This is due to their ability to access information and to take part in public decision-making processes, and more particularly, to be involved in campaigning and in competing for seats or appointments in the legislative, executive or judicial branches of government.

The latest data from the Centre for Legislative Development (CLD) in Metro Manila states that three (13%) out of the currently existing 24 senators, 37 (17%) out of the 211 House of Representatives (HoR) members, 2,198 (17%) out of the 12,665 city council members, 10 (13%) out of the 77 deputy governors, 192 (12%) out of the 1,548 deputy mayors, 15 (19%) out of the 74 governors, 241 (15%) out of the 1,635 mayors, and one (6.7%) out of the 15 chief prosecutors, are women. The great number of women holding strategic positions in the three institutions is a sign of the progress of women's political participation in the Philippines.

In general, the political participation of the Philippine people can be seen during elections, whether for mayors, regional and national representatives, governors, or the president. They welcome this particular democratic process joyfully, holding hope for changes after a candidate has been elected. Political participation is also seen in the supervisory activities of the work of the executive, legislative, and judicial institutions. The social groups actively carrying out this supervisory activity include labourers, farmers, youth, and women, as well as professionals, educators, NGOs and the Church. They also have representatives in the legislature.

The Philippines is still a part of the Asian region and has many similarities to Indonesia, in terms of their very pluralistic and multicultural societies. Obstacles for women's participation in politics among others come in the form of cultural barriers, most notably the stereotyping of women with their domestic roles and responsibilities, the Church's influence that places women as good mothers, obedient and loving wives, and the negative perception of politics. Structural obstacles faced by women come in the form of the electoral system, economic barriers and educational factors. Besides the similarities between the two countries, there are also differences, for example, in the electoral systems.

In Indonesia, the prevailing electoral system is the PR system, or representation through the legislative institution. In contrast, the Philippines uses a parallel system (FPTP) of

PR where candidates compete fiercely with one another. The similarities and differences found during the study visit were analyzed by every participant, the clusters of similarities and differences were then discussed and summed up to obtain a final conclusion whether they could be applied or not in the context of Indonesia. Previously, it was mentioned that women's political participation in the Philippines could also be seen from the activities of overseeing the process of formulating public policies, whether through the executive or the legislative institutions.

For example, the passing of the bill on anti-violence and anti-trafficking cannot be separated from the role of social groups, particularly NGOs. They actively lobbied the Senate and the HoR to ensure that the bills were promptly ratified. Prior to this, they actively approached various other social groups by promoting their ideas about those bills through group discussions. After receiving support from the public, they then pressured the legislative bodies. Finally, the HoR ratified those bills. The NGOs involved among others were Pilipino, one of the women NGOs existing in the Philippines since 1981, and the Democratic Socialist Women of the Philippines (DSWP).

The close cooperation between NGOs and other social groups is quite significant in influencing public policy-making in the Philippines. This requires responsiveness of the government to public aspirations and needs which also applies to addressing women issues. Although there is no Ministry for Women's Empowerment in the Philippine administration, the in 1975 government established the National Commission on the Role of Filipino Women (NCRFW). This national commission functions to give counsel to the President and help the cabinet in policies and programs for women's development.

Its main interventions in policy are channeling particular acts like the Act on Anti-rape, influencing the legislative agenda to become more gender-responsive and to prioritize legislative agendas for women. It also tries to increase public awareness on Gender and Development (GAD). The mechanism works by organizing the legislative groups, whether in the Congress or women NGOs as lobbyists. To take a concrete example, the Bulacan Province is led by Josefina de la Cruz, a female governor. She is one of the 15 female governors among the 24 governors in the Philippines. Governor de la Cruz' concern about women issues in her region prompted her administration to establish a Women's Centre.

Operating under the supervision of the National Commission, it is the only women's institution established at the local level. The selection of people - mainly from NGOs - to be involved in the Women's Centre was very tight. Out of the 200 NGO activists who registered themselves, only 24 were selected. These 24 people were further reduced to 12, and it is these people who are now involved in the Women's Centre. The duty of this institution is to directly serve the public, especially women, including offering medical aid. Creating a relationship between civil society and political institutions in the context of developing a responsive government, as has been illustrated above, can be achieved by strengthening cooperation among social groups.

With close cooperation among those social groups, civil society can reinforce its bargaining position *vis-a-vis* the government. In this way the government will heed and consider voices that constitute the aspirations of the public before making or launching a public policy. Sharing the same vision before submitting a concept to the government or the legislative institution is the root of all advocacy activities, thus the importance of close cooperation among social groups. Why? Because both the executive, i.e. the government and the legislature will only make a public decision after careful consideration. Whenever there are two different streams of opinions concerning an issue, revolving around a bill for example, then that will hinder and block its ratification.

This happened in the Philippines when there were two different streams of opinion concerning a bill on reproductive rights and a bill on anti-rape. In the former, one of its points mentioned abortion, and the Church opposed this. In the latter, the point of contention was that of domestic violence. Some felt that the bill applied only to those who are married, while others felt that the law applies also to couples who are not officially wed. In the end, both bills were delayed in their ratification. On the one hand, when certain social groups fought for a seat-quota of 30% in the legislative institution, they did not receive a positive response from female legislators who felt they did not need any special treatment.

These women MPs felt they could achieve their goals following 'normal' procedures, by relying on their individual capacities and competing with their male colleagues. On the other hand, outside of the party and among NGO activists they feel that Philippine women's lack of opportunity to stand and compete in elections is due to several factors, among others: local culture, resistance from the Church, and the image of politics itself. In particular, the main obstacle was the direct electoral system whereby those who possess popularity and wealth are able to obtain many votes. For those owning neither capital, popularity nor wealth, they are beaten in the middle of the competition, even though they may be sufficiently capable.

Unsurprisingly, female politicians holding positions in the legislative institution in the Philippines are artists (who can bank on popularity gained in the entertainment sector), and those who come from wealthy families, etc. In general, it can be said that the success of these female politicians is also derived from the fact that they hail from certain powerful and wealthy clans, even if they claim that their success was due to their capabilities. It is thus understandable that the issue of quotas was not considered important for these socially privileged female politicians. However, several women NGOs and political parties continue to actively fight for quotas, despite the fact that 12 years of struggle have failed to make it a reality.

The dynamics of public empowerment in Indonesia through the strengthening of social groups has much in common with the conditions in the Philippines. Many NGOs have emerged and conducted advocacy and empowerment for the public. These include their goal to affect the public policy-making process. They contend that they are truly on the side of the people. Considering that the conditions are not too different from Indonesia, the success and weakness in the advocacy activities of civil society groups in the Philippines could be used as comparative material for learning. The successes can add to their strategic tools as steps that could be adopted, whereas the weakness can be used as a means for introspection.

In the context of creating a relation between civil society and political institutions to develop a responsive government, helping social groups to avoid interna! conflict is much needed to avoid that these conflicts becoming obstacles in determining central issues and strategies in advocacy. This does not mean that these kinds of strategies have not been applied in Indonesia because Indonesian NGOs have also adopted similar struggles in strategies. Although advocacy takes a long time in the Philippines, at least by finding common conditions, it can become a mirror for reflection about the importance of a united vision of social groups to bring down the absolutist power of the state. In conditions of weak social solidarity, toppling the absolute power of the state becomes impossible.

In the Indonesian context, the following measures could be taken to empower social groups:

- Conduct a program on building awareness of civil society's political rights in the form of advocacy and campaigns.
- Conduct political discussions, training and workshops.
- Mobilize civil society groups to organize themselves into a unified and independent community to struggle for their rights and to resist State domination.
- Formulate a united vision among social groups.
- Create alliances for advocacy and to reduce state power.

The next stage would be to attempt to induce transparency in the government for the purpose of involving the community in public policy-making. It is this kind of public involvement that can develop a public sense of belonging and help unify people in facing societal and political problems. The increasing complexity of problems faced by women nowadays demands them to increase their participation in political decision-making. The belief that it is women who truly know what they really need makes the above demand a necessity. When a policy related to women is made without consulting a sufficient number of their representatives it could affect them adversely and produce counterproductive results.

Take for example, the forced use of female contraceptives that are dispensed without due consideration of the users' health. Women's groups also believe that hostile decisions and policies such as war, etc., are a result of the dominance of 'macho' power structures which are devoid of a 'feminine and motherly touch'. The fact that women make up over 50 per cent of the entire human race is another reason why their equal representation in decision-making institutions should be attained. One agenda of paramount importance in the women's movement today is to increase women's political participation. This makes it possible for them together with their male counterparts to formulate decisions at the legislative, executive and judicial bodies at all levels.

A number of policies and action plans have been designed to achieve this end, such as the increasingly popular discourse on the need to achieve a 'critical number' which is often referred to as women's quota for legislative seats. In connection with this growing discourse, the author had the opportunity to take part in the Asian Study Visit program to the Philippines from 31 August to 7 September 2002. The visit was aimed at enabling the participants to closely observe women's political participation in the Philippines, the process of drafting and enacting laws, the electoral process, the obstacles encountered, and the role played by both the government as well as NGOs in addressing the need to enhance women's political participation. The author would like to present some of her findings from the Philippine study tour, and will try to adopt them, wherever relevant, to the Indonesian context.

The Philippine Constitution provides a bicameral legislature which is directly elected. Compared to Indonesia, political parties in the Philippines are less dominant: any candidate can go directly to the public and run for, say, president. In order to win, a candidate needs money, close relations with political figures, and above all, popularity. Anyone having these 'qualifications' is likely to be the next winner. A number of women politicians and public officials that we met had these qualifications.

The Philippine Party List Law reserves 20 per cent of seats in the House for marginalized groups such as peasants, fishermen, women, youth groups and disabled people as long as they are able to obtain a minimum vote of 25 for each seat reserved. In 1998, the Adbanse Pinay, a feminist political party, won one seat, but lost support during the 2001 elections. The 30 per cent quota for women is still debated heatedly in the Philippines. Most women House members that we spoke to, still disagree on this topic, asserting that women deserve seats in the legislature for their eligibility and capability, and not because of a reservation or a quota system.

On the other hand, such groups as *Akbayan Muna* and *Adbanse Pinay* (both new parties), the NCRFW (the National Commission in the Role of Filipino Women, a government organisation), the DSWP (Democratic Socialist Women of the Philippines), *Pilipina* and *Gabriela*, two feminist NGOs, are aggressively fighting to achieve this quota. Women candidates have a fair chance of being elected as local officials. Councillor Vicky Vega was elected by an absolute majority as a member of Angeles City Council. Several other women made their ways to Barangay Kagawad seats (equivalent to the *kelurahan* village council in Indonesia).

These women gained victory due to their concrete action in the community where they live. Prior to their political service, they had worked as midwives, schoolteachers, and church activists. It was due to their past activities that their local constituents fully supported them and even helped finance their campaigns.

This fact indicates the serious need to politically empower Indonesian women. We should however not take a narrow view that women's political participation can only be measured by their number in institutions and ignore their 'political participation' in other sectors. Women acting as mothers who give birth to their children nurture them and prepare them as future leaders should also be considered to be engaged in a form of political participation. The bravery demonstrated recently by Indonesian housewives protesting against the increase of the cost of electricity should also be seen as a form of political activism. Women's political participation should be seen from a wider perspective, so that the quest to improve their image, to boost their intelligence, and to make them more aware of their vital role that will improve their lives, the lives of the family and the community, should be supported by everyone.

The electoral law passed in February 2003 by the Indonesian House of Representatives indicates that the future elections will feature PR open list system. This means that political parties still retain their role as 'kingmakers' in the legislature, even though nowadays voters can directly access and contact their favourite candidates. Similar to their Philippine colleagues, many Indonesian women politicians enjoy advantages brought about by their close connections to popular politicians and their access to wealth. Women candidates need to process this reality and make use of it if they desire to come forward and win in the competition.

The demand to have a quota system implemented for women in parliament is conditional on the capability of the political parties to support each candidate. A major political party may not find it difficult to reserve 30 per cent of seats for women in their party structure, but there is the danger that the women could be manipulated in the prevalent practice of corruption, collusion and nepotism (korupsi, kolusi dan nepotisme, KKN) in Indonesia. Small political parties may only be able to allocate 10 to 15 per cent of seats for their women candidates. What is more important is how the aspirations and interests of women can be understood and fought for by all parties, not just women legislative candidates.

Problems faced by women should be seen as being the problems of humanity, so that everyone should feel called upon to find a solution, whatever their sex or gender. Another challenge related to the quota policy is the need to improve the quality of women parliamentarians. Often we hear people complain about the limited ability of women parliamentarians who are unable to deal with 'hard' problems in the area of state management and the economy. To make sure that this quota scheme does not act as a boomerang against women, women parliamentarians should be given time to increase their knowledge and hone their skills so that they can perform as qualified politicians ready to give their very best for the country.

Another point that should be noted is the fact that women leaders do not always support women's causes. This is something that our Philippine friends deplored. Thus the crux of the matter is not the mere existence of women officials in state institutions, but how they fight for the interests of the women they purport to represent.

In light of this reality, training women politicians, officials and parliamentarians to adopt a comprehensive gender perspective is of paramount importance. In fact, possessing knowledge and an understanding of gender issues should be considered a criterion of political recruitment. For local and regional elections, women should be encouraged to show their true abilities and achievements to gain support from the people who would then defend, choose and even campaign for them because of their belief in their candidates' abilities. To achieve this, women should attempt to learn as much as they can about the conditions and problems of the locality where she lives.

Borrowing from the Philippine experience, it is best to adopt a PR system or mixed method for choosing a village head (*lurah*) or sub-district head (*camat*) elections in Indonesia. There have to be guarantees that the whole process be conducted in a fair and transparent manner and which also allows room for criticism. The elected leaders should be the best candidates who have the ability to solve problems faced by the people regardless of their sex.

THE POLITICAL PARTICIPATION AND EMPOWERMENT OF WOMEN

Many Filipino women have just began to realize their political rights. Although the increase in the number of women holding positions in the government has yet to reach a significant amount in numbers, the political participation of women has begun to emerge. They realize that the political rights they own do not only make them voters but also potential political candidates.

This can be proven with the existence of government organizations or non-government organizations which are beginning to care and think of the importance of the political participation of women at policy-making level, among others: the Center for Legislative Development (CLD), the House of Representatives (HoR), the Senate, the Akbayan Party, the Center for Asian Women in Politics (CAPWIP), the National Commission in the Role of Filipino Women (NCRFW), the Governor of Bulacan Province, Councilor Vicky Vega and female officials at the local levels, specifically in Angeles City. Last but not least is the enthusiasm of village women to participate in the political arena is present even though they commence at the lowest level, namely, the village.

To empower women, Filipino women have exerted various efforts, among others:

- Educate voters and citizens;
- Train female candidates;
- Improve the political participation of women through the media, namely in the form of training them on how to make news imbued with a gender perspective and training women to speak, particularly through the mass media;
- Organize women in communities, especially young women;
- Advocacy skill and public speaking training for organization members in all regions;
- Establish relations with other parties (with various professions) to become aware of gender perspectives, for example with physicians, teachers etc.;

- Raise various gender issues in forums/seminars;
- Promote the 30 per cent quota through forums/seminars;
- Disseminate information related to gender balance.

Seen from the data above, it is evident that men dominate politics in the Philippines. Women serving in policy-making positions are not more than 10 per cent though the majority of the voters are women. Issues on violence against women (not only physical violence, but also sexual violence and economic exploitation), on the trade in women and children and on reproductive health, have instigated the majority of Filipino women to join forces to attempt to influence policy makers so that public policies made do not discriminative against them. This is proven by their perseverance in proposing several bills five years ago concerning women problems such as trafficking. These proposals are scheduled to be approved no later than the end of this year.

Subsequently, the Anti-rape Law and the Domestic Violence Law are also being currently proposed.

- The *Akbayan* Party, being the only party that still maintains its goals for the achievement of the quota of 30 per cent for women, puts forward its aspirations through one of its members serving in the legislature. Although the representative of *Akbayan* is not a feminist, the party can still channel its aspiration through that person by way of giving materials on the importance of increasing the number of women in the legislature.
- The CAPWIB, being an NGO existing at the national level, has its own strategies, namely, by way of gathering persons or groups from different backgrounds to understand their problems. Subsequently, the problems are included in their agenda. Basically, they work first at the local (field) level and then put forward women's aspirations at the legislative level.
- The issues raised do not concern women problems only, but also general public ones such as economic problems.

THE BIGGEST BARRIERS FACED IN THE EMPOWERMENT OF WOMEN'S POLITICAL ROLE

Cultural Barriers

- Although the majority of women play roles as mothers and wives, the decision-making in families is still dominated by men. In the political realm, women politicians are also often harassed by male politicians. Relations in patriarchal culture reduce the women to inferior beings.
- The existence of a negative perception toward politics is also a barrier. Some women do not want to participate in politics because politics is deemed to be full of nasty games.

Structural Barriers

- To become a politician one must have popularity.
- Politics is expensive and consequently women must posses a lot of money in order to engage in it.
- The existence of family/dynastic relations also poses problems.
- Most politicians are men and the majority of them oppose the representation of women because they are often seen as threats.

Successful Strategies/Campaigns

- Women must show their capability.
- Put up posters along the roads to attract attention.
- Approach women door-to-door.
- Develop a good personal image in the community.
- Always improve the level of professionalism and increase self-confidence.
- Get in touch with fellow activists in NGOs to get moral and material support.
- Seek funding support by making a list of names of those who can be contacted. This is conducted by directly meeting the person concerned or by sending an SMS and lobbying over the telephone.

- Use funds to the best of their ability and by being selective.
- Always shake hands with the community members they met.
- Aim to be popular.
- Always give good service to the community. This could be done by performing direct social service in all sectors of the community (women, the handicapped and youth).

Lessons Learned from Unsuccessful Strategies and Efforts

- Do not neglect constituents.
- A good relationship with the community must always be developed for the public to base future interactions on.
- There is not much support for women, hence it is necessary to seek support by lobbying and approaching key persons at the grassroots to jointly put forward their aspirations to the policy-making level.
- Genuine and strong lobby and advocacy skills.
- Women are very often defeated in a campaign due to money problems. A special strategy needs to be devised in seeking and regulating finances.
- Effective fund raising is a priority for susess.
- Women need to always improve their own capabilities and professionalism, so that men do not denigrate their existence in politics.
- Ned to constantly upgrade skills.

4

Community-based Movements of Japanese Women

Since the early 1980s the Japanese have talked a lot about the internationalization of their society. Through the word "internationalization" they have discussed the importance of bilateral communications between Japan and foreign countries, for example, saying that the Japanese should pay greater heed to the global situation, and try to make themselves better understood by people overseas. Some went on to say that the Japanese had to learn the "international" ways of thinking and behaving, and Japan become a real member of the global community.

Bioethics was no exception. Modern Japanese bioethics began in the early 1970s. The Japanese women's liberation movement started in 1970, and they fought against an anti-abortion movement that was led by the government. This was the beginning of Japanese bioethics. Japanese bioethics started as feminist bioethics. This is a very important theme, but we do not have enough time to discuss it today. Women's fight against the government has continued from the 1970s into the 1990s.

In the 70s, they argued three points, namely, (a) the state should not interfere with the individual in women's sex and reproduction, (b) abortion was a freedom and right of women, (c) we will have to create a new society where women want to give birth of their own will. Their fight was mainly against the Japanese government. They did not necessarily know much about world wide women's liberation movements. (And, of course, western feminism knew nothing about Japanese feminism in the 70s.)

Their main attention was focused on raising consciousness among Japanese women and strengthening solidarity. Japanese feminism itself began in the early 20th century. They have continued a long fight for women's rights throughout this century. The 70s women's lib movement was a contemporary version of this historical Japanese feminism. Discourse among the pro-choice movement of Japanese feminism underwent a slight but profound change in the early 80s. They started to speak of freedom of abortion under the name of "fundamental human rights" of a woman.

In this they were influenced by the world wide feminism movements of the time. In 1975, the first International Women's Conference was held in Mexico; leaders of Japanese feminism took part and brought back information from around the world. They were faced with women's conditions in the third world. Some of them were shocked by the fierce debate between women from advanced industrial countries and women of the third world. In 1980 the Treaty for the abolishment of discrimination against women was adopted in Copenhagen. In that treaty women's rights in sexuality and reproduction were confirmed.

Japanese feminism, influenced by these world wide movements, started to assert that a woman's reproduction should be based on the "fundamental human rights" of a woman. For example, a women's lib group, SOSHIREN, said in 1982 that freedom of choice whether to give birth or not should be a "fundamental human right" of a woman. And they emphasized that their movement was linked with contemporary world wide feminism. The Japan Association for family planning asserted the same thing in 1983 and stated that this issue must be discussed and reconsidered based on the contemporary world wide consensus.

They looked overseas and found in the international standard "fundamental human rights" a strong tool for the development of their movement. This occurred in Japanese feminist bioethics in the early 1980s. During the same period, Japanese male scholars began to know of the word "bioethics" as medical ethics through American bioethicists. They invited bioethicists from the United States and began exchanges with them. From the mid-80s a fierce debate on brain death and organ transplants. The boiled up Japanese people showed strong concern about this controversy. Some people said that we had to learn western bioethics and introduce it into Japan.

Others said that Japan had a long history of traditional ethics, and hence we had to create a "Japanese" bioethics different from the western one. For example, many people said that the Japanese put greater importance on human relationships, not rather than human rights, and hence they needed a relationship-based bioethics different from the rights-based one. One of the interesting points was the completely different interpretation of the concept "internationalization" held by these two parties.

The former, who think the Japanese have to learn western bioethics consider "internationalization" as following the international basic standard, such as "fundamental human rights," and contributing to worldwide ethical rule-making. On the other hand, the latter, who think the Japanese should go their own way consider "internationalization" as advocating an local ethical tradition, and by so doing, contributing to global diversity among cultures and religions etc. Interestingly, those who like to speak of "East Asian bioethics" seem to look at the issue through an "East-West" paradigm, and say that eastern or Asian countries need a new type of bioethics different from the western one.

Even in western countries there are a many people who have strong antipathy towards modernization. Similarly, in Japan, there are many people who have sympathy toward modernization. Let us go back to "internationalization." Japanese bioethics, since 1980s, has tried to internationalize itself, but has continuously been faced with a difficult problem: "at heart what is internationalization?"

It is not following the United States' standard. For instance, with regard to global environmental problems such as regulation of CO_2 emission, the United States still refuses to accept an "international" standard. In the bioethics field, ethical standards concerning reproductive technologies are vary even among European countries.

If we pursue rigorously international standards, the concepts remaining in our hands would be a very few, such as "human dignity," "love," "compassion," and so on. Even "fundamental human rights" can be rejected by certain religious groups in some contexts. This means that in this global age we have to think about ethical issues based on very few shared ethical standards. In conclusion, I want to distinguish three concepts, "Westernization," "modernization," and "internationalization."

These three concepts are completely different, but are often used mixed up. Internationalization is not the same as Westernalization nor modernization. But, of course, it is not the same as resting on traditional values. Internationalization may be a difficult goal, particularly for non-western countries that are undergoing a rapid process of modernization.

It is such an irony that those who claim for Japan's full participation in the US-led "war for democracy" are the same people who deny legitimacy of the democratization that took place after the defeat of the imperial military regime in 1945. They denounce the democratization which included disarmament and women's liberation as "forced upon" by the occupiers, and represent the process as "feminization of the nation", which only resulted in all kinds of modern social problems such as increase in crimes, divorces, prostitution, selfish youths, and lesser childbirth.

In fact, granting equal rights of women in civil life and in family affairs was one of most critical reforms in the democratization process, over which nationalists have deeply regretted. It should not be regarded merely as a gift from western liberators for poor repressed Japanese women, considering that in most of western countries women did not enjoy suffrage at that time. To understand the important meanings women's liberation had in the democratization of Japan, one has to remind how patriarchic family system functioned in the former military regime.

In the imperial military rule, Emperor was God - Father, untouchable absolute authority, and individuals as his children were encouraged to abandon self-autonomy to be a part of the nation as a big family that is bonded by "natural" respect and love. Family, each of which had a small emperor-father, was major institution through which the state exercised control over individuals. It suggests that liberation for women could not be achieved just by granting them civil rights, but requires confronting with militarism and nationalism that is closely connected to patriarchic family systems.

It was this recognition from which Japanese feminists started questioning how women were mobilized by the state as mothers and wives for colonization and invasion, while women in occupied territories were forced to be subject to brutal rapes and sexual slavery. Contrary to the claim of the revisionists, Japanese people who were tired of suppressive military rule eagerly welcomed the "forced democratization" 60 years ago. However the US soon betrayed its own ideals of achieving peace through disarmament and democracy, as they reconciled with the ruling elites of the old regime, in order to transform Japan into the major fort of the military-economic block against communism in Asia.

In spite of the dominant discourse that the Imperial Japan was successfully transformed by the US into a democratic, peaceful and pro-women state, the old empire has never gone. It was saved by the new empire that utilized its legacy to exercise power over Asia throughout the "Cold War", in which freedom of speech and association was suppressed, thousands were killed, and victims of the sexual violence were silenced.

While nationalists put blame on feminists for destructing family, it was rather development of capitalism that has played major role in retreat of traditional family systems. In the War on Terror which emerged from the uneven development of global capitalism, the state is re-finding political values of family. As the North Korea is represented as another "evil state", the whole Japanese nation is encouraged to identify with the families of the victims abducted by the North Korea.

On the contrary, when peace activists were taken as hostages by an Iraqi armed group, the government and mass media shamelessly sponsored right-wing attacks against the victims and their families for being critical to the state policy of supporting the US occupation. I think it was very suggestive that the government used the neo-liberal term "self-responsibility" when they asked the hostages to pay back the costs for rescuing them.

While welfare state is supposed to assure economic security and social rights of citizens, it is assumed that neo-liberal state owes limited responsibility for protection of life and assets of citizens. However, this case suggests the fact that there is no more unquestioned category of "citizens" who can unconditionally expect even minimum protection of life from the state. The War on Terror is in fact a process through which citizenship is redefined in terms of royalty to the dominant systems.

Unlike wars between nation-states, the boundary between citizens to be protected and "enemies" to be killed is intentionally left vague in this war, contributing to increased anxiety and fear. And it is this anxiety and fear that calls the old empire back, which demands royalty to the nation that is represented not as union by contracts but as naturalized community of an extended family. A few weeks ago, the ruling party of Japan suggested to drop gender equality from the Constitution to enshrine family as the foundation of the nation.

While the old empire attacks feminism that reveals the fiction of family and nation as union by unconditional affection, the new empire blatantly takes credit of women's liberation to distinguish between "civilized" and "barbaric" nations. What should we do to these two empires? Fighting against the attacks on memories should be central in our struggle against nationalisms and imperialisms, since the new imperialism has direct interest in monopoly of history, as it distinguishes itself from the old empire.

As we face the War On Terror that is turning our daily life into the battlefields everywhere, we need to share not only memories of the past war, but also how we have differently experienced militarization, occupation, existence of military bases, "high-level security", economic development or underdevelopment, in order to get back our words and public spaces from the empires. Although they attempt to define democracy and women's liberation by power and interests, we shall be able to define democracy by nonviolence and gender equality.

And we shall not confuse women's suffrage with civilization, or universal norms with imperialism. It is not Bush, Osama bin Laden or Emperor to determine basic principles of gender justice. They must come from on-going dialogues within transnational women's movements based on solidarity and respect to each other's lived experiences. This ch will discuss Japanese women and their involvement with the traditional craft movement and production within Japan. In order to understand Japanese women and their relationship to this movement, one must look at the social context and historical placement of women throughout Japan's lengthy history.

Starting with the Tokugawa or Edo period (1615-1868), a strong sense of proper place within society and community was in- stilled in men and women living in Japan. Historically and contemporarily, the family, which is an extended part of the community, ranks first in a woman's obligation and overrides other more individual pursuits such as the arts. Within traditional craft and fine craft production communities, women's roles still reflect the idea of community harmony through cooperative work.

Most traditional craft and fine craft products cannot be produced by one individual alone and, oftentimes they require several different stages for the final product to be made. Thus, it is women who fill the niche in the craft movement by processing of clay, lacquering paper, or the weaving of fine fabrics for the making of kimonos. This does not mean that women do not themselves produce traditional and fine crafts in Japan. Several women have been named National Living Treasures for their knowledge of and production of various crafts in Japan.

Women hold apprenticeships with master craftsmen, placing them within the forefront of craft production, if not the producers of the final products. It is the final showing of the craft piece in a gallery or department store with the main artist's name on it that shapes the worth and personality of the art works, hiding the multiple hands that shaped the actual piece into its final form. At the same time, there is a contradiction between the appreciation of those products produced by women and some women's status as National Living Treasures. Historically, women have had little access to the Japanese world of art, or have only been exposed to certain types of art thought fit for women to produce.

Few women have broken free from their social obligations as wives and mothers to immerse fully in artistic endeavors. During the Edo period (1615-1868), Japan was ruled by a series of shoguns from the Tokugawa family. This particular family provided Japan with more than 250 years of peace and security after the country's civil war This security led to the stimulation of Japan's industry and commerce led to be emerge a materialistic culture, a trend that had begun in the preceding Momoyama period of 1568-1600" Townspeople and artisans soon became prosperous and were able to find a consumer base for their products.

Early in the seventeenth century Toku gawa leyasu enforced the division of the populace into four major social classes from the highest rank of the samurai, then farmer, artisans, and lastly merchants. Mobility within this system was restricted because it was felt one was born into a class. The peasant farmer held the highest ranking after samurai because it was thought of as the only profession that truly de something Artisans merely changed the form of goods already produced by peasants.

Merchants were ranked below the artisans because Lisans pro-controlled the land on which they worked. "It was quite common for peasants to supplement their meager incomes by handicraft work done in their homes. Although the authorities did their best to see that this domestic Industry fields, this type of cottage industry eventually surpassed the output of artisans in the castle towns and cities. Some peasants even engaged in trade in the countryside". Artisans and merchants enjoyed great prosperity even though they were regarded as lower classes. Merchants developed what was called the putting-out system in which merchants made advances on raw materials and equipment rather than pay money to producers. Provincial merchant and peasant landholders adopted this system to industrialize the farm communities with subcontractors supervising the subsidiary handicraft "In trades where operations were both complex and numerous, the merchants assumed responsibility for dividing the work in its various stages among the producers.

This system produced large amounts of raw silk, cotton and silk textiles paper, mats, lanterns ... by the end of the Tokugawa period". Women within this four-tiered system remained low with little legal or social freedoms. The feminine image suffered with the introduction of Buddhism, Confucianism, and the growth of feudalism.

In Japan including Shinto have contributed significantly to the development and maintenance of separate gender roles and gender equality. "These religions have encouraged these people to accept a nation of ethos which proclaims that people are born with differing abilities and into different statuses within society, thereby serving to maintain the prevailing social order". "Many Buddhist texts taught that women's nature was inherently evil associating them with attachments to the sensual world as opposed to the spiritual realm". Because of a woman's supposed evil nature they were given very little freedom to explore themselves.

At a very early age, a girl learned that she would be taking care of her own family and later the family of her husband.

Women had to follow three obediences in which they had to obey their fathers as a daughter, obey their husbands when married, and obey their son if widowed. Women could not become independent under Buddhist teachings, and those promoting these teachings did not wish for them to be. Nunneries in Europe were usually thought of as a place where women could find educational freedom.

Faced with either marrying or getting a religious education, some women chose not to get married but in Japan even the nunneries were places of male domination. "The nunneries had such a dependent status that they were referred to as the 'laundry room of monasteries' in the Ninon sandol jitsuroku, a record from the ninth century. The nunneries were subordinate to the monasteries and the nuns were expected to serve the monks. The monastery and nunnery relationship paralleled that of the Japanese household or family system.

"While the monks lived atop the holy mountains conducting various religious affairs in service of the nation, their wives, mothers, and sisters resided in a separate community at the foot of the mountains under the protection of the monks, leading a religious life and performing their assigned roles - sewing and washing the monks' clothing and preparing their meals".

With the introduction of Confucianism, women's status within the Japanese society dropped even lower. "From the seventeenth century on the to Kugawa government fervently promoted Confucian teachings which generally regarded women as inferior to men, reinforcing the doctrines of Buddhism". Sentiments that women were lower than men originated from the Chinese patriarchal society were.

These notions of male superiority over female inferiority surfaced in the elements of Yin and Yang Yin and Yang through their interaction created the universe. Yang embodies the positive, bright, male principle and yin the negative, dark female principle. A husband and wife symbolize this union of vang and yin or heaven and earth. Women are to regard their husbands as heaven.

The samurai class mainly carried out the doctrines of Confucianism Women within these classes was supposed to set examples for women in other classes. Therefore, women in samurai classes, even though they were considered higher on the social ranking, had even less freedom to deviate from their roles as good wives and mothers. Women from the other social classes were given greater responsibilities within the families occupations.

They were often called upon to assist in running the family business and at times went beyond merely helping their husbands and became imaginative entrepreneurs". The influence of various religious teachings, as well as the strict structures set up for people to live, shaped Japanese thought and identity. An individual consciousness became subordinate to that of the group consciousness

A shogunal ordinance in 1649, proclaimed that a peasant wife's duty was to work at the loom. The more influencing patriarchal system within the samurai classes also urged women to concentrate on the art of sewing. The act of women weaving and sewing during the Tokugawa period serves as an indicator of social standing and placement of women within the Tokugawa work force.

"The 'iconicity' of women at work, then, points to several discourses in Tokugawa society that include working women among their objects, and which were in part concretized in specific literary genres". Moral instruction books were written during this time giving rules for how men and women should live. All were based on Chinese versions, the earliest written during the Han dynasty. Primarily women in China wrote these moral instruction books, but in Japan they were written by men who reinforced a woman's duty to the home and caring of their families and the pursuits of certain labor.

Professional artists during the Edo period were by and large males, since women were supposed to fulfill certain household duties before leisure 'activities. Two exceptions to this rule were Kiyohara Yukinobu (1643-1682) and Sasakishogen (active late seventeenth-early eighteenth century)

who both became famous for their painting and calligraphy. "For the wives and daughters of the upper class (shogun, court nobility, and daimyo), personal artistic interests could be indulged only when they did not interfere with family duties, but we know that some of these women did devote considerable time not only to reading but also to writing poetry.

Women born into high-ranking families were likely to receive training in calligraphy and in composing the traditional Japanese form of poetry known as *waka*. One of the most prestigious positions for a woman of samurai class was a lady in waiting for the imperial palace in Kyoto, or in one of the many castles in Japan. Families competed for these positions to secure for their daughters prestigious placement for marriage and to strengthen political and economic positions within the family.

Women within these positions also had the benefit of being surrounded by cultivated women and could devote a certain amount of time to artistic pursuits. *Waka* became the most suitable written form for women, and during the seventeenth century several female *waka* poets were recognized. Otagaki Rengetsu, was one such woman who was a member of the elite samurai class who had connections to *waka* and other artistic pursuits. She is most known for her unique pottery that she inscribed with poems.

After being married twice, she decided to become a nun. She turned to pottery to support herself, creating utensils for use in the Chinese-style form of tea drinking know as *sencha*. She seems to have been self-taught, crafting her pots by hand and adding her own *waka*. It should be noted that pottery is not considered even presently as something that women do in Japan at the master level. Louse Cort has pointed out that Rengetsu's popularity was linked m part to her identity - the fact that she was a woman Lher than *oZ* of the countless professional male potters.

The craft community sees effort by all members of the household as contributing to the production of a ceramic item; the outside community seeks out the individual for praise in producing a unique art form. In reality, the naming of individuals as living cultural treasures fails to compensate for the lack of recognition for those who help and produce particular portions of what will become the finished product. Japanese society has always placed boundaries around what is considered the social unit such as the *ie* as being *uchi* inside and *soto* outside of the social unit.

"Tradition is seen to grant a local community strength in communal participation and action by providing the locality with a sense of solidarity and unity. In other words, in the Japanese 'folk' theory of traditionally, community-wide activities are both indicators and products of the power of the community which (in turn) is still based on its 'past' legacy". The rural communities of Japan, whether or not they still hold on to their traditional ways of life are associated by urban and city dwelling Japanese as the holders of traditional truths and antiquated life styles.

It is only by going to these particular communities that one can get a sense of what truly is Japanese. As Ayano Chiba pointed out, 'I'll explain our work as many times as you like, but you'll never understand it until you do it. The *uchi* and *soto* system also keeps women in a state of being outsiders themselves within their own communities. Historically, as in the example of nunneries, women hold a position separate from men in the *i.e.* which is transferred when they become an outsider residing in their husband's. Insider and outsider knowledge within women's worlds and men's worlds contributed to the engendering of specific craft items, or the inaccessibility of certain craft production to women.

Outside of the craft communities, women still duplicate the traditional *ie* system in that they are responsible for taking care of the family. Roles are changing slowly within the family structure in Japan, with men contributing more to household and family care and women entering into the full time positions with companies. The *ie* system and associations with *soto* and *uchi* still prevail as a primary system of seeing the structure of the traditional household has changed in some respects from that of the entire unit acting to produce the same products.

With the decline of farming and the economic necessity of survival, rural communities have turned to traditional crafts and performances to draw the nostalgic Japanese public into their communities. Now, a collective effort is put forth in the production of craft items for tourists. The passing of farming techniques is still prevalent. Its educational approach has been used by those in the craft movement who continue the apprenticeship model of passing on certain cultural skills and techniques in craft production. Women often do the bulk of the work in preliminary craft production.

And, since the full knowledge and mastery of each craft item requires years of work and observation, it could be said that women will soon fill areas where men used to reside as the prestigious repositories of the actual knowledge and expertise. Still, women's contributions to raising the family and farming have blocked many women from fully participating within the craft movement. Women find that when they no longer have the responsibilities of childcare that they can explore traditional art forms. Women historically have been the main element in the preservation and continuance of certain traditional art and craft forms within Japan.

These women tend to be of middle class origin with grown children who wish to get back in contact with their traditional roots. "The traditional arts such as *chadc* are popular ways for women to spend their leisure time because these arts affirm traditional views of women as nurturing and supporting others in society. At the same time, they allow women to pursue personal goals of self-expression, artistry, the development of managerial skills". Changes within the Japanese family structure and household duties such as in the Edo period have encouraged women to look to the traditional arts for personal growth and enjoyment.

"The traditional arts have a special appeal for middle-class women in that these arts advertise themselves as providing self-improvement and educational opportunities that enhance a woman's abilities as wife, mother, and hostess. Women are encouraged to take up traditional arts in order to learn Japanese cultural practices and pass [them] on to their daughters". Traditional crafts and arts again are seen to symbolize that of a proper and past way. It is this relationship which complicates women's relations to traditional crafts in Japan and the society's overall assessment of the relationship that women have with craft production.

Though women in rural communities reliant on craft production lead different lives from women who live in urban settings, the same rules set up in the beginnings of the Tokugawa period still apply to them. The outside community's interpretation of women's worth in their production of tradition craft items contributes to the lack of acknowledgment of women's true contributions to the craft industry.

The inside dynamics of the craft labor system incorporate women's activities into the collective process of craft production emphasizing the process over the item. Japanese women still tend to gravitate towards traditionally female-based crafts or do not make the actual finished craft items. When women do excel at making a certain craft product, they are elevated to high status, but often ignored as achieving status with their male counterparts.

It is the Japanese system of separate worlds of men and women and the social structure that dictates what women can and cannot do, placing them in an uneasy relationship within the craft world of Japan. What needs to be examined is the relationship between outside urban influences based on traditional values and inside rural perspectives also based on traditional values, and how they collectively place women in contradictory roles of producing and not producing craft items within Japan.

5

The State of Gender in the Sathya Sai Baba Movement in Malaysia

The Sathya Sai Baba movement is inspired by South Indian guru Sathya Sai Baba (1926) who teaches the unity of all religions. Some followers of him have faith in his claim to be a *purna avatar* (full divine incarnation) of Shiva and Shakti, who is believed to have been predicted in the *Bhagavad Gita*.

This means that some of his followers see him as a God. They are engaged in singing devotional songs called "bhajans" and selfless service (seva). Its official organization is the Sathya Sai Organization. However the Sathya Sai Baba movement extends beyond the organization. An important aspect of the faith of adherents is the miracles attributed to Sathya Sai Baba. The number of adherents is estimated between 6 and 100 million.

OFFICIAL LIFE STORY OF SATHYA SAI BABA

The official biography of Sathya Sai Baba was written by Narayana Kasturi. Additional sources for the official life story are Sathya Sai Baba's discourses. Sathya Sai Baba was born on 23 November 1926. His followers believe that as a boy, Sathya Sai Baba performed many miracles (levitating, materializing fruit, sweets, pencils etc., clairvoyance).

At approximately the age 14 Sathya Sai Baba made a claim that he was the reincarnation of the fakir Sai Baba of Shirdi. To validate his claim it is alleged that jasmine flowers were dropped onto the ground and that they miraculously arranged themselves into the words "Sai Baba" in Telugu. It is claimed that he performed a number of miracles including healings, materializations, and more spectacularly, making his face appear on the moon and proving his omnipresence.

In 1963 he declared to be an incarnation of Shiva and Shakti. In a 1976 interview he claimed to be a full divine avatar. Sathya Sai Baba gained followers in India since the 1930s. Outside of India, he only became popular since the 1960s and 1970s. The number of Sathya Sai Baba centres in the United Kingdom grew during the period 1970 until 1983 from 2 to 51. Several of Sathya Sai Baba's activities are considered debatable.

PRACTICES IN THE ASHRAMS

The popularity and the donations by followers have enabled Sathya Sai Baba and his organizations to build an ever-increasing ashram called Prashanthi Nilayam near the once poor and isolated village of Puttaparthi. An important practice in his ashram in Puttaparthi is the *darshan* (spiritual sight) that Sathya Sai Baba gives. During *darshan* Sathya Sai Baba walks among his followers. He may listen to a few chosen persons, accept letters, or materialize and distribute *vibhuti* (sacred ash). He says that his *darshan* has spiritual benefits for those who attend it.

Usually people wait hours to get a good place for *darshan*. Sathya Sai Baba sometimes invites people for a group interview with him in a room in the *ashram* 's *mandir* (Hindu temple). Followers consider it a great privilege to get such an interview. Sometimes a person from this group is invited for a private interview. Sathya Sai Baba's manifestations of vibuthi emphasizes his claim to be a reincarnation of Shirdi Sai Baba who used to take ash, called *udhi*, from an ever-burning fire, called dhuni. Vibuthi is an ancient Hindu symbol, among others associated with Shiva.

Sathya Sai Baba resides much of the time in his main *ashram* Prashanthi Nilayam ("abode of peace") at Puttaparthi. In the hot summer the guru leaves for his other ashram called *Brindavan* in Whitefield, India (sometimes called Kadugodi), a town on the outskirts of Bangalore. He has left India only once for a visit to Eastern Africa in 1968. He is a prolific orator in his native language of Telugu, and also speaks passable Tamil. He claims to be the *Kali Yuga purna avatar* (full divine incarnation of this era) of Lord Shiva and Shakti.

He says that he is omniscient, omnipotent and omnipresent and can create matter from mere thought. He also stresses he is free from desires, and that this is the state that one should aim to attain, consistent with the Vedic teachings. He plays down his claims about being an incarnation of God by saying that everybody is God but that only he realizes and experiences this fully. In correspondence with his perceived divinity, followers often capitalize references to him in their writings ("He", "Him" etcetera).

Sathya Sai Baba has prophesized that he will reincarnate again in the 21st century as Prema Sai Baba to finish the spiritual transformation of the world, starting with India, where his previous and current incarnations have begun. He has said that he will die after he has become 93 years old but there is no official statement for the popular belief among followers that he will die when he is 95 years old (96 according to Indian counting). Sathya Sai Baba has stated that his three incarnations will help to usher in the Golden Age of mankind that will come soon.

Sathya Sai Baba has said that he performs miracles to attract people and then to transform them spiritually, telling his followers *not* to focus on his miracles. He can be seen in person to perform these miracles in the form of materializations of small objects, for example jewelry such as bracelets, rings, watches and especially *vibhuti* (holy ash). He said in a 1976 interview that these trinkets have symbolic value, and offer the owners protection by reminding them of his protecting powers when in danger.

Occasionally, at Maha Shivaratri, he publicly produces lingams that come out of his mouth that devotees claim materialize in his body. He says that he can heal the diseases of his devotees by either his spiritual power or by taking on the disease himself. There is anecdotal evidence that supports this claim. Babb wrote in a 1983 article that "the miraculous are absolutely central to this religious movement" and that the plausibility of these miracles "seems to pull people into convictions ostensibly at odds with what their own subculture deems to be common sense and considered judgment."

He wrote in that article that his observations are based on his contact with the local following of Sathya Sai Baba in Delhi that according to Babb included a sophisticated and cosmopolitan elite. Babb further wrote in that article that the energy of Sathya Sai Baba's "magic" can have "life-transforming effects on devotees." Sathya Sai Baba has said that all of his acts have meaning and significance.

So many followers interpret the acts and sayings of the guru as teachings, sometimes even as personal teachings. Some followers, especially in the ashram, attribute coincidences to Baba's will and try to find a sometimes hidden meaning in them.

Babb wrote in a 1986 book that some devotees tend attribute every event to Sathya Sai Baba's will and tend to see the world as an *enchanted garden*. He says that when a person dreams about him then this is because of his will and this is a form of his communication with people. Followers report dreams that contain messages from the guru to them. Some people became devotees after having such a dream.

Teachings

The Sathya Sai Baba movement advocates the unity of all religions. Sathya Sai Baba says that all religions lead to God and that followers should continue to follow their original religions. He says that those who follow his teachings will find themselves exampling their own original faith more fully, i.e. that will make Christians become better Christians and Hindus better Hindus, et cetera. The five basic human values that he advocates are: Truth (Sathya), Right Conduct (Dharma), Peace (Shantih), Love for God and all creatures (Prema), and Non-violence (Ahimsa).

He teaches a rather traditional but eclectic form of Hinduism that come from many sects and movements including *advaita,* occasionally drawing from other religions like Buddhism, Sikhism, and Christianity. He says that he has come to restore faith in, and the practice of, the Vedas. He says that a very important way a person can emancipate oneself is through selfless service to ones fellow man (seva).

Sathya Sai Baba has repeatedly stresses the importance of *sadhana* (Hindu spiritual exercises) for example by meditation. He asserts that sadhana is important for achieving *moksha*or kaivalyam (liberation from ignorance and from the endless re-births due to karmic consequences). Sathya Sai Baba teaches the importance of *Bhakti yoga* (Hindu devotion to God).

He preaches a strict morality with regards to sensual desires (including food, sex, meat, alcohol). Some of his exhortations are to put a ceiling on desires. By this, he seems to mean that followers should not waste time and money. He teaches that the world is just *maya* , that only God is real and that the seeming diversity of all life is another illusion. All life is one, he says. The meaning of life is to experience this oneness with God and other living beings.

Followers attribute many miracles to him which they witness in his presence and in their own countries, like spontaneous vibhuti manifestations on the pictures of the guru in their homes, and bilocation, the appearance of Sai Baba in their own presence while he is also in another place. They also report that he has materialized out-of-season fruit several times. He says he performs these miracles to attract people and then to transform them spiritually.

Sathya Sai Baba said that he does not speak through other people in a discourse in 1962. In spite of this, the British author Lucas Ralli claimed that he received messages from Sathya Sai Baba and wrote in his books that his claim was endorsed by Sathya Sai Baba in an interview. His books with messages from Sathya Sai Baba are sold by the Sathya Sai Book Center of America. The anthropologist Lawrence Babb wrote that he considered the teachings of secondary importance in the cult when compared to the emphasis on the miraculous.

Babb further wrote about the Sai doctrine that "there is little relatively to dwell upon, or at least nothing very distinctive. His philosophical views are simplistic, eclectic, and essentially unoriginal." The anthropologist Alexandra Kent notes that this lack of originality is in correspondence with Sathya Sai Baba's claim to revive old truths. The British newspaper the Times described Sathya Sai Baba's teachings in 2001 as "a collection of banal truisms and platitudes."

ACTIVITIES IN LOCAL SATHYA SAI BABA GROUPS

Globally, local Sathya Sai Baba groups assemble to sing *bhajans* (devotional songs). Baba says that concentration on the name of God with the help of *bhajans* will easily lead to concentration on God and to higher devotion. *Bhajans* are sung at nearly every meeting. Bhajans are simple verses. One line is sung by a lead singer and is then repeated by the rest of the group.

In those bhajans the name of traditional Hindu deities have sometimes been replaced by the names of Sathya Sai Baba. In addition they study Sathya Sai Baba's teachings and the holy books of the various world religions. They also perform community service, which they call *seva*. The greeting *Sai Ram* is used by followers.

Organizations

There are both independently founded Sai Study Groups worldwide, and also local *Sai Samithis* (Sathya Sai Baba groups) are part of a hierarchical structure called the Sathya Sai Organization. As of 2007, the chairman of the organization is the American Michael Goldstein. The logo of the Sathya Sai organization is a stylized lotus flower with the text of the five human values written in each petal. These are Love, Truth, Peace, Righteousness and Non-violence. This text version has replaced the old logo with the symbols of the main 5 or 6 world religions in the petals.

The charter of the Sai Organization says that every member should undertake *sadhana* (spiritual discipline) as an integral part of daily life and abide by the following nine-points code of conduct.

1. Daily meditation and prayer.
2. Devotional singing/prayer with family members once per week.
3. Participation in the educational programmes conducted by the Organization for children.
4. Attendance at least once per month at group devotional programmes conducted by the Organization.
5. Participation in community service and other programmes of the Organization.
6. Regular study of Sai literature.
7. Putting into practice the principles of "ceiling on desires", utilising any savings thereby generated for the service of mankind.
8. Speaking softly and lovingly with everyone with whom one comes into contact.
9. Avoiding talking ill of others, especially in their absence.

Sathya Sai Baba is the figurehead to a number of free educational institutions, charitable organizations and service projects that are spread over 10,000 centers in 166 countries around the world. The Sri Sathya Sai Institute of Higher Learning in Prashanti Nilayam is the only college in India to have received an "A++" rating by the National Assessment and Accreditation Council (an autonomous body established by the University Grants Commission).

Besides this institute, there is also an Institute of Music and an Institute of Higher Learning in Anantapur, which is a women's college. The Sri Sathya Sai Institute of Higher Medical Sciences in Puttaparthi (also known as the Super Specialty Hospital) is a 220 bed facility providing advanced surgical and medical care free of cost to the public. It is situated 6 kilometers from the guru's ashram and was inaugurated by the then Prime Minister Narasimha Rao on November 22, 1991 and was designed by the Prince of Wales's architectural adviser, Keith Critchlow The Sri Sathya Sai Institute of Higher Medical Sciences in Bangalore is a 333 bed facility with advanced operation theatres, ICUs and CCUs meant to benefit the poor.

The hospital was inaugurated on January 19, 2001 by the then Prime Minister Atal Behari Vajpayee. Other eminent participants were Abdul Kalam, Michael Nobel (distant relative of Alfred Nobel), Noah Samara and Anji Reddy. The hospital has served 250,000 patients, free of cost, from January 2001 to April 2004. The Sri Sathya Sai General Hospital was opened in Whitefield, Bangalore, in 1977 by Sathya Sai Baba to provide free care to poor local villagers. Since that time, the general hospital has grown to a 35,000 sq ft (3,300 m^2) building that provides complex surgeries, food and medicines free of cost.

The hospital has, since its inception, treated over 2 million cases. The Sri Sathya Sai Central Trust runs several general hospitals, two super specialty hospitals, dispensaries, eye hospitals and mobile dispensaries and conducts medical camps in rural and slum areas in India. It was in the year 2000-2001 the largest recipient of foreign donations. The Trust has also funded several major drinking water projects. The first drinking water project, completed in 1996, supplies water to 1.2 million people in 730-800 villages in the drought-prone Anantapur district in Andhra Pradesh.

The second drinking water project, completed in 2004, supplies water to Chennai (formerly known as Madras) through a rebuilt waterway named "Sathya Sai Ganga Canal". The Chennai water drinking project was praised by Tamil Nadu Chief Minister, M Karunanidhi. Karunanidhi said that although he is an atheist, he differentiated between good spiritual leaders like Sathya Sai Baba and fake godmen. The third drinking water project, expected to be completed in April 2006, would supply water from the Godavari River to half a million people living in five hundred villages in East and West Godavari Districts.

Other completed water projects include the Medak District Project benefiting 450,000 people in 179 villages and the Mahbubnagar District Project benefitting 350,000 people in 141 villages. In January 2007, the Sri Sathya Sai Central Trust revealed that it would undertake another drinking water project in Latur, Maharashtra. His Educare (formerly called Education in Human Values) program seeks to found schools in all countries with the explicit goal to educate children in the five human values and spirituality.

The Sri Sathya Sai Books and Publications Trust is the official publisher of the *Sathya Sai Organization*. It publishes the international monthly magazine called Sanathana Sarathi in English and Telugu. According to their website, they shelve over a thousand books and provide Sai-related literature in 40 languages. The book trust also supplies CDs, DVDs and audio tapes. In various nations, similar publication trusts are maintained in their own native language.

On November 23, 2001, the digital radio network "Radio Sai Global Harmony" was launched through the World Space Organization, USA. Dr. Michael Nobel (distant relative of Alfred Nobel and one of the patrons for the radio network) said that the radio network would spread Sathya Sai Baba's message of global harmony and peace.

CELEBRATIONS AND COMMEMORATIONS

The most important celebrations and commemorations are:

- Maha Shivaratri the great night of Shiva, date is based on the Hindu calendar.
- *Easwaramma* day on May 6 Celebration and commemoration of Sathya Sai Baba's mother.
- Sai Baba's Birthday 23 November.
- Guru Purnima date is based on the Hindu calendar. Gratitude and devotion to the guru is shown.
- Christmas.

CONVERSION AND MISSION

John D. Kelly, as of 2006 a professor of anthropology at the University of Chicago wrote in an article about Hindu mission in Fiji that the Sai Baba movement was missionary. In contrast, Dr. Kim Knott who worked as of 1997 at the department of theology and religious studies of the University of Leeds untagged in a table the "Sathya Sai Baba Fellowship" as missionary. Sathya Sai Baba has discouraged publicity and proselytism for him in a public discourse. (23 November 1968)

CHARACTERIZATIONS AND CLASSIFICATIONS

Knott tagged in a table the "Sathya Sai Baba Fellowship" as devotional, charismatic authority, reformist, and including non-Asian membership. Untagged were revivalist, missionary, and caste-related. Kent describes the Sathya Sai Baba movement in Malaysia as a "Hindu Revitalization movement." Babb favours the label cult over the label movement, because of what he sees as its highly individualized focus on miracles instead of a focus on a world view.

Kelly wrote that the Sathya Sai Organizations reject the label Hindu. According to Kelly, they its founder as the "living synthesis of the world's religious traditions" and prefers to be classified as an interfaith movement. Kelly further wrote when comparing ISKCON with the Sai Baba mission (he does not write which Sai Baba mission he means) that the Sai Baba efforts in Fiji are ambiguous where ISKCON is dogmatic and structured, proliferating where ISKCON is planned and controlled, self-contradictory where ISKCON is clear, gentle where ISKCON is stern, and to put it most broadly, open where ISKCON is closed.

Kelly further stated that the Sai organization in Fiji does not ask its members to undergo initiation or to commit themselves to obey particular leaders. Former followers Nagel asserts that the atmosphere surrounding Sathya Sai Baba is clearly Hindu, in spite of Sathya Sai Baba's claim to foster and unite various different religions and that he dropped all Muslim elements that Shirdi Sai Baba practiced.

EDUCATIONAL INSTITUTIONS, CHARITABLE ORGANIZATIONS, HOSPITALS AND SERVICE PROJECTS

Sathya Sai Baba supports free schools and other charitable works in 166 countries. The Sri Sathya Sai Institute of Higher

Learning in Prashanti Nilayam is the only college in India to have received an "A++" rating by the National Assessment and Accreditation Council. His charity supports the Institute of Music and the Institute of Higher Learning in Anantapur, which is a women's college. The Sri Sathya Sai Institute of Higher Medical Sciences in Puttaparthi is a 220 bed facility that provides free surgical and medical care and was inaugurated by the then Prime Minister Narasimha Rao on November 22 1991.

The Sri Sathya Sai Institute of Higher Medical Sciences in Bangalore is a 333 bed hospital meant to benefit the poor. The hospital was inaugurated on January 19 2001 by the then Prime Minister Atal Behari Vajpayee. The hospital has provided free medical care to over 250,000 patients. The Sri Sathya Sai General Hospital was opened in Whitefield, Bangalore, in 1977 and provides complex surgeries, food and medicines free of cost. The hospital has treated over 2 million patients.

The Sri Sathya Sai Central Trust runs several general hospitals, two specialty hospitals, eye hospitals and mobile dispensaries and conducts medical camps in rural and slum areas in India. The Trust has also funded several major drinking water projects. One project completed in 1996 supplies water to 1.2 million people in about 750 villages in the drought-prone Anantapur district in Andhra Pradesh.

The second drinking water project, completed in 2004, supplies water to Chennai through a rebuilt waterway named "Sathya Sai Ganga Canal". Tamil Nadu Chief Minister M. Karunanidhi praised the Chennai water project and Sai Baba's involvement. Other completed water projects include the Medak District Project benefiting 450,000 people in 179 villages and the Mahbubnagar District Project benefitting 350,000 people in 141 villages. In January 2007, the Sri Sathya Sai Central Trust said it would start a drinking water project in Latur, Maharashtra.

Sai Baba's Educare program seeks to found schools throughout the world with the goal of educating children in the five human values. According to the Sai Educare site, schools have been founded in 33 countries. The Times of Zambia states, "The positive influence of Sathya Sai is unprecedented in the annals of education in Zambia. Sai Baba's education ideals as embodied in his human values-based approach in education are an eye opener to educationists in Zambia."

On November 23 2001, the digital radio network "Radio Sai Global Harmony" was launched through the World Space Organization, USA. Dr. Michael Oleinikof Nobel (distant relative to Alfred Nobel and one of the patrons for the radio network) said that the radio network would spread Sathya Sai Baba's message of global harmony and peace. In January 2007 the Baba was given a big felicitation in Chennai Nehru stadium organised by the Chennai Citizens Conclave for thanking him for the 200 crore water project which brought water from the River Krishna in Andhra Pradesh to Chennai city.

Four chief ministers attended the function. The notable news about this event was that Sai Baba was sharing the same dais with Karunanidhi (Chief Minister of Chennai) who is a very well known hardcore atheist against Hindu gurus / godman and that Karunanidhi was felicitating Sai Baba. This was covered in all newspapers.

Demographics

According to the Sathya Sai Organization, there are an estimated 1,200 Sathya Sai Baba Centers in 130 countries worldwide. The number of adherents is estimated between 6 million and 100 million, predominantly people of Indian ethnic origin. In Nordic countries and the Netherlands followers defected after 2000 due to negative publicity about him. Simon Weightmann who worked as of 1997 at the department for the study of religions at the University of London wrote that Sathya Sai Baba is one of the most popular gurus, both in India and in the Hindu diaspora and that as a consequence of his inclusivist stance he has a large following among the urban middle class.

Professor Harold Coward who worked as of 1997 as a professor for the centre of religious studies at the University of Victoria wrote that Sathya Sai Baba, together with several other modern Indian gurus, has attracted more occidental than South Asian Canadians. A significant fraction of the movement in Malaysia is of Chinese extraction, though the majority there is of British East Indian Hindu origin. The situation of women in Malaysia has improved over time, much thanks to women's increased access to education and awareness of their constitutional rights.

Legal amendments in order to eliminate any discrimination against women have been made continuously, but still there is no clear definition of such discrimination. Customary and traditional practices continue to make a distinction between the sexes: each ethnic group in Malaysia is influenced by Asian values, which determine the role of women in the domestic/ private sphere while men dominate the public sphere (CEDAW, 2004). The population is predominantly Muslim (60%), but there are also significant groups of Buddhists (19%), Christians (9%), Hindu (6%) and various traditional Chinese beliefs (3%). Regional differences also exist and women's civil liberties appear to be more restricted in the state of Kentalan than elsewhere.

FAMILY CODE

Family matters are governed by a combination of civil, customary (*Adat*) and Islamic (*Sharia*) law. The civil Law Reform Act (LRA), which entered into force in 1982, sets the legal minimum age of marriage to 16 years for women and 18 years for men and concludes that all marriages shall be based upon mutual consent. The same principles are set forth in the Islamic Family Law Act (IFLA) of 1984, but for a marriage to be fully recognized it also requires the consent of the wali, i.e. the woman's guardian.

With regards to early marriage, the UN (2004) estimates that 5 per cent of Malaysian girls between 15 and 19 years of age are married, divorced or widowed. Polygamy is illegal under the LRA, but polygamous marriages that had been contracted before the law came into force are recognized. Islamic law, in turn, allows any Muslim man to take as many as four wives, provided that he will treat them fairly and can support them financially.

The government nevertheless tries to control the practice of polygamy and will only grant a man permission to have multiple wives if the proposed marriage is just and necessary. It was only following amendments to the Infants Act in 1999 that parental authority was granted equally to both parents. Previously, only the father was recognized as the legal guardian of an infant's person and property. The law is applicable to all non-Muslims, and to Muslims in those states that have adopted the law (four out of thirteen states in 2004).

A cabinet directive was issued in 2000 to allow all mothers, irrespective of religion, to sign any documents related to their children. In the event of divorce, the LRA give men and women the same right to custody and the welfare of the child is central to the court's decision. Islamic law generally considers the mother to be best suitable to care for children under the age of seven. Inheritance for non-Muslims is governed by the Inheritance (Family Provision) Act of 1971 and the Distribution Act of 1958.

Before 1997, the Distribution Act discriminated against women insofar that when a man died intestate, his wife was only entitled to one-third of his property if they had children and one-half if they were childless. By contrast, when a woman died intestate, all her property was awarded to her husband, irrespective of if the marriage had produced any children or not (CEDAW, 2004).

Today, however, the law is gender-neutral on this issue. Islamic law provides for detailed and complex calculations of inheritance shares. A woman may inherit from her father, her mother, her husband, her children, and under certain conditions, from other members of her family, but her share is generally smaller than a man's entitlement. A daughter, for example, inherits half as much as a son. This is commonly justified by the fact that a woman has no financial responsibility towards her husband and children.

PHYSICAL INTEGRITY

There is no clear picture of the prevalence of female genital mutilation (FGM) in Malaysia, nor what form the practice takes. Muslim women in the state of Kelantan have admitted to having undergone circumcision as infants, but no clinical injury has been detectable. It is thus uncertain whether FGM in Malaysia is symbolic non-cutting rituals, similar to those found in Indonesia, or a form of clitoridectomy. Violence against women is not uncommon and includes sexual and spousal abuse.

The issue is addressed in a number of laws, most notably in the Domestic Violence Act of 1994. By penalizing violence within the family, the law contributes to eliminate a culture that gives men the authority to abuse his wife. Some state Islamic laws generally prohibit wives from disobeying the "lawful orders" of their husbands and present an obstacle to women pursuing claims against their husbands in Sharia courts. Muslim women can, however, also file complaints in civil courts.

Provisions in the Penal Code criminalize rape and assault, but enforcement is sometimes difficult. The concept of spousal rape is not recognized by the law. Klasen et al (2003) indicates that there is some occurrence of missing women. The sex ratio at birth is 1.07 and 1.01 for the total population.

CIVIL LIBERTIES

Women enjoy freedom of movement, although locally imposed restrictions based on Sharia may apply in certain areas. For example, there are gender-segregated cinemas in Kelantan. The rural-to-urban migration of young females in the 1970s and 1980s signaled a change in previously established societal norms against the movement of unaccompanied young women.

All persons above the age of 18 have the right to apply for a passport. There are no nation-wide restrictions on women's freedom of dress, but local authorities in Kelantan enforce the wearing of headscarves by Muslim women and imposed fines for violators. All female police officers, including non-Muslims, are required to wear headscarves during public ceremonies.

OWNERSHIP RIGHTS

The Constitution gives men and women equal rights to inherit, acquire, own, manage or dispose of any property, including land. Within the matriarchal Minangkabau community, women are actually favoured as ownership of heredity or tribal lands is restricted to women. A married man and woman may have separate property, but any assets that have been acquired during the marriage shall be considered joint property and, as such, divided equally in the event of divorce.

A Muslim woman can claim one-third (in some cases one-half) of the value of the land and property if her husband dies or divorces her. Similarly, women have the legal right to apply for bank loans and enter into any type of contractual relationships. Access to credit, however, depends on the level of income and poverty in Malaysia is more prevalent among women than men. In the public sector, both male and female officers have equal access to government housing loans under the Housing Loan Fund Act of 1971 (CEDAW, 2004).

6

Gender and Religious Legitimacy in Thailand

With the arrival of the 21st century, the goal of gender parity throughout the world remains unfulfilled, and particularly so in the political arena. Despite some progress made in various parts of Asia, the ability of women to participate as policymakers in the political process remains limited. In Thailand, as in most other Asian countries, politics has traditionally been a male preserve. Compared to men, women have not been visible in governance and politics. Although Thailand was among the first Asian countries to grant the right to vote to women, after almost seven and a half decades' of slow, incremental gains for women in politics, the representation of women remains no more than a blip on the political landscape dominated by men.

Women have a long way to go before reaching the critical mass needed to produce women-oriented policies. Since women are grossly underrepresented in political bodies, the interests of women are not adequately represented in the legislature or in government. As a result, the country is deprived of the benefits, which accrue from women's expertise and experiences. There is still little analysis on the participation of women in politics at various levels of government in Thailand and research to date is fragmentary. However, interest in this field is growing in light of the development of democracy with the introduction of the new constitution in

1997, as well as changes in civil society. In this ch, the case of Thailand is used to achieve three main objectives.

First, the position and advancement of women in the Thai parliament will be analyzed in order to contribute to research on women's political representation in the developing world. Second, the case of Thailand will be used to test some of the assumptions and theories developed in the advanced industrialized democracies of Europe and North America concerning the impact of women in public office. Third, the major barriers facing the entrance of women into the national parliament in Thailand will be examined to see whether the Thai case is consistent with research findings on women and politics in industrial democracies of the West. Thailand constitutes an interesting and significant context for studying women's political representation.

First, the country is undergoing fundamental changes in her political system as a result of constitutional reform in 1997. Thailand is an example of a relatively stable, transitional democratic country. Since the new constitution, or the "People's Constitution" as it is sometimes called, Thai democracy is moving from a system with traditional patriarchal characteristics of governance toward one with greater accountability and greater transparency. Second, Thailand's economic development since the 1960s has gradually transformed it from a poor agrarian society to a more industrial one. This has changed the preconditions for democracy and civic society. Thus, Thailand provides an interesting test of the consequences of economic development and industrialization for the status of women. Third, the strong patriarchal tradition of Thai society and women's subordination has carried over into the contemporary period.

If significant improvement in the political participation of women can be seen in Thailand, it would mean that the barriers to women's political underrepresentation are surmountable in a strongly patriarchal society. One of the important questions concerning the low proportion of women in the Thai national legislature is whether or not their numbers can make a difference with regard to the types of bills introduced and passed. Female politicians who constitute a small minority may not be able to express their distinct preferences and priorities until their numbers approach a "critical mass". Hence, some questions come to the fore.

What can account for the relatively low proportion of women's representation in the parliament in Thailand? What are the major obstacles facing the entrance of women into the political arena? In the following section, Thailand's case will be analyzed in order to examine whether women parliamentarians are more committed than their male colleagues to the pursuit of women's issues in the context of the country's low level of women's political representation in the Parliament. We know very little about the various factors inhibiting women's advancement in electoral office at the national level in Thailand and almost nothing regarding whether policy outputs differ due to women's participation in policymaking.

Realizing that any analysis of the legislative priorities of women legislators in a single session is unlikely to give a complete picture of the extent of their involvement with legislation affecting women, additional data was gathered. Data on the legislative agendas of female and male members of the House of Representatives in the Thai parliament was collected for several legislative sessions beginning from the advent of the government led by Thaksin Shinawatra, the leader of the Thai Rak Thai party, in 2001 to September 2003, in order to examine their policy priorities. In my analysis, women were compared to men serving in the House at the same time. Given the small proportion of women in the House of Representatives and the small number of bills initiated by the MPs, all types of bills were included in the analysis. The data were obtained from the Thai parliament, which maintains records of all bills and their fates.

In 1932, women acquired the rights to vote and stand for election in Thailand following the change from the absolute to constitutional monarchy. Although Thai women were among the first in Asia to gain the franchise, their situation in the political arena did not substantially change after women obtained the right to vote. Career opportunities in electoral politics were culturally closed to them. It was not until 1949 that the first woman was elected to parliament. In the 1952 elections, four women were elected. In 1955, a law requiring candidates in parliamentary elections to belong to political parties was enacted. In the election that followed in 1957, there was little space for women and only one woman was elected. During the five decades between 1949 and 2000, there was little growth in the representation of women, and women's participation in electoral politics continued to remain minimal, although women consistently exercised their right to vote.

The number of female parliamentarians has not kept pace with the considerable advances women have made in other areas. Women are often not recruited to run for elective office and are therefore unable to accumulate the experience and expertise needed to make them a viable force in politics. Thai women face numerous obstacles in their struggle for political representation. The under-representation of women in legislatures is a serious problem because it runs counter to the ideals of democracy. The reasons for women's absence from the arena of electoral politics are many. Is it because women are prevented from seeking and winning election, or is it because they have simply chosen not to enter the political arena?

Research in this area suggests several possibilities. Women's sex-role socialization has inhibited their participation in formal politics. Women and men are conditioned by society to play different roles. Men are more active in the public domain while women are more active in the private realm. The concept of socialization encompasses the development of the stereotypical belief that only certain patterns of behavior are suitable for women and that politics is not included in these behavior patterns. Women also encounter this problem with the dual role as mother/wife and politician, which can be difficult to combine. The lack of self-confidence among women has also reduced many women's desire to participate in politics.

The corruption of politics and the role of money have additionally limited many women's participation in the formal political arena. There is a complex interaction of structural, institutional and cultural variables that have had the effect of establishing the political realm as a near- male monopoly. During the last 15 years, Thailand has undergone an extraordinary transformation. It has changed from an authoritarian regime to a multiparty democracy in which politicians are chosen in regular elections. In the late 1990s, a range of new institutions was established. The new constitution has been heralded as one of the most important events in the democratization of Thailand's political systems, which witnessed tne transformation of parliament and significant changes in the electoral system.

The new constitution of 1997 has provided a significant enabling framework for gender rights. Article 30 states that women and men shall enjoy equal rights, this is a first step towards giving women more opportunities to participate in the male- dominated political arena. It was the women's movement that has continually emphasized the gender-based capsizing of political institutions. Nevertheless, Thai women's role in politics continues to be minimized to tokenism in their ascent to political power. The slow incremental increase in the numbers of women serving in the Thai parliament raises important questions concerning the impact of women in public office. If more and more women enter public office, what are the consequences likely to be for the content of politics? Does women's representation in the Thai parliament lead to women-friendly policies?

It appears that women do have some specific priorities, and evidence especially from the U.S. and Nordic countries has demonstrated that women representatives actively seek to promote their agendas. When we look at the national level of government in Thailand though, the question of women's representation becomes more problematic because women's representation in the parliament has remained at the range of level of tokenism for almost the entire period since women were granted the right to vote and hold office. In the late 1960s, for example, there were only six women in the House of Representatives, or a mere 2.8 per cent of the total House membership.

This gradually increased to about 4 per cent during the 1980s and jumped to 6 per cent after the 1992 elections. In the 2001 general elections, women occupied only 9.2 per cent of the seats in the lower house of the Thai parliament, a figure that is considerably below the Asian average of 14 per cent. The proportion of women in the lower house increased to 10.6 per cent in the 2005 general election, the highest ever in Thailand. In addition, women occupy only 10 per cent of the 200 seats in the Senate. This dismal record at the national level is also apparent at lower levels. Women legislators are markedly absent from provincial and local assemblies.

The local level is often seen as the level where women can move into the political arena with relative ease. Despite some factors that may positively affect women's representation in local government (i.e. less competition for positions available, possibility for women to participate in politics alongside employment and family responsibilities, and increased acceptance of women's involvement in local-level government), it remains difficult for women to break into electoral politics, even at the local level. Women's recruitment to local and provincial assemblies may be of interest because it provides a good training ground for women wishing to pursue political careers at higher levels of government, in addition to providing a future pool of women candidates for the Thai parliament.

Frequently local governments can serve as stepping-stones for women aspiring to parliament. However, the current low proportion of women elected to provincial and local assemblies provides only bleak prospects for the representation of women in parliament and other higher political positions in the future. Unlike many other countries, the representation of women in Thailand has been somewhat higher at the national level than at the local level until quite recently. One of the main reasons why fewer women are represented at local and regional levels than at the national level may be that most local political bodies comprise rural areas, which are predominantly influenced by traditional views of women's public and private roles.

The political sphere is reserved for men, and in many rural areas there exists strong prejudice against active participation by women in politics. Moreover, at the local level, power has traditionally remained vested in the hands of local worthies, and women have generally been marginalized in the affairs of villages and communities. Female political representation on the local level varies considerably depending on the degree of urbanization. In the Bangkok area, for instance, the proportion of female politicians on the local level is considerably larger than on the national level. The literature on women and politics suggests two major perspectives on political representation, namely, the descriptive and the substantive.

From the perspective of descriptive representation, electing more women serves the symbolic purpose of gender equality, and renders legitimacy to the political system. It argues for increasing women's representation in legislative bodies so that it better reflects their proportion in society. The substantive perspective claims that increased representation of women in parliament would make a substantive difference because women and men have different experiences and different priorities in political issues. Thus, it is considered important to incorporate women's interests and perspectives that lead them to advocate issues that are either marginalized or excluded, especially in times when legislative bodies are dominated by men.

Women officeholders are often assumed to act on behalf of women, working to introduce and pass legislation that improves their political, economic and social positions. The numerical presence of women presumes that female legislators will bring to politics perspectives, values and issues that are poorly represented. The presumption of female legislators acting on the behalf of women, or representing women's interests, constitutes a crucial part of many arguments in favor of gender parity in public office, and the legislature in particular. The substantive representation of women's interests implies that female politicians have a gendered awareness that leads them to act in certain ways.

Can we assume that female politicians have a shared experience and perspective that unites them because of their gender? There are differences among women politicians based on ideological, ethnic, religious, economic, social, or other differences. There will always be women legislators who deny gender as a factor in shaping their priorities in policy issues. There are important factors such as party policy and party discipline that influence their political behavior. There also exist male politicians who advance women's interests and form alliances with women politicians to promote those interests. In order to understand the question of whether women are in fact representing other women, it is important to keep in mind the possibility that women politicians represent differences among women.

WOMEN'S LEGISLATIVE ACTIVITIES AND POLICY PRIORITIES

Despite the recent increases of women in the national legislature in Thailand, we still know very little about these women. Who are they, and what motivated them to seek public office? Very little research has systematically explored the careers and the policy contributions of these women. Compared with female legislators in the 1990s, women parliamentarians now have a far better educational background. The demographic and social characteristics of representatives have changed over time. The newly elected legislators of the House of Representatives in 2001 were younger and decidedly better educated than their predecessors. In terms of education, female and male parliamentarians do not differ much.

Candidates have been required to have at least a bachelor's degree or its equivalent, but in comparison with those elected in the 1996 general elections, representatives with a master's degree increased by nearly 24 per cent, and from 17 to 41 per cent in the House of Representatives. The increase was particularly noteworthy among those elected in the party-list system: 43 per cent of the deputies had a master's degree and 17 per cent had a Ph.D. The majority of female legislators had been actively employed before becoming representatives. Indeed, they were predominantly women who were already involved in the public sphere in one way or another, either as professional or business women, local officeholders, or members of women's organizations.

Some entered politics from a civic worker or volunteer background. Female parliamentarians are more likely than their male colleagues to come from advantaged backgrounds and from political families. Both male and female parliamentarians are drawn disproportionately from the best educated in Thai society. However, women enter into national politics later in life than their male colleagues because women often have to fulfill responsibilities as mothers and wives before entering politics. My interviews with female politicians complemented by other data, show that women in parliament overwhelmingly tend to come from the middle and upper classes, and in many cases belong to prominent political families.

Many of them became politically active by being exposed to politics through family life or by joining organizations. Although some of the women politicians are feminists and have made efforts to advance women's causes, most of them are virtually indistinguishable from their male colleagues in their background, performance, and policy agendas. Do women legislators in Thailand serve as role models for the women of their country? Since the women parliamentarians in Thailand are from the same socio-economic elite as their male colleagues, it can be difficult for them to serve as role models for the masses of Thai women. Family ties in Thailand, as is the case elsewhere in Asia, is a key variable in the determination of political networks and success in public life.

Turning to an examination of the motivation of female legislators for becoming a political candidate, there is some diversity among the female politicians. The women were questioned about their motivation for entry into the national legislature: all expressed a motivation for entering politics that could be characterized as civic-inspired (they wanted to help the constituency, society or country in general, a goal which was coupled with a sense of public service), and some also expressed an opportunity-based motivation (such as they were encouraged to seek office, recruited to run, wanted to enter politics, or had previous political experience).

Most of them said that they received encouragement from their family circle to enter politics. Several female legislators entered political life through civic and volunteer activities, usually motivated by a sense of civic duty and a desire to make their constituency a better place. Two conclusions may be drawn from the interviews. First, women senators put more emphasis on civic-inspired motivations than their female colleagues in the House of Representatives. Second, women legislators of both houses of parliament pointed out that women in politics make more responsible choices, guided by civic-oriented considerations, rather than career or other opportunity-oriented motives, than their male counterparts.

A study of twenty senatorial candidates carried out by the Women in Politics Institute (2000) found some diversity among the respondents. When women senators were asked about their motives for seeking office, all respondents gave civic-oriented reasons. The most common motivational theme was to help solve the country's problems and create a better society. Interestingly enough, many female candidates did not emphasize the issues of women and other underprivileged groups in Thai society. Some of the respondents gave a more opportunity-based explanation, such as they were supported by various organizations, friends or their families. Moreover, all respondents were influenced in one way or another by the fact that the Thai political system was changed by the adoption of the new constitution.

THE IMPACT OF WOMEN POLITICIANS

Do women legislators in the Thai Parliament have some specific policy preferences and interests different from those of male legislators? This question of women's representation becomes more problematic as a result of the small number of women in the Parliament. It is expected that the priorities and interests of female and male politicians are relatively similar because, as long as women in a legislative body constitute a small minority, they tend to adapt to existing conditions and act more like their male colleagues than their female colleagues.

In the international literature on women and politics, there has been a great deal of discussion on questions concerning the relationship between the numerical presence of women in politics, sometimes referred to as descriptive representation, and the expression of women's interests, or substantive representation. Many researchers interested in determining the impact of women on the policy process argue that issues pertaining to women would be better represented if there were more women legislators. They believe that the more women legislators elected, the more likely it is that women-friendly policies would be enacted.

Electing more women potentially translates into increased substantive representation of women as an interest. However, there is no guarantee that increased descriptive representation would lead to enhanced substantive representation. If women and men politicians in general have different attitudes and perspectives on many issues, then it becomes important to elect more women to look after issues of specific interest to women. Past studies in this area indicate that women do not hold distinctive policy preferences as do men, except on a few issues. Recent research, however, indicate that there exist differences in attitudes and behavior between the sexes.

Studies of female politicians, especially from state legislatures in the United States, show that they have distinctive priorities and interests, especially when the numbers of women legislators increase beyond token levels. Female politicians are more attentive to issues of special interest to women such as families, children, health, education, and social issues. One of the questions regarding the small proportion of women legislators in Thailand is whether or not female politicians make a difference in their impact on Thai politics. If the Thai parliament increased its amount of women legislators, could we expect then a shift to issues that reflect women's concerns? Would politics with a high proportion of women politicians lead to policies which are different from those enacted by a strongly male-dominated political system?

Will the nature of Thai politics change with the increasing share of women in political bodies? Much has been written about the impact women have on issue areas of traditional concern to women in established democracies in the West. Many recent studies done on women's legislative activities tend to suggest that female legislators approach their work from a distinctive perspective based on their experiences as women. Indeed, the existing literature is rich with respect to the policy priorities and preferences of female legislators, especially in the Nordic countries and the United States. A number of studies claim that women have different policy agendas and priorities compared to men.

Moreover, these gender differences are determined by the very differences in their socialization and life experiences. Once elected, women politicians are expected to legislate differently to men. For example, female legislators are more concerned with issues related to traditional areas of interest to women, such as families, social welfare, education, women's rights, children, environment, and health care. Their male colleagues are more likely to be concerned with "men's issues" such as economy, finance, business and defence. A survey of nearly 200 female parliamentarians in 65 countries by the Inter-Parliamentary Union (IPU) showed that women have different priorities and interests compared to those of men.

Nearly 82 per cent of the respondents believed that women hold conceptually different ideas about society and politics. A very high proportion of respondents to this survey agreed that women's involvement in politics makes a difference. 86 per cent of respondents believed that women's participation in the political process changed the nature of politics by bringing about positive changes in form, political behavior and traditional attitudes, substance, processes and outcomes. Moreover, an overwhelming majority, nearly 90 per cent, felt they had a responsibility to represent the interests and views of women (Inter- Parliamentary Union 2000).

The theory of critical mass, when applied to gender relations in politics, suggests that when women remain a distinct minority within a legislative assembly, they tend to conform to the prevailing norms, but once the numbers of women reach a certain size, there will be a change in the nature of political discourse and policy agenda as the minority begins to act distinctively and challenge the patterns of gender interactions. It has been argued that "critical mass" numbers of women are crucial in transforming policies and politics. Few women do not represent a broad base for change, nor can they represent women of diverse backgrounds. Dolan and Ford, for example, argue that "[t]here is a variety of evidence to support the 'critical mass' thesis-that women act more distinctively once their numbers reach a certain threshold" (1998:77).

Many others claim that it is difficult to keep women's substantive concerns on the agenda in the absence of a strong presence of women within Parliament. In a study of the Arizona state legislature, Saint-Germain concluded that women do make a difference in state legislatures. She found that when women were present in small numbers in the legislature, the proportion of bills proposed by women and men with regard to areas of traditional interests to women was not noticeably different. However, once women captured more than 15% of the seats in the legislature, women changed their legislative behavior-they were more likely than men to propose such bills.

It has been said that, with the proportion of women below 15 per cent of a legislative assembly, women members may be relegated to token status. As Taylor- Robinson and Heath argued, "The problem for token women is that they may not feel that they have enough support to rock the boat and bring up topics of interest to women, because such topics may be criticized or ignored by the male super-majority" (2003:81).

The existing literature seems to suggest that as more women become elected, there will be more evidence of gender-based differences in policy priorities in legislative bodies, since an increase of women would include other life experiences with alternative lenses through which to view issues, problems, and policies. Some scholars claim that a critical mass of women legislators will be needed in order to pursue a women's agenda in the legislative body.

Norris and Lovenduski argue: When a group remains a distinct minority within a larger society, its member will seek to adapt to their surroundings, conforming to the predominant rules of the game...But once the group reaches a certain size, critical mass theory suggests that there will be a qualitative change in the nature of group interactions, as the minority starts to assert itself and thereby transform the institutional culture, norms and values. One of the most convincing evidence of the "critical mass" thesis comes from Sue Thomas's (1994) study of female and male politicians in 12 state legislatures in the United States.

In states where the proportion of women in the legislature was below 15 per cent, women were reluctant to take a high profile on women's issues. However, in states where the proportion of women was 20 per cent or more, female legislators gave priority to legislation that addressed traditional women's interest areas as well as increased their legislative activity and success at obtaining enactment for their proposal in such areas.

It is important to note, as Sawyer points out: "to increase the number of women in parliament, or even to increase the number of feminists in parliament, is insufficient to ensure that 'women' are better represented". Nevertheless, previous findings on the policy priorities of women in respect to men have proved to be rather inconsistent. Some studies have found little evidence of gender differences in priorities and agendas due to party discipline, which tends to inhibit the manifestation of any gender differences in legislative behavior. A critical question was whether female legislators can make a difference in a predominantly male institution like the parliament in Thailand.

The scarcity of women in the parliament has made it difficult to evaluate the policy impact of electing women. Indeed, with 21 women serving in the Senate, compared with only 46 in the House of Representatives, it seems unlikely that they would "act for" women. It is difficult to test the "critical mass" proposition-that women act more distinctively once their numbers reach a certain threshold, since the proportion of women in Thailand is far from attaining a sufficient critical mass to enable them pursue a different legislative agenda than men. For women politicians in both chambers of the national assembly, the idea of a critical mass ranging from 15 to 35 per cent women is of little relevance.

The percentage of women in these bodies remains well below 15 per cent. In any case, one can ask the question; do women politicians in the Thai Parliament legislate differently than men, even if they are in a token position? As mentioned previously, research on gender differences in policy priorities have focused on the U.S. and Nordic legislatures. These studies have shown that, in many cases, women do pursue a different legislative agenda to men. Research that goes beyond highly advanced industrial democracies is rare.

Taylor-Robinson and Heath (2003) have extended the research on gender difference in policy priority beyond the U.S. and Nordic countries to Honduras. Their research does not support the generalization that women legislators tend to place a higher priority than men on legislation relating to issues of traditional interest to women such as children and family issues. They found no gender-based differences in policy priorities on these themes.

Yet they found that the results of their study support the contention that, as with women legislators in advanced democracies in the West, women politicians in the Honduran Congress put a higher priority on women's rights than their male colleagues, even when they have only token representation: ...even in an inauspicious setting, where women have only token representation in the legislature, and economic and social forces make the task of women in politics difficult, women still legislate differently than men.

Particularly when it comes to women's rights issues, even token women representatives play an important role in bringing legislative attention to women's concerns. In looking at women's legislative activities inside the Thai parliament, I focused on committee service activities. In Thailand, as in many other countries, committee positions play an important role in the legislative process. Given the importance of committees in determining what issues get placed on the legislative agenda, the appointment of more women to relevant committees may increase the openness of the parliament to take up women's issue legislation. Previous research in Western democracies found female legislators serving on committees dealing with traditional "women's issues", such as education and health and social welfare.

Thomas (1994), for example, wrote that female state legislators in the United States were more likely than their male colleagues to hold seats on committees related to their traditional role as caregivers. Either by choice or discrimination based on sex-role stereotypes, women rarely serve on committees dealing with finance, budget, or science and technology. The women legislators in my interviews were involved in various careers, including the health field, education, business, and social work. Their educational and occupational background proved important in determining what these women will select in regard to committee assignments once they are in office.

In looking at committee assignments in Thailand, I found that female legislators in both houses of the parliament focus much of their legislative activity on issues of traditional interest, but not to the exclusion of all other issue areas. Not surprisingly, nearly 65 per cent of the members of the House Committee on Children, Youth, Women and the Aged consisted of women, areas where women have traditionally borne disproportionate responsibility. Further, women constitute 24-29 per cent of committees such as Tourism, Public Health, and Social welfare.

Yet, as compared with the situation in the past, women were no longer exclusively confined to a narrow set of committee assignments since women have recently made their way to the more traditional "male" committees, to a certain extent. Almost 24 per cent of the committee members on Science and Technology and nearly 18 per cent of the Foreign Affairs Committee in the lower house are women. Despite their small numbers, women who did succeed in getting elected were no longer dominantly swayed along sex-stereotyped lines into 'women's committees'.

With this said, women are much less likely than men to sit on business committees. In committees such as Communications and Telecommunications, Armed Forces, Economic Development, Monetary Affairs, Finance and Banking, either there was only one woman or none sitting on the committee. The picture is also quite similar in the Senate. The data on committee assignments appear to indicate that these women parliamentarians pay considerable attention to issues of traditional concern to women.

It would be misleading, however, to conclude that Thai women parliamentarians as a group are exclusively concerned with issues having an impact on the needs and lives of women to the neglect of other issues. What about women's leadership activities inside committees? The chair is the focal point of committee activities and an important source of legislative power through controlling the agenda and the flow of discussion. The gender pattern in committee assignments is much more pronounced in the profile of women committee chairs.

Only three women in the lower house held committee chairs in 2003, all within the traditional "women's committees" of Children, Youth, Women and the Aged, Consumer Protection, and Social Welfare. Despite the increase in the number of women MPs in the 2001 House election, the proportion of committee chairpersons who are women is much less than the proportion of legislators who are women. As for the Senate, the proportion of chairpersons who are female is the same as the proportion of female legislators. Only two women held a chair position in the standing committees on Public Health and Labor and Social Welfare. Why have women's membership and their leadership been concentrated on certain types of committees?

There are several plausible explanations. One is that women legislators may have been steered toward areas of interest to women because of stereotypical views about their expertise. Another plausible explanation is that women may have chosen "female-oriented" committees because of their interest in these issue areas. It is out of their own choice rather than outright discrimination that this gender disparity in committee assignments occurred. In short, appointments to committees tended to be based on the expertise and interests of the legislator. To examine the role of these issue concerns in the legislative career of female legislators, we also have to look at their legislative behavior.

In contrast to committee assignments, women legislators did not specifically target women's issues in their legislative focus. Although nearly all the female legislators of the Thai Parliament I interviewed expressed women's common interests and concerns, they differed in the extent to which these concerns were salient. Judging from these interviews, it seems that both men and women have supported bills promoting issues related to women's interests in many instances. Yet, female legislators have appeared to be more concerned with women's interests than their male colleagues, even though they felt did not feel any "obligation" to represent women's interests.

To explore further whether female politicians behave differently to male politicians, where women have only token representation in the legislature, I examined the legislative agendas of both female and male legislators in the House of Representative from the time Prime Minister Thaksin formed the government. The bills were grouped into six categories by subject area (children, education, environment, health care/

public health, welfare-social security, and other). The data was obtained from the offices of the House of Representatives, which keep records of all bills proposed and the bill's fate. It is difficult to assess the impact of women's political presence in national legislative assemblies such as the House of Representatives in the Thai parliament due to the small number of women MPs, as well as to the strength of party discipline.

Are women legislators more likely than their male colleagues to attach priority to legislation concerning women? Women MPs have had an impact on a number of content areas. The presence of women legislators has made a difference in the number of bills introduced and passed dealing specifically with children and welfare-social security, the areas where women have traditionally shared a disproportionate responsibility for the rearing of children and for the care of those who cannot care for themselves.

Proportionally speaking, the single subject of children has received an unusually large amount of legislative attention. However, there is no significant gender-based difference in the numbers of bills relating to children proposed. It is possible that male legislators in Thailand have become more diverse and knowledgeable about the issue of children than their forefathers. Contrary to my expectations and patterns of the long-established democracies in Europe and the United States, where women legislators tend more often than men to prioritize issues such as the environment, public health and health care, women legislators in Thailand did not introduce and work on legislation specifically relating to these areas.

In sum, with respect to the issues of children and welfare/social security, even token female legislators play an important role in introducing and pushing those issues through the legislative process. Perhaps the increased presence of women legislators will make a significant difference in the types of bills to be introduced. Several explanations arise as to why women legislators did not introduce and prioritize of issues important to women through the legislative process. One possibility is that they may find themselves pressured to conform and fit in to an overwhelmingly male-dominated institution.

Why do we need more women in leadership positions? Generally speaking, female political leaders in Thailand appear to believe that women are a force for good governance. Pavena Hongsakul, former minister of the Prime Minister's Office, said: "Women tend to be more concerned with creating a just society. And 99 per cent of women are clean (not involved in corruption)". Similarly, Sudarat Keyuraphan, the first woman to hold a ministerial post in the Interior Ministry, claimed that if half the Cabinet was female, there would be far less corruption in Thailand: "And by tackling the issue of corruption we could make a major contribution to improving just about everything in our society".

In addition to women's sanitizing and cleansing influence on politics, some female leaders have emphasized women's distinct approach to problem solving. Women legislators are more likely than their male colleagues to conceptualize issues and policy problems more broadly. For example, Dhipvadee Meksawan, director-general of the Office of the Civil Service Commission said: "Generally, men tend to particularise problems while women's way of thinking is more holistic. On average, women are less overbearing and are therefore more capable of paving the way to a democratic society as opposed to a pyramidal or hierarchical social structure". Other female leaders in Thailand were convinced that women legislators have shown to be more sensitive to issues most directly affecting women, families, and children than their male colleagues.

For example, Laddawan Wongsriwong, a former deputy secretary general to the prime minister, said: "They are more concerned about the quality of life, about children, education, AIDS and the environment". The former Deputy Education Minister Kanchana Silpaacha was of the opinion that "men may give more importance to issues other than those directly related to the needs of women and children". Supatra Masdit and Pavena Hongsakula acknowledged that female leaders have distinct interests, but emphasized that they shouldn't confine themselves to "women's issues.

In addition, in my interviews, female parliamentarians expressed the belief that women bring a different perspective to the legislative process. However, only one of respondents felt a sense of responsibility to represent women. Some of them were concerned about being pigeonholed as exponents of women's issues. There was a feeling that if they devoted themselves to women's issues, they could experience this as an obstacle in their political careers, by becoming closely associated with "soft" issues with a low status. Employing data on bill introduction, this study shows that female legislators in the Thai Parliament do advocate a "female agenda" in the areas of children and welfare/social security, but no significant gender differences were found in other issue areas considered to be of traditional interest to women.

Even though record numbers of women were elected to the House of Representatives in 2001 and 2005, they were still a very small minority of members. Women MPs have also faced problems because many of them were relative newcomers, lacking relevant expertise and experience. Although the new electoral system did help to facilitate the election of women to the House of Representatives, it also acted to reinforce party dominance. Consequently, women legislators in the House feel more accountable to their party than to any potential groupings outside the parliament, such as women. Women do not behave differently than men with regard to a number of "women's areas", as long as they constitute a small minority.

The impact of party is stronger than the impact of gender. Although most of the women legislators I interviewed recognized shared concerns among women and had a gendered awareness that women and men's life experiences give them different perspectives, only a few felt that women should speak up for matters that affect women. Increased women's presence in national assemblies may not necessarily lead to improved representation of women's interests and issues. "Changing the gender composition of elected assemblies," Ann Phillips argues, "is largely an enabling condition...but it cannot present itself as a guarantee" (1995: 83).

In other words, increased descriptive representation does not automatically lead to enhanced substantive representation.

The extent to which a relationship exists between the numerical presence of women and the representation of women's interests, however formulated, is an empirical question. Women legislators may additionally disregard women's interests and behave like their male counterparts. It has been said that the token status of women in public office keeps them within the mainstream of politics. It seems that while some female legislators are sensitive to the needs of women and pay considerable attention to so-called women's issues, it does not easily translate into an improved representation of their interests.

They said that their role was not different from that of their male colleagues. It became clear, both from my conversations with the respondents and my observations of political women in Thailand, that as far as members of the House of Representatives are concerned, women's political loyalties rest with their political parties and constituents rather than with women *per se*. Even among women of the same party, it seems that their solidarity and loyalty rest primarily with the party, their constituents, and political patrons-not with the other women in the party. At the same time, female legislators pointed out that if some gender solidarity could be developed, then so much the better. There is strength in numbers.

Some female politicians told me that their goal is to reach the "critical mass" stage that will allow them to advance their political position and gain influence in the policymaking process. Forging alliances with other female politicians across party lines can be one opportunity for women to promote their interests. But alliances are not necessarily exclusively gender based. In many cases, alliances have been forged with male colleagues in order to bring about positive outcomes. Even if the percentage of women were to exceed a certain threshold, for example 15 per cent or more, it is not likely that this would have any significant impact on female solidarity within the House of Representatives, given the relatively high level of political partisanship, which exists in that body.

More women parliamentarians do not necessary mean better representation of women's interests. Attempts to forge unity among women MPs in the past have been prevented by the claims of party loyalty. Existing research tends to suggest that the presence or absence of an organized women's caucus can influence the extent to which women legislators actively discuss and work on legislation that affects women and have a positive influence on the passage of such bills. Moreover, the presence of a women's caucus provides female legislators with additional resources beyond their numbers. In an effort to provide a focal point for women legislators of all parties, the Women's Parliamentarian Club, consisting of women members of the lower house and senators, was established in 1992.

In the Thai context, women legislators come together more as an informal group than through a formal legislative caucus. It was intended as a forum for women legislators in both houses of the national legislature to meet together and provide encouragement and support for efforts that they make on behalf of women. Although it is the only formal space for women legislators, the Club has not been very successful in forging unity. Unfortunately, a majority of women legislators are infrequently involved in the activities of the Club. It seems that women legislators in the parliament do not have a strong collective sense of group membership since women are not a homogenous group. Its core membership consist of only about twenty members and, in the absence of a feminist identity or orientation among Thai parliamentarians, it meets quite infrequently and informally.

OBSTACLES TO INCREASED FEMALE REPRESENTATION

What obstacles do Thai women encounter when they try to get elected into political office? In a patriarchal society like Thailand with a strong emphasis on the dominant role of men, the obstacles to women's candidacy and representation are many and extremely difficult to surmount. Women who attempt to run for elective office experience considerable difficulty. There are many factors that combine to preclude women from elected office in Thailand, thus the lack of women in political bodies cannot be accounted for by one single factor.

Such an explanation for the lack of women in Thai politics is multi-faceted and requires some space for discussion.

Various factors that underlie women's representation, or lack thereof, in advanced industrialized democracies are well researched and understood, while our understanding of women's representation in developing countries is much poorer. Moreover, Matland (1998) found in his study on women's political representation in developed and developing countries that none of the significant variables promoting women's representation in established democracies, such as electoral systems, women's participation in the labor force, the cultural standing of women and the country's level of development, has a statistically significant and consistent effect in those of less developed countries.

His research seems to indicate that a minimum level of socio- economic development is needed to create favourable conditions, such as the development of electoral systems and women's participation in the labor force, in order to have any positive effects on the representation of women. Otherwise, anything below the minimum threshold has very minimal impact on factors favoring the representation of women in developed democracies. Pippa Norris (1987) argues that women candidates must overcome three major barriers to get elected to public office. First, they must be willing to become candidates for office. Women's political representation would increase if more women were willing to become candidates.

Women are underrepresented because most of the candidates for office are men; it is impossible to get a woman elected if no woman runs. Second, the party gatekeepers must choose those women who desire to run as candidates. The attitudes of political parties toward women in politics can be a source of great difficulty for women in their efforts to overcome barriers that hinder their representation. Third, the voters must select the female candidates. The sex of the candidates plays a factor in whether a woman is selected, since women candidates can face difficulties in winning approval from voters due to the prevalence of sex-role stereotyping.

In other words, in most political systems women need to overcome three concrete barriers in order to be elected to parliament. These three barriers are eligibility, selection and election. The process of legislative recruitment involves the availability of individuals who are first, simultaneously interested in political activities and have the resources to get involved in politics; second, willing to come forward and to run for elective office; and last, who are selected among the pool of aspirants by the gatekeepers casting the final decisions over who is to stand for election. This supply and demand model is not unique and has been applied to established democracies.

RECRUITMENT PROCESS

In this section, various factors that influence the parliamentary representation of women in Thailand will be examined. Through the recruitment process of eligibility, selection, and election, I will attempt to delineate the different variables responsible for women's access to the Thai parliament in order to provide a better understanding of the obstacles women face in political participation.

What variables inhibit the mobilization of women as parliamentary candidates? The first step is to be eligible to stand for elections. Eligibility as such refers not only to the basic democratic rights such as the right to vote and right to stand for elections, but also enumerates the informal requirements for candidacy. Such legal requirements for the eligibility of candidates include nationality, age, residence, holding public office, and education. After the enfranchisement of women, the formal requirements have not appeared to present any particular barrier to women in running for public office in most political systems and, therefore, do not seem to work to the disadvantage of women, relative to men. But, how do the formal rules of eligibility affect women in Thailand?

The legal eligibility requirements are the same for men and women, and thus fail to explain the paucity of women in the Thai parliament. The informal rules and norms of Thai society, however, may be seen to present severe obstacles, given the lamentable social and economic position of women in Thai society. Generally speaking, parliamentarians are part of the socio-economic elite and are recruited from occupations in which there are few women; they are additionally distinguished by their high levels of education. Similarly, women who do aspire to stand for national elections often come from influential political families.

SOCIAL AND CULTURAL OBSTACLES

It is commonly assumed that socio-economic variables, such as the ratio of women's literacy, the ratio of women's participation in the work force, and the ratio of university-educated women, have an effect on women's political representation in the public arena. A recent study, for example, concludes that women's representation tends to increase when women approach the same level as men in areas of literacy, labor force participation and university education. In Thailand, when compared to other countries in Asia, the ratio of women's employment outside the home is high. In fact, Thailand has one of the highest participation rates of women in the labor force in Asia, accounting for nearly half of the working population.

However, such activities apparently do not have the effect of stimulating women's participation in politics. Women are concentrated in workplaces that are traditionally considered female and within these work places the overwhelming majority of women hold low-ranking jobs. Women are rarely found in high-level positions in economic structures where men acquire the skills and behavior patterns necessary and advantageous in the formal political arena. Although economic and social developments have liberated Thai women in many ways, and their participation in the paid labor force has increasingly become more visible, politics remains, on the whole, a male activity. At all levels of government, women are fewer in number, and if anything, occupy marginal positions in the formal political arena.

The paucity of women in the Thai legislature cannot be attributed to the level of women's participation in the labor market. What then can account for the extremely low proportion of women candidates? Studies on the relationships between socioeconomic changes and cultural values have resulted in the development of two contending schools of thought. The modernization school has argued that industrialization brings about pervasive cultural change. For instance, Ronald Inglehart (1997) argues that systematic changes in societal culture and its value system take place as a result of the shift from pre-industrial to industrial society, and additionally from industrial to post-industrial society. The other opposing school emphasizes the enduring nature of traditional cultural values and attitudes despite rapid socioeconomic changes, and claims that traditional values tend to persist in the industrial era and have an autonomous impact on society.

Thailand has experienced rapid social, economic, and political changes in recent decades. How have these changes affected societal culture and its value system in Thailand? The case of Thailand does not support the central tenet of modernization theory that economic development is closely associated with major changes in traditional values and beliefs. According to this theory, industrialization leads eventually to changes in gender roles, attitudes toward authority, and political participation. Traditional values persist in today's Thai society, despite the rapid socioeconomic changes that have taken place in recent decades.

The political culture in Thailand has a traditional negative attitude towards the participation of women in political life. It is still common to see politics and women constructed as each other's antithesis. Traditional political culture in Thailand has been essentially elitist and non-egalitarian, thus many traditional views on the role of women continue to prevail. The role of women has long been primarily confined to that of wife, mother and housekeeper. The demands of domestic and parental obligations and the social separation of the sexes have prevented women from participating in the public arena on the same equal basis as men. As result, women have thereby not been able to obtain the experiences that are required for a political career. In addition, tradition can be a powerful force and religion further plays a key role in the lives of the great majority of Thai people.

The deep and broad cultural heritage of Thai society, and more particularly its religious elements, has left an imprint on cultural values, despite modernization. In short, traditional values continue to exert an independent influence on the process of modernization in Thailand. According to cultural explanations, women in traditional societies tend to be reluctant to become candidates for elective office. They may not come forward because they anticipate being discriminated against. Moreover, if they run for office, they are disadvantaged relative to male candidates.

Women's chances for election to parliament are generally not as good as men's, and studies in the past have for the most part failed to present systematic evidence confirming the relationship between cultural variables and women's representation in elected office, since it is difficult to test empirically the influence of culture on women's representation. However, there is now strong and persuasive evidence that cultural factors constitute a key factor in explaining women's entry into elected office.

Pippa Norris and Ronald Inglehart (2003) have put forward the argument that prevailing political culture affects women's political recruitment. Voters in a traditional political culture are more likely than those in an egalitarian culture to perceive women as less qualified than men to run for public office. In fact, systematic cross national evidence has shown that egalitarian attitudes toward women as political leaders are strongly related to the proportion of women elected to public office.

One of the most important cultural factors in explaining women's under- representation in politics is sex-role socialization. According to theories of sex- role socialization, women and men are socialized to accept gendered assignments to different kinds of roles in life. For instance, women's domestic roles are viewed as incompatible with the toughness and assertiveness that politics and political leadership require; thus politics is perceived as a male domain. As a consequence, such stereotypical attitudes influence whether women are prepared to run for office.

What is discovered in many societies with traditional cultural values is that women may be reluctant to come forward as candidates for elected office. In a survey of nearly 200 female parliamentarians in 65 countries by the Inter-parliamentary Union (IPU), many respondents (76 per cent) cited hostile attitudes toward women's political participation as an important obstacle to running for parliament. The exclusion of women from public life in Western cultures also reflects the warp and woof of Thai culture. The influence of a hierarchical and authoritarian culture in which women's roles are defined by Thai Buddhism, which is circumscribed by more or less non-egalitarian attitudes towards women's political role, has subsequently led to the low participation of women in political life.

Throughout the history of Thai culture, two primary beliefs about men and women have prevailed. First, women have been viewed as the inferior sex and second, that men and women are fundamentally different psychologically and sexually. Furthermore, both male dominance and the male/female dichotomy are conceived in religious terms and Buddhism, for instance, has repeatedly legitimized women's subordination by providing a rationale for containing women in the private world. Women in Thailand today, as in many other Asian countries, still live in a shadow of a long tradition of female subordination, with a rigid division between the public and private emanating from Brahmanism. Women are prohibited from being ordained as monks and as a result, they are frequently considered to be 'merit deficient'-unable to obtain merit as monks.

While women can become nuns, the status of nuns is held as inferior to that of monks. However, a woman can at times obtain merit through a son who has been ordained; hence upon entering monk hood, sons can pass on the merit to their mothers. In the spirit of Thai Buddhism, women are viewed as 'polluters', and there is fear that women will "contaminate and lessen the sacredness of Buddha images, and especially holy amulets worn by men". Any physical contact between women and monks is forbidden.

There is a widespread fear that, upon entering the public sphere, women may drain strength from men. In short, the pattern of male supremacy and women's subordination in Thai society is underpinned by Buddhism. This religious influence can additionally be found in the legal codes of the country through, for instance, the many laws relating to labor and family, which have been discovered to be discriminatory. Consequently, the potent influence of Thai Buddhism tends to reinforce traditional social roles assigned to women, reinforcing cultural values that continue to marginalize women's political interests.

EDUCATIONAL OBSTACLES

One of the important reasons for the paucity of women in the Thai parliament has been their under-representation in the eligibility pool of the population from which candidates for the national assembly are drawn. It has often been said that women's educational, occupational, and socio-economic status is important in determining the eligibility of women for elective office. Women often lack the "appropriate background" to be chosen as a candidate. Despite the fact that the educational level of women in Thailand has risen substantially in recent decades, the formal requirements for candidacy in the Senate and the House of Representatives, requiring the minimum of a bachelor's degree, seems to work to the disadvantage of women, relative to men.

This recent requirement has reduced the number of prospective politicians, which correlates with claims made by many potential women candidates who cite a lack of higher education as a significant factor. Many women leaders at the local level who do not have a university degree became disqualified from running for elected office at the national level. The high educational profile of parliamentarians has thus only served to reinforce elitism in national politics.

Orathai Kokpol observed that the requirement of a bachelor's degree for candidacy discriminates against women: [I]t has a negative impact on social groups with a low level of education such, as farmers, industrial workers and informal sector workers, because it excludes the majority of them from the right to stand as a candidate in an election. This has reduced the already low representation of these groups even further. In contrast, this requirement favours civil servants as the most educated group in Thai society... The fact that under 10 per cent of Thai people with passive voting rights hold bachelors' degrees brings into question whether this requirement for candidacy obstructs democratic representation.

OCCUPATIONAL OBSTACLES

Women are also handicapped when the question of occupation is considered. Women are scarcely found in the professional, administrative, and managerial occupations that often lead to political careers. Women's occupational backgrounds are often not as "suitable" for elective office as those of men; hence recruitment of potential politicians to the parliament in Thailand emphasizes a certain strata of the population. In the 2001 general election, three types of occupational backgrounds were prominent among candidates and elected members of the House of Representatives. They were primarily politicians, businessmen, and civil servants.

As a result of the high educational requirements, bureaucratic positions have now become a significant channel into parliament. The proportion of candidates with bureaucratic backgrounds dramatically increased from 6 per cent in the 1996 election to 24 per cent in the 2001 election for the House of Representatives. It is also interesting to see the decrease in the number and proportion of candidates with political backgrounds dropping from nearly 18 per cent in 1996 to 12 per cent in 2001. It is not clear whether this change can be attributed to the requirements of a bachelor's degree.

Businessmen have always been an important component of the pool of candidates, but the percentage of candidates with business backgrounds has decreased to 24 per cent in the 2001 election, lower than previous elections. The occupational backgrounds of the candidates for the 2005 general election appeared similar to candidates in the previous election; when examining the backgrounds of senatorial candidates, it was found that civil servants (38%), lawyers (17%), and candidates with business backgrounds (16%) were amongst the most prominent. Since women are found to be in few numbers in such "suitable" occupations, this has only further reduced their opportunities of securing a political career.

THE SELECTION PROCESS

The second stage consists of the selection process whereby potential candidates can be identified and selected for elections. One of the most significant factors that may increase the proportion of women's representation is the willingness of women to put themselves forward as candidates. The decision to run for elected office can be influenced by a number of factors that operate at the individual level. On the supply side, these include such factors as the resources and motivation of potential candidates. These resources include financial backing, human resources needed to run the campaign, education, availability of time, organizational affiliation, and established networks. Generally speaking, fewer women possess these necessary resources.

In interviews female parliamentarians mentioned poor self-esteem, lack of experience, and lack of resources as some of the major reasons why women do not want to run for office in Thailand. Women often do not have the experience necessary for a political role, as well as lack the confidence deemed appropriate for running for public office. Women's perception of their own self-worth is shaped and reinforced by prevailing male-biased social norms and beliefs. It may be the case that women additionally may lack information and knowledge about the procedures and mechanisms involved in politics.

One Thai study argues, however, that Thai women's interest in politics is not less than that of men and that they are even more knowledgeable about politics than men. Another reason women have been slow to enter the arena of electoral politics is related to their view of politics. Female values are viewed by many women as incompatible with the money schemes and corruption associated with Thai politics. For a woman aspiring to stand for election, her perception of politics is important. In Thailand, as in many other developing countries, it is often assumed that the political game is too dirty for women to play because of their supposed moral superiority, an excuse often used by females not to enter politics.

Politics is viewed as representing an arena for dishonesty in which politicians do not shy away from bribery and corruption and frequently pursue their own selfish interests. According to people's attitudes and the self-conceptions of women legislators in the Thai parliament, women as symbols of innocence and virtue contrast with corrupt Thai politics. Almost all female parliamentarians I interviewed emphasized that women's distaste for abuse of power and money in cultivating influence has made it difficult for many women to be part of political life. But at the same time, it is pointed out that the participation of women in politics is important because of their sanitizing influence on politics.

They were optimistic about the future as well as convinced that voters perceive women candidates as a new alternative in the tarnished political scene dominated by men. Voters believe that men and women alike would increasingly vote for women candidates as they tire of the corruption that has riddled Thai politics for years. This linkage between the self-conception of women as symbols of innocence and moral superiority and the voters was also evident in an interview with Sudarat Keyuraphan, a woman MP of the Thai Rak Thai party, conducted by the Far Eastern Economic Review. As she explained, "I deeply believe that most voters would like to elect women politicians at both national and local levels. They have strong confidence that women politicians have better intentions and are less corrupt than male politicians".

Thai elections feature frequent vote-buying, vote-rigging and cheating. The high level of vote-buying and malpractice in Thailand is a deterrent to women coming forward as candidates. The political reforms in the second half of the 1990s were meant to put an end to the corruption and vote-buying which had marred elections in Thailand for decades. The 1997 Constitution included several provisions designed to fight corruption. One such provision incorporated compulsory voting in an attempt to make the electorate so large that vote buying would become extremely expensive. Another provision worked towards greater transparency of political contributions. Moreover, it included the creation of a mixed electoral system in which 100 members of the House of Representatives are elected under a party-list system while 400 members are to be elected in single-member constituencies.

Nonetheless, as the elections of 2000, 2001 and 2005 show, vote-buying and other election irregularities persists as a reminder of the continuing deficits of Thai democracy. While it is difficult to assess the level of vote-buying, the practice seems to exist in all parts of the country, although it is most common in rural regions. Since candidates cannot distinguish themselves by a set of distinctive party policy stances, they continue to rely on their own vote-mobilization apparatus with vote canvassers. This means that candidates have to foster personal networks for a support base through district services and by building up a large campaign war chest. It was estimated that despite the new regulations to eliminate vote-buying and corruption, a total of 20 billion baht in bribe money was circulated during the election campaign, with the price of votes ranging anywhere from 50 to 1,000 baht in the 2001 elections to the House of Representatives.

The Senate election in March 2000 was seen by many Thais as the first test of political reform under the 1997 Constitution, which attempted to broaden citizens' participation in politics while limiting the influence of traditional money politics and corruption. There were hopes that Thailand's first Senate election would bring about a change in the country's corruption-riddled, fragile democracy. However, there were numerous reports of electoral corruption and malpractice, such as vote buying and voting irregularities, including accusations that political parties were financing candidates behind the scenes. As for other individual-related factors, financial resources have come to play a determining role.

The electoral contests in Thailand, notwithstanding the official ceilings imposed by the National Election Commission, are very costly; this gives an undue and unnecessary advantage to candidates with large sources of funds available to them, over those whose resources are more limited. Women, due to lack of financial resources, often find these measures prohibitive and unhelpful. There is very little reliable data available thus far that assesses the use of campaign funds under the new system, but it is still more than likely that a successful candidate needs huge amounts of money. In 1995, for example, a politician in a typical constituency in the northeastern region spent 20-25 million baht.

In the 2001 House of Representatives election, it was estimated that the total amount spent by a politician was within the range of 30-50 million baht, and in some cases up to 70 million baht. Where do these funds come from? Candidates draw upon their own and family resources and from whatever wealthy, personal connections they may have in the constituencies. In the case of candidates for the House of Representatives, some economic support for approved candidates comes directly from their parties. The fact that candidates need much financial resources to get elected has rendered political office at the national level, especially in the House of Representatives, beyond the reach of many politically ambitious women.

Electoral and financial rules for the Senatorial elections forbade candidates to belong to a political party and further regulated how the money should be raised and spent. In many cases, candidates for the Senate had to raise the bulk of the money themselves. Although candidates for the Senate are not permitted to conduct election campaigns, money still proved to be an important asset for election. Personal support organizations, based on networks of vote canvassers for politicians, are a key factor for the high cost of electoral politics in Thailand.

In order to buy votes, candidates rely on a network of vote canvassers, who usually consist of influential individuals in the villages. Despite the campaigns against vote-buying, its practice is an important factor in making election campaigns very expensive, and thus prone to corruption and bribery. A would-be politician's first tasks are to form a supporters' organization, and then do everything possible to obtain the support of voters. In order to cultivate a supporters' organization that will ensure election and re-election, candidates use enormous amounts of money in presenting gifts of money to their constituents.

The larger the supporters' organization, the greater the amount of money required. When it comes to elections, it is not so much the stand on specific issues candidates take, but the strength of the candidate's support base that assures electoral victory. Women are often at a disadvantage in the patron-client system of Thai electoral politics because they often do not have access to the patronage network machinery for election campaigns. Men have stronger links with established political party machines and patronage networks.

Even if women succeeded in establishing support structures, men have larger networks from which to draw support than women. In many cases, women have been unable to win because of their relative isolation from the world of patronage politics. If women are to win in elections, they would have to rely on the male- dominated network. In fact, successful women candidates are often linked to the patronage system through kinship political networks established by the woman's political family and the family of her husband.

POLITICAL PARTIES AND WOMEN CANDIDATES

The selection of potential candidates also involves the process through which individuals are selected by the party. In many countries, party leaders, party officials, and faction leaders play the role of gatekeeper in the nomination process. In some countries, non-party selectors, such as local notables, financial sponsors, and interest groups play a crucial role in selecting candidates. Norris (1996) distinguishes between the bureaucratic and patronage systems of candidate selection. In a bureaucratic system, the selection process is highly institutionalised and based on legalistic authority in the Weberian sense; and it is determined largely by party rules that are detailed, explicit, standardized and followed by party officials.

In contrast, in a patronage-oriented system, the selection process can be relatively closed and characterized by patronage led by power brokers at various levels. Such a system is built upon either traditional or charismatic authority. One important aspect of the relationship between parties and women is whether the parties encourage women as electoral candidates. It is commonly believed that parties do not provide women with opportunities to run for elected office. In the past, it was quite common for women candidates to face discrimination by party elites in long-established democracies.

Party leaders did not recruit women to run for office while they directed those women who desired to run for election toward seats in which they were sacrificial lambs, thus failing to support women's candidacies. As a consequence, women have difficulty in fund-raising and in being perceived as credible candidates by the media and by voters. More recent studies in advanced industrial democracies, on the other hand, have shown that such bias against women candidates has diminished significantly. In the case of Thailand, one of the most important causes of the failure to mobilize more women candidates to the House of Representatives is attributable to the inability or unwillingness of party leaders and other selectors to recruit a substantial number of women candidates.

Thai political parties are still very much male-dominated institutions and the party gatekeepers who choose the candidates are similarly predominantly men. Although an increasing number of women have become members of political parties, they are largely excluded from governing bodies in political parties and occupy less than 10 per cent of high positions in political parties. In Thailand, where the selection process takes place in the context of a patronage-oriented system, non-party gatekeepers such as financial supporters, provincial and local notables as well as various interest groups also play a role as selectors.

Political parties in Thailand as a whole have done little to encourage women's electoral candidacy. Indeed, it is widely known that political parties in Thailand are responsible for failing to nurture the emergence of women as candidates and leaders, whatever their public stance. The traditional cultural conceptions of women's social roles are deeply embedded in political parties. Several female MPs I interviewed blamed the male political culture in the parties for the parties' failure to nominate women. Women candidates received less support than men from party leaders, faction leaders and local leaders.

Moreover, they mentioned that women were less likely than men to be asked to stand for election. The few women who have managed to attain parliamentary seats have usually had family ties to a male party or faction leader. Thai political parties are less likely to nominate women candidates for the winnable seats in the House of Representatives. An analysis of the 2005 general election results clearly show that women were nominated for hopeless contests more often than men. With the exception of the Thai Rak Thai Party, the success rates for women candidates were low. The Democratic Party put up 52 women candidates, but only six were elected.

Among the 35 women candidates from the Mahachon Party, only one was elected. The Chart Thai Party nominated 40 women candidates, but only two were elected. As for the Thai Rak Thai Party, the success rate of its women candidates was extremely high. 44 out of the party's 51 women candidates were elected, reflecting the unusual, but favorable political atmosphere for the governing party. One of the most important characteristics that distinguish women's recruitment in Thailand is the very different party environment in which it takes place. In contrast to some of the new democracies in Asia,

Thai political parties tend to have weak structures, without clear-cut ideologies and policies.

Moreover, many parties do not survive very long and, generally speaking, voters appear to be less interested in the programs of political parties than in obtaining the benefits brought to the constituencies by politicians. This is especially so in rural areas where the failure of parties to formulate concrete policies to benefit the rural poor led other factions and individual politicians to "seize the initiative in promising benefits to rural voters, and claiming personal credit for improvements delivered". In the historical development of Thai politics, political parties played a peripheral role in electoral politics for a long period because there was a lack of firm legal basis.

From the moment that Thailand entered the modern era, political parties have evolved as de facto institutions and neither their organizational forms, their position in the political system, nor their basic functions have ever been explicitly defined in legal terms. Indeed, the legal status of political parties in the system of government in Thailand has been vague and indefinable. This is in part due to "the absence of continuous political development and the frequency of military coups"; it was not until the adoption of the political party law of 1981 that political parties became more important in electoral politics at the national level.

Today, as in many other countries, political parties play an important role in the Thai national-level political system. Party membership is mandatory for candidates running for the House of Representatives, and parties (and other selectors) decide which individuals will have the opportunity to become their candidates at the national level. Nevertheless, the weak institutionalised nature of political parties in Thailand favor those who have accumulated political capital, i.e. resources based upon political connections, party experience and external group support. At the lower levels of government—provinces, districts, *tambons*, and villages—political parties do not play any significant role in politics. Instead, informal political groupings of local politicians dominate the political arena.

On the surface, it appears that most Thais do not feel alienated from the political parties, and their affiliation appears to be very high compared with that of other Asian countries. Judging from statistics on party membership, many Thais belong to a political party. In December 2001, the 15-plus parties had altogether more than 20 million members. The five largest parties had garnered more than 18 million and the Thai Rak Thai Party accounted for 6.8 million of them, followed by the Democrat Party with 3.7 million. The other large parties are Chat Pattana with 3.6 million, New Aspiration with 3.1 million, and Chat Thai with 1.6 million.

Fewer women than men participate in political parties; however it should be noted here that it is difficult to obtain reliable statistics on party membership. Despite the seemingly impressive membership figures, many political parties are weakly institutionalised and lack firm organization. From the very beginning, Thailand's parties were formed around personalities, not around particular issues.

Even today many of them essentially are still loose coalitions of factions and individuals organized around influential political leaders or bosses. As one analyst of Thai politics argues, "parties have always had to rely on factions, and individual MPs, to establish their own electoral networks". Parties are largely based on patron-client relations as they form, merge, split, and disappear with the political fortunes of these patrons.

The weak party system has encouraged national level candidates to rely on the support of local elites for election campaigning. At various local levels, parties are largely absent, thus allowing traditional networks of politicians and local bosses to dominate Thai electoral politics. Networks are highly important in terms of the vote-getting structures that are necessary for candidates to make the leap into the parliament. Structures that successfully acquire votes include a group of vote canvassers.

Such necessary structures are generally based on networks of influential leaders who need vote canvassers to get elected and "they seek contact either with individuals who have contact to local individuals or with local notable themselves, whom they might incorporate in their cliques to enhance the chances of being elected in the next election". Local political cliques (known also as *phuak* or *phakphuak*), or networks of local bosses, play a powerful role in mobilizing support. Local bosses usually consist of notable local politicians, such as village headmen, tambon headmen, members of the Tambon Administrative Organizations (TAO), and as well as local and provincial councillors. These informal groups are all-powerful within their domain and serve as henchmen for the MPs.

The last hurdle in the process of becoming a parliamentarian is being chosen by the voters. An obstacle for women seeking to get elected is that voters discriminate against female candidates due to gender stereotyping. Voters are more influenced by preconceived notions about males and females than each individual's personal merits. While female candidates are still perceived in terms of their private and domestic roles, male candidates are viewed in terms of their public and occupational roles. Voters tend to perceive women as less qualified and less suited for politics than men. There exists empirical evidence that voters' stereotypical view of gender has negative consequences for female candidates and that women candidates would be more successful if they were perceived as possessing masculine traits such as assertiveness and toughness.

Evidence of voter discrimination has not been conclusive and an increasing number of studies in advanced industrialized democracies have questioned the findings that voters react negatively to female candidates. These studies have found that the gender of the candidate has no or only little impact on voting, and that women do as well as men in garnering votes. Some indicated that voters' gender stereotypes had some negative impact on women candidates when running for parliament, while others said the gender of the candidate did not have any significant impact on voting and that voters are just as likely to vote for women.

This particular lack of support for women candidates reflects the predominant perception of women's role in Thai society, where men exercise the official power and women are confined to exercising power behind the scenes. I was told by several female parliamentarians that, in election campaigns, female candidates had experienced difficulty in being taken seriously, and had often been subjected to humiliating comments and derogatory remarks. They had to convince voters that they were competent and possessed masculine traits. Unfortunately, comprehensive and systematic surveys of voters' perceptions and attitudes do not exist in Thailand. Nevertheless, available studies seem to indicate that some stereotypes related to women still persist, and that female candidates have faced difficulty in winning voter approval.

THE EFFECTS OF ELECTORAL SYSTEMS

According to the existing literature on women and politics, the characteristics of an electoral system in a country is one of the most important factors affecting women's representation in national assemblies, especially in long established democracies. The effects of the electoral system cannot be explored in isolation from the broader institutional and socio-economic context of a society. The literature tends to support the contention that women have higher levels of representation in legislatures in countries with party-list systems than in countries with single-member majoritarian electoral systems.

Under the proportional representation (PR) system, women are often included to broaden the party ticket in order to appeal to as many different segments of voters as possible. Rule's study (1987, 1994) found that the PR system was the major determinant of women's political representation, even when socio-economic, political, and contextual factors were controlled. Nations employing mixed systems, combining both PR and majoritarian electoral systems, were shown to elect more women by proportional vote than by district vote.

Studies have also found that there is a direct relationship between women's representation and district magnitude (i.e. the number of representatives per district), hence the larger the district, the higher the women's turnover. It should be noted here that the relationship between type of electoral system and women's representation is not automatic. Some studies question the argument that PR systems are better suited than majoritarian systems in increasing women's representation in national parliaments.

Chapman, for example, argues that "before the sudden improvement of recent times, proportional representation systems had already existed for decades in Norway and Denmark with the same infinitesimal proportion of women legislators as everywhere else" (1993: 6-7). It has also been argued that some majoritarian systems have elected more women than some PR systems. Can the paucity of women politicians in Thailand be attributed to the way in which politicians are elected? Can theories about the relationship of electoral systems and women's electability, developed in the advanced industrialized democracies in Europe and North America, explain women's under-representation in Thai politics?

Thailand has recently undergone a transformation of its electoral system since the country experienced widespread dissatisfaction with the existing political system in the 1990s. This resulted in a new constitution and a new electoral system. What happened to female representation when Thailand changed from a plurality system, in small multi-member constituencies with multiple voting, to a mixed system of single-member constituencies and proportional representation? In mixed systems, such as in elections to the Japanese House of Representatives and the German Bundestag, far more women have been elected through proportional representation than through single member districts.

Will the relationship between the type of electoral system and female representation hold true for elections to the Thai House of Representatives in Thailand? Before the introduction of a new constitution in 1997, direct elections were held only for members of the House of Representatives, based upon the relative majority system. During the period of 1978-1997,

Thailand had a unique type of majoritarian electoral system. While most majoritarian systems have single-member constituencies where each voter has only one vote, Thai voters were permitted to cast ballots for as many candidates as there were seats in a constituency.

In other words, a plurality system in small multi-member constituencies with multiple voting was used for elections to the House of Representatives in Thailand. In the pre-1997 electoral system, party labels were weak and candidates tended to rely on their own vote-getting mechanisms, rather than on parties, in election campaigns. This was because, in two and three seat constituencies, it promoted contest, not only between competing parties but also between rival candidates from the same party. As a consequence, well-organized personal vote-getting networks of individual politicians served as the most important mechanism for mobilizing votes.

The previous electoral system for the Lower House, based on multi-member constituencies and a multiple vote plurality system, did not facilitate women's representation. The 1997 constitution provides for a mixed electoral system whereby 400 members of the House of Representatives are to be elected on a single- member constituency basis and the remaining 100 elected on a party-list basis forming a single nationwide constituency. It was expected that those elected in the national constituency would need far more than solely local appeal and thus need to represent larger interests, as against short-sighted local interests.

Cabinet ministers are further chosen from the party-list MPs, forming a mixed system that is partly based on the German electoral system. The electoral threshold on the proportional side of the election is 5 per cent nationally. This new mixed system was first applied in the general election of 2001, producing results which, in terms of the representation of women, were higher than the election which preceded it. It was presumed that certain features of the new electoral system had the potential to facilitate more women into public office.

The first feature was the creation of new seats in the House of Representatives in Thailand which increased from 392 to 500. This new change was perceived as allowing for the election of more female candidates; however, this increase was not at all matched by substantial increases in the number of women candidates. The oft-described reason for the paucity of women legislators at the national level is the low level of turnover among the legislators. A high level of turnover can facilitate women's entry into parliament. In the 2001 Lower House election, for instance, there were more newcomers than ever before. Since it was the first general election under the new electoral system, there were suddenly more new open seats available than before.

Half of the 400 constituency MPs and 36 of 100 MPs from the party-list system were newcomers. Another feature of the new electoral system allotted 20 per cent of the seats in the House of Representatives to a party-list system. It was anticipated that this particular feature would facilitate the election of more women. However, the Thai political parties have yet to nominate a sizeable number of women in winnable positions. Although only a few female candidates were placed within the top ranks of party lists, there were some differences in the recruitment of women candidates between political parties.

The Thai Rak Thai Party, the Democrat Party, and the Chat Thai Party were very poor in nominating women candidates. Each of them had only one woman candidate in the top twenty slots while a number of parties, such as the New Aspiration Party and the Chat Pattana Party, were marginally better and had two candidates. Altogether, the two largest parties, the Thai Rak Thai Party and the Democrat Party, fielded a total of four and nine candidates on their party lists. The differences between the political parties cannot be explained on the basis of ideological differences. As Orathai Kokpol (2002: 94) commented, "no party paid serious attention to the promotion of the role of women in politics in recruiting candidates."

The change of electoral systems from multi-member

districts to a mixed system, in turn, affected women's legislative recruitment. The new electoral rules resulted in much smaller single-member constituencies, making it possible for candidates to focus their election campaigning on a more limited area of influence than in previous elections. Consequently, these smaller constituencies favored those candidates who had close contact with their home districts, thus enhancing the significance of local politicians in influencing elections, and especially members of provincial assemblies and their vote-getting networks. For political parties, these provincial politicians were interesting as potential candidates for the House of Representatives.

As Nelson explains, "Having succeeded in their attempt to be elected to the provincial council means...that these people command solid networks of local leaders...who provided them with the villagers' votes they needed to win their seats". The traditional system of patrons and clients has continued to influence voting. The new electoral system continues to push candidates to campaign on the basis of personal qualities and constituency services. Candidates have to raise their own money and form their own support organizations based on networks of vote canvassers.

A low number of women candidates participated in the January 2001 election for the House of Representatives. 352 (12.65 %) of the 2,782 candidates competing for the 400 seats in the constituency election were women, while in the party-list election 148 (15.74 %) of the 940 candidates vying for the 100 seats were women. The number of women candidates was lower than in the previous general election of 1996. A mere 11 per cent of women candidates in the single-member constituencies were elected, while 4.7 per cent in the proportional representational side of the electoral system for the House of Representatives were successful.

In the 2005 general election, as in previous elections, far more women were elected through single-member majoritarian systems rather than via party lists. About 11 per cent of women candidates were successful in single-member constituencies and only 6 per cent in the party-list election. In other words, women were more successful in single-member districts, a format that commonly restricts women's success at the polls, than in party-list districts. This is contrary to the existing literature on women's representation, in that women are more likely to get elected in PR systems than single-member majoritarian systems.

In examining women's representation on the parties' lists of candidates, I found that women were over-represented in those list positions that do not have a realistic chance of getting elected. Some studies pointed out that there are three types of candidate positions: sure, marginal, and hopeless seats. The sure seats are those which a party is sure to keep, even if they experience a poor electoral showing. The hopeless seats are those a party is certain to lose even if it has a good election. Marginal seats are those between the above two types of seats, namely, seats a party will win in a good election but lose if it experiences a poor election.

For the party-list election for the House of the Representatives in Thailand, women were represented disproportionately in marginal, and more especially, in hopeless seats. The Thai case is consistent with past research findings. If women's political representation in descriptive terms is to be improved, it is necessary to increase women's nominations to winnable seats. In fact, a number of female MPs pointed out in interviews that it is important to get women into positions high enough on the party list to be elected. Unlike its predecessor, the new Senate was to be entirely elected. The electoral reform under the new constitution provides for direct elections for the 200 senatorial seats from 76 provinces.

The new Senate has become more powerful than the previous one. In the past, Thai senators were political appointees and acted as rubber stamps for the government. But, what expectations did the framers of the Senate hold with regard to its function? First, the Senate was considered essential to a system of checks and balances. It was expected to act as a check on the House of Representatives and the government. It has the power to recommend the removal of persons holding political posts including the prime minister, cabinet members and MPs.

The constitution calls for an elected Senate to act as a watchdog over the country's political arena. Second, it was expected that the Senate, like the party-list members of the House of the Representatives, would represent larger national interests as opposed to the partisan and parochial local interests represented by the members of the House of Representatives. Thus, senators are required to be non-partisan. Since the Senate, unlike its predecessor, was to be elected, the framers had to create an electoral system capable of yielding the desired result. Instead of the 400 single member districts that elected representatives, there were only 76 districts for the Senate, one for each province (*changwat*).

The larger constituencies designed for the Senate were one means. It was assumed that the Senate would provide for alternative elements, unlike those elected through the electoral system of the House of the Representatives. Hence, it was hoped that persons elected from the larger constituencies would be different in character from partisan politicians. A further expectation was that the Senate would, most probably, provide stability and continuity. The Senate with its independent and longer term of office (six years) would give stability to the political process of the Thai political system. The 2000 election to the Senate was unusual in many respects, with voter turnout particularly high in the Thai context. 70 per cent of all eligible voters voted in the election.

The constitutional requirement of compulsory voting, with penalties for those who fail to exercise the right to vote, and the provision for advance voting, appeared to be reasons that drove people to the polls. Senatorial candidates are not permitted to engage in "normal" election campaigning. They were only allowed to introduce themselves to the voters. The 2000 Senate elections under the new electoral rules took a long time to implement, requiring five rounds to complete, due to voting irregularities and fraud. The fact that the senatorial election excluded the role of parties further raised expectations regarding the number of women willing to run, since it was perceived that non-partisan politicking would protect women from being subjected to discrimination by party elites.

Even though candidates for the Senate were not allowed to have backing from political parties, it was estimated that a majority of the senatorial candidates, that is 70 per cent, had close connections with political parties. This was also confirmed by a number of senators I interviewed. Among the candidates for the Senate seats, a dominant group was made up of figures from the military and bureaucracy (39.5 per cent). Research, particularly in the United States, has shown that the paucity of women female legislators at the national level depends on the power of incumbency and that open seats are advantageous to women.

Women's chances for winning elections are not so great because most female candidates for the U.S. House of Representatives have to run against incumbents, not for new or open seats. Since the 2000 election for the Senate was the first opportunity in Thai history for candidates to be directly elected by the people, all seats were open seats. However, despite the expected surge of women to participate in the election in addition to the reformist atmosphere in which the constitution was drafted, the electoral results were disappointing. Women's representation in the Senate did not improve under the new Constitution. The new Senate contained a slightly larger proportion of women representatives than the outgoing Senate whose members, by contrast, were appointees. What was surprising was the very low number of women who did decide to run.

There were no women candidates at all in 28 of the 76 provinces and among the total number of 1,523 candidates for the senate, only 115 candidates were women (7.6 per cent), and only 20 women were elected out of a total of 200 elected (10 per cent). In the Bangkok area, a mere 26 women of the 265 candidates ran for Senate, only one was elected. One important means by which women entered parliament in Thailand was what is called "the kinship route." Women who successfully run for parliament are often members of families with a well-established political base. Indeed, the role of kinship in the electoral success of women candidates is significant in Thailand.

As mentioned previously, it is difficult for women to create a personal support organisation without patronage from influential leaders in the party. Very few women wishing to enter into national politics have an independent support base, and many women legislators owe their seat to being the wife, daughter, sister, niece or granddaughter of a former politician or government official. It was estimated that approximately two- thirds of the new female senators were wives and relatives of politicians or former government officials.

Among the successful candidates for Senate seats are the wives of former interior minister Sanan Kachornprasart and justice minister Suthas Ngernmuen. The Thai case defies most accepted explanations prevailing in the literature concerning related factors facilitating increases in the representation of women in parliament. According to common belief, the Thai party-list system should have brought about the election of more women to the House of Representatives. Thailand's experience serves as a caution against common expectations that the adoption of proportional representation will lead to greater legislative opportunities for women.

The number of women elected to the Thai Parliament remains minimal. On the whole, it is difficult to discern any significant influence that the new electoral system has had on women's electability. It will most likely require a number of elections before the new electoral system will bear any fruit. When a new electoral system is introduced, there is quite often a transitional period before the electorate and parties come to terms with its logic. Hence it is not realistic to expect that it will deliver immediate results.

The Thai people have barely had a chance to familiarize themselves with the new electoral system, let alone acquire any experience with its operations. Moreover, there is no guarantee that the electoral system changes will have an immediate effect. Matland (2002), for example, has urged caution in attributing too much significance to the effects of the PR system on women's political representation in the developing world. He argues that PR systems do not help to increase the numbers of women legislators in developing countries, while Norris also claims that the role of the electoral system is "independent of levels of political and socio-economic development".

Although the existing literature on women's representation tends to find electoral systems as being positively influential, the impact of the electoral system concerning the representation of women in Thailand has not resulted in any significant changes in both the single-member constituencies and the PR multi-member constituencies. In fact, it is fair to say that the electoral system has played only a minor role in shaping the political opportunities for women in Thailand. What is of more significance are the cultural, socio-economic, and political factors that have a daily impact on women's lives. Hence, as far as women's representation in the national assembly is concerned, the main problem in Thailand lies not with the electoral system per se, but with the dearth of women candidates and the absence of women selected to run in winnable seats.

7

Consciousness-raising Among and Beyond Women's Movement Activists in China

The most remarkable change in historical studies in China during the last two decades has been the rise of new social history. It challenges the traditional historiography in three ways: in the objects studied, in the sources used, and in methodology. Social historians have shifted the focus of their research from the so-called "elite history" to "mass history." In addition to studying the lives of rulers and social elites, they are concerned with subjects preciously neglected- which include but are not limited to women, ethnic minorities, and working class people.

Social historians contend that Chinese history should not be based only on the examination of a series of significant political events, dynasty changes, ruling ideologies, governmental policies, and institutional systems, but also on the understanding of human behavior, peoples' daily lives, and their feelings and experiences. New social history is also characterized by using new materials for research. Unlike traditional Chinese historiography whose primary sources are mainly from officially compiled historical books and documents, social historians also use oral history, folk literature, and materials from field investigation as primary sources for their research. Their new theory and methodology encourages an inter-disciplinary framework and the borrowing of conceptions and methodologies from anthropology, sociology, psychology, and related academic fields.

Social historians also emphasize the significance of studying history from the perspective of the people being studied. For example, to study women, one should examine their behavior from the point of view of women not of men. Consequently the rise of new social history has profoundly impacted women's history in China. For thousands of years, Chinese history has been basically men's history. The main reason women were ignored related to their political, economic, and social position in the society. Being dominated by Confucian ideology that promoted the ideas of female inferiority and separation of sexes, women were generally excluded from formal education and participation in policy-making, the military, and other activities in public spheres. Their place was mostly inside the household, acting as mothers, wives, and daughters.

Therefore, women's lives and contributions to society were considered insignificant by most traditional historians. After 1949, when mainland China was ruled by the Communists, historians applied Marxist theory in their studies. Marxism emphasizes the significance of economic structure and class struggle but is blind to gender differences and ethnic distinctions. As a result, the mainstream of historiography in Communist China was studies on peasant uprising and political and economic systems. This approach unfortunately ignored family, marriage, women, and minorities.

Women's history has become an important new field of social history in China since the mid-1980s. In 1983, Li Xiaojiang, one of the pioneers of Chinese gender studies, published her article "*Renlei jinbu yu funu jiefang*" (Progress of mankind and women's liberation), which is the first scholarly publication in women studies. Two years later, the first non-official women's professional organization, Association of Women's Studies, was founded and in the same year the first academic conference concerned with women's studies was held in Zhengzhou. Since then women studies in China has developed rapidly.

The primary sources used by traditional historians were officially compiled historical books. The main references to women in these multi-volume collections of dynastic history are the chapters about empresses and imperial concubines or a few chosen exemplary women. When discussing the problem of using these sources, Susan Mann points out that "valuable as they are to historians of women...these biographies written by men grow opaque when we try to understand what women themselves thought or believed." The rise of social history has opened new channels of sources. Some valuable materials available in China are to be found in literature (poems, novels, diaries, personal jottings, and folk songs), in archives (court records, land leases, marriage contracts, etc.), in visual arts and materials, and in personal interviews.

These previously ignored sources provide historians opportunities to get information about common women's lives, which is crucial to the development of women's history in China. In recent years, Chinese historians have made great efforts to collect primary sources of various kinds and to use these sources to study women's history. Ding Yizhuang's book, *Zuihou de jiyi: shiliu wei qiren funu de koushu lishi* (The last memories: the oral history of 16 Manchu women) and Li Xiaojiang's series *Rang nuren ziji shuohua* (Let women's voices be heard) are good examples of collecting primary sources from personal interviews. Their books are based on interviews with women from diverse social backgrounds, and provide valuable information about women's experiences and feelings in the male dominated society.

Guo Songyi's book, *Lunli yu shenghuo: Qingdai de hunyin guanxi* (Ethics and life: marital relations in the Qing dynasty) and Wang Yuesheng's, *Shiba shiji Zhongguo hunyin jiating yanjiu* (Marriage and family in China in the eighteenth century) use a great quantity of archives, personal jottings, and literary sources to examine women's lives and the marriage system in the Qing dynasty. Deng Xiaonan's research on Tang and Song women is a representative work that uses archaeological sources and field research findings in historical studies. It is seen that, as a new field of social history, recent scholarship on women use a great deal of materials from archives, literature, and personal interviews as the primary sources to make up what is missing in the official data.

These efforts of social historians contrast with traditional Chinese historiography, which shows women as passive objects as revealed by men's writing brushes where they often appear in footnotes because the main text treats social norms in a male-dominated society. For example, the records of "exemplary women" in the collections of dynastic history primarily reflect men's expectation of women and the narrative was designed to promote Confucian doctrines in the society. After the Revolution of 1911 buried the Qing dynasty, followed by the New Cultural Movement, many new ideas were introduced into China from the West that challenged traditional culture and the old social order. Among other changes, efforts were made to redefine women's social status and roles in response to the feminist movement in the West.

However, since the feminist movement in China was led by elite male intellectuals, women were still in the position of "passive object," being represented and criticized by men. Male feminist activists wrote about women primarily from men's perspectives, using women's problem as their weapon to condemn Confucianism and the feudal system, ideas and institutions, which were the main targets of the New Cultural Movement. Still, they did call for women's liberation, including the abolition of foot binding and encouragement of women's education and employment, and they advocate "a new woman" who would be "educated, employed, independent, concerned with public life, and attentive to the plight of women more oppressed than she."

Books and articles in this period emphasized the suppression of women and the fact they were victims of the feudal system. However, women's subjective perceptions and the roles they played in constructing the society were overlooked. Recent research on women has showed a tendency to approach women's problems from women's points of view and demonstrates a strong sense of needing to reveal women's actual life experiences. Ding Yizhuang's *Manzu de funu shenghuo yu hunyin zhidu yanjiu* (Research on lives and marriage patterns of Manchu women) is a good example. Based on solid historical sources collected from Manchu archives, this book attempts to explain the changes in women's lives and marital behavior from a woman's perspective and challenges some mechanistic grand theories.

The way in which some social historians apply a multidisciplinary approach in their studies is illustrated by Guo Songyi's book on ethics and marriage relations in Qing China which uses new methodologies borrowed from sociology, statistics, ethics, and psychology. A multidisciplinary approach such as this is especially significant for women's studies and gender relations because it enables an author to explain marital and family history from a comprehensive point of view. In addition to the books mentioned above, two other books require our attention. They are *Funu xue he funu shi de bentu tansuo: shehui xingbie shijiao he kua xueke shiye* (The native exploration to the women studies and women's history: gendered perspectives and interdisciplinary views) by Du Fangqin and *Lishi, shixue yu xingbie* (History, historiography, and gender), edited by Li Xiaojiang.

Both are concerned about methodology, framework, and the direction of development of women's history in China. Li's book, *Lishi, shixue yu xingbie zuotanhui* (Forum on history, Historiography, and gender), is a proceeding of a conference that was held in Dalian, China in the summer of 2002. This conference invited the most popular Chinese scholars of social history to reflect on the current trends in the development of women's history and gender studies in China. The conference illustrated the two issues which are the main concerns of Chinese scholars in the field. One is the definition of women's history and its position in traditional historiography. What is women's history? How should we understand its significance in the field of historical studies? Some scholars believe that women's history is just a new research area in the field which makes women an object of research.

In other words, women's history simply studies women in the past. They admit that women have been ignored by historians for thousands of years and argue that now it is the historians' mission to study women's experiences in the past and their contributions to society. To these scholars the rise of women's history is not in conflict with traditional historiography, but just adds a new subject to it. Other scholars argue that the rise of women's history and gender studies is a revolution in the methodology of historical studies because it not only introduces a new subject but demands a review or re-thinking of the whole history of China from the perspective of women. Since this new perspective places women at the center of historical analysis, it forces a critical re-examination of all the assumptions and conclusions historians had made before they integrated women into their scholarly works.

For example, Qing studies in the past have focused on political, economic, and military systems, areas men were mostly involved in. Studying the changes of these areas after the Manchu conquest might lead historians to conclude that sinicization (*Hanhua*) was the key to Manchu success in China. However, if we reexamine Qing history and the Manchu conquest by placing women at the center of the analysis, an approach which would examine the Manchu society from a more personal level, we can see that many old Manchu traditions continued. Therefore, we may have a different conclusion about Manchu-Chinese acculturation and the reason for their success in China. This example illustrates the second, more revolutionary definition of women's studies and Chinese scholars are not agreed upon which to choose.

Another issue of concern to Chinese scholars of women's history is how to evaluate and accept the tendency of academic globalization. Compared with the accomplishment of women's studies in the United States and Europe, Hong Kong, and Taiwan, women's history in China is still a developing field. China's opening to the West since the 1980s has provided scholars a great opportunity to learn new methodologies and to broaden their theoretical views in women's studies. As a result, many new terms and theoretical frameworks used by Western historians in their research, such as "feminism," "postmodernism," "post structuralism," etc, have been directly introduced into the field of women's studies in China. In this respect, Chinese historians who received their degrees overseas and went back to China for conferences or other academic reasons have played a crucial role in shaping some frameworks of social history in China, including women's history.

Their research is well-recognized by Chinese scholars who realize that a combination of Chinese tradition in historiography and the new theories and approaches can be significant to the development of women's history in China in the twenty-first century. However, with more and more Western theories introduced, Chinese historians have started to worry about so-called "*lilun zhiminhua*" (theoretical colonization). They argue that the significance of indigenization (*ben tu hua*) should be emphasized in the field of Chinese history and that it is especially important in a new field like women's history. Since the situation of Chinese women is different from that of women in the West, some terms, frameworks, and perspectives that are used by Western scholars in women's history may not work perfectly for China. For example, the term "gender," which is widely used in Western works in women's studies, does not have a fixed Chinese equivalent.

In one article, Li Xiaojiang points out that Chinese scholars "respect Western-based feminist theory, and yet they still believe that Chinese women's studies has its own background and circumstances unique to Chinese history and social reality. Western feminist theory is certainly valuable as a rich source of reference, but Western feminist tradition can hardly provide a standardized answer to all Chinese women's questions." The unique circumstances and background of women's studies in China refer to the reality that the feminist movements in Chinese history were "male oriented" movements because they were mostly led by men and saw women as a passive objects being liberated by men.

Therefore, Chinese women lacked the sense of self-representation and self-consciousness of their situation as victims. Other Chinese scholars also have questions using women's writing as a primary source in women's studies, which is emphasized by Western scholars in the recent years. Using women's writings, including diaries, novels, poems as primary sources helps historians to know what women themselves felt and thought about the world, and indeed, some scholars have made significant achievements in this field. But Chinese scholars claim that these sources are very limited, especially in pre-modern Chinese history, due to the unique situation of China.

The issue of "theoretical colonization" was one of the main themes discussed at the conference of 2002 and has been a contentious topic in China's academic field since then. According to critics, when some Chinese scholars return from overseas, they ignore the differences of women's situation in China and in the West and make a fetish of "foreign things." This makes scholars in China worry about the future of Chinese women's history because it is facing the danger of "colonization," which will "ruin the foundation of women's history in China." Another Chinese scholar observed:

The greatest sorrow is that our history is being interpreted by other people (referring to foreigners) as they please. If our history is defined by other people within their framework, then the whole story of our nation and people is in doubt. Of course, other people do not change the order of dynasties in our history. What they do is to take away the firewood from under the cooking pot (*fu di chou xin*)—study our men and women and then rewrite the contents of our history.... When other people's voice is recognized as a standard language and when we use this language to study our history without hesitation, we easily become 'outsiders' in our own land—this is how the process of post-colonization is accomplished.

She also believes that no matter how much the world is integrated as a whole in the future, the study of history must be local. As a new field of social history, women's history in

China is still in its infancy. There are at least two areas that need to be further developed. First, current works on women's history, especially in the pre-modern period, primarily focus on family life, marriage, childbearing, and sexuality. Needless to say, these are indeed the important areas women make their dramas, but the study of women's lives and their contribution to society should go beyond the inner-quarter. Women's roles in society at large, such as women's labor, education, and religious practices, should also be studied.

Another problem in the field is that some historians are still using a Sino centric approach to conduct their research and overlook ethnic distinctions among the people of China. It is not uncommon that a book bearing the title of "Chinese" women or women in some specific dynasty actually discusses only the experience of Han women. Like all other social groups, women in China are not monolithic. When studying Chinese women in history, one should understand and view them as diverse ethnically. Women's identities and behaviors can be very different according to the diversities of ethnicity and social status.

For example, a stereotypical impression of Chinese women is that they had their feet bound after the Song dynasty (960–1279). But when we view the women of China in all their diversity, we learn that actually only some Han women practiced foot binding. Manchus, Mongols, Tibetans, Hmongs, and other ethnic minorities did not bind their women's feet. Moreover, even within the Han community not every woman had small feet—those from poor families did not do it because they needed a pair of "normal feet" to work in the field. In addition to the practice of foot binding, Han women's lives differ from those of their counterparts of other ethnic minorities in many other respects, including the position within the family, the roles in social production, in marriage, in gender relations, and so on. In recent years, scholars in the United States have argued for a construction of gender that is attentive to both class and ethnic identity.

It is an important approach for women's studies in China because neither men nor women lived in a vacuum; instead, the historians should indicate the class and the ethnic group they belonged to. In conclusion, while I believe that as a new field of social history, Chinese women's history has a very bright future, its development must be based on a deep understanding of Chinese history and culture, solid primary sources, and an open-minded attitude to new theories and methodology. Chinese women have more of a say in politics, with over 200 of them now in highly prized positions such as governors and cabinet ministers, a senior official announced.

The proportion of female officials at various levels of government and state institutions has risen to 40 per cent, said Huang Qingyi, vice-president and first secretary of the All-China Women's Federation Secretariat, speaking at a press conference. "The participation of women in politics has increased enormously," Huang remarked, noting that currently there are nine female state leaders. These important women include Wu Yi, vice-premier and member of the Political Bureau of the Communist Party of China (CPC) Central Committee, State Councilor Chen Zhili, along with He Luli, Gu Xiulian and Uyunqimg, all vice-chairwomen of the Standing Committee of the National People's Congress, the country's top legislature.

Since 2001, five women have been promoted to high profile positions, Huang added. At the end of 2005, there were 241 women in ministerial posts, key provincial decision-making positions, or in equally important posts at state agencies. China has a long history of preference towards men and only a few women managed to squeeze themselves into positions of power during the country's feudal past. Generations of Chinese women were once forced to bind their feet, a kowtow to the weird culture at the time that appreciated the "beauty" of deformed small feet. The position of women in Chinese society started to rise remarkably since the Communist Party came to power, under Mao Zedong's claim that, "Women should hold up half of the sky." This opened opportunities for women, even from the grassroots of society, to climb up the political ladder. Huang, 63, was a good example herself.

She was an ordinary horticulture technician in central Henan Province back in the early 1980s. Over the past two decades, she has held positions as a gardening researcher, the vice head of an agricultural science institute, the vice secretary of the Party Committee in Henan, and the vice director of the Organization Department of the Communist Party. Today, Huang is also the vice chairperson of the National Working Committee on Children and Women under the State Council and a member of the CPC Central Committee. The National People Congress is also expected to enroll more female lawmakers during its five-year reshuffle in 2008, in a bid to ensure that men do not take up more than 78 per cent of the nearly 3,000 seats available at the top legislature, Huang said.

In addition to political rights, women in China have made inroads into the problem of employment discrimination. Currently 45 per cent of China's working population are female, with more than 4 million women living in rural areas being lifted out of destitution, Huang said. "However, Chinese women still face some difficulties. Their quality of life still varies between the cities and the rural areas and among regions," Huang added. Huang said that China's efforts in promoting women's development and safeguarding their rights were recognized by the United Nations. Ten years ago, Jia Junqiao became the first woman village head of Longju in North China's Hebei Province. She won the village election to become head of the village committee - the grassroots administration for farmers' self governance.

In the past 10 years of Jia's leadership, the first road has been built, wells have been dug and the local primary school has been repaired, a job put off for years by her male predecessors. Jia, 50, shared her decade-long experience last week at a forum in Beijing of rural Chinese women who have won prizes for creativity in rural life from the Women's World Summit Foundation. Since 1995, a total of 34 rural Chinese women have been awarded the prize, for their efforts in improving the lives of people in rural China. Jia's story is but one of the many shared by rural Chinese women today as they try to play a more active role not only in improving their own livelihood but also in local public affairs.

In fact, increasing rural women's political participation has become an objective for a three-year gender and development programme jointly conducted by the China Association for NGO Co-operation (CANGO) and the local women's federation in Linqu County, East China's Shandong Province. The programme was granted a US$210,000 donation from the United Nations Development Fund for Women (UNIFEM). According to the description of the programme on CANGO's website, only women's equal participation in politics can achieve democracy and equality between women and men; help establish a rational democratic system; guarantee the representation of different interest groups; broaden the scope of issues concerning public welfare and prevent the waste of human resources.

"Women have made great contributions to economic development," said Zhang Hongman, a UNIFEM official in China and organizer of another forum last week in Beijing. It is especially true in the past few years as many of the young and middle-aged rural men have gone to cities for work. The women, who remain behind, tend to the farm and take care of the children and elderly. Rural women have become the backbone of agricultural production and family life in rural areas, Zhang said. "However, this will not automatically bring about an increase in the participation of women in politics," Zhang added.

CHANGES IN LINQU

UNIFEM and CANGO could not have picked a better place to attempt their programme than Linqu. Linqu County is located in the middle of Shandong, where women make up 49 per cent of the total population. "Shandong is the home of Confucius (551- 479 BC). The doctrines of Confucius and Mencius (372-289 BC), which disapprove of women's participation in public affairs, still have enormous influence on rural people there," said Yin Xiurong, chairwoman of the Linqu County Women's Federation, who has taken direct charge of the programme.

Yin and the other programme staff carried out surveys in villages, talking with township and village heads as well as villagers, women and men alike, to learn about their views on expanding women's participation in local public affairs. "Many women had a strong desire to play a part in discussing and deciding public issues," Yin said. "Some said they'd be willing to take up administrative posts if the channels were open. "However, most men said local women already enjoyed a pretty high social status. They grumbled, 'Isn't it already high enough'?" Yin recalled.

Women's voices are largely unheard or are rejected outright when it comes to decision-making in rural China. It is common to see a whole bunch of men enveloped in a haze of cigarette smoke discussing village affairs such as how many seeds to buy next year while the women chat in their homes and courtyards. The project took the form of a series of interactive training courses on gender and development, in the county seat as well as in villages. The courses were open to both women and men. Classes usually started late and ended early during the farming low-season, so the women still had time to finish their housework.

Every class included two co-ordinators and 25 students at most, so all students had a chance to voice their concerns. During the courses, participants shared views on such issues as how women identify themselves and how they see their villages. They discussed and argued, or even drew pictures to illustrate their views when writing proved difficult. They also learned some fresh ideas about gender equality as opposed to the traditional Confucian ideology. More than 3,000 women and men - including officials and business people - in Linqu participated in the courses.

"Many women said they have become more positive in decision making after the classes," said Han Henan, a professor with Beijing-based China Women's University, who acted as a co-ordinator in a few sessions. Apart from discussions on gender issues, the organizers also invited agronomists and other experts to talk about new agricultural technologies and management skills. "It is good to see many women begin to feel they can be as outstanding as men in both farm work and public affairs," Yin Xiurong said.

A number of local male officials were also invited to participate in the interactive programme. "They are becoming aware that there is a gender equality issue in formulating policies and they said they would take such an issue into consideration," said Zhang Huiyu, vice-chairwoman of the Linqu County People's Political Consultative Conference. Linqu County recently announced a series of affirmative plans, among them making sure that every grassroots committee of a village with a population of above 1,000 has at least one woman member.

Despite the progress, people involved in the project believe there is still a long way to go before the ideas of gender equality take root in Linqu, as well as the whole country. "The project has ended. Yet there is still a long way to go for us to further promote mainstream gender equality and women's participation in politics in rural areas," said Zhang Hongman.

LARGER ROLE FOR WOMEN

As head of the village, Jia Juntao also organized a tree-planting group composed of women villagers in Longju. Not only did they have to fetch water from the mountains 1.5 kilometres away every day. They also braved men's laughs and ridicule and put up with the loss of tree saplings at night. They persisted and have turned the Rocky Mountains surrounding their small village into a green sea of fruit trees. They have earned both the money and the respect from the men of the village, Jia said. Moreover, Jia sees changes in the village women.

A growing number of them are becoming more independent, Jia said. In the past, women often listened to their husbands during elections for the village chiefs, Jia said. Now they make their own decisions, and can even become candidates for roles leading the village. "Rural women are an untapped source. The world would be totally different if all their potential was exploited," says Xie Lihua, chief editor of the Beijing-based *Rural Women Knowing All* magazine. Sharon Chiang stamped her ballot on March 22 and dropped it into the ballot box. A member of the first generation in Taiwan to grow up with neither war nor martial law, she was helping select Taiwan's next president. It is a signal of how much has changed in Taiwan that Chiang and other young women found their participation completely unremarkable.

In dozens of conversations with nineteen to twenty-six-year old women in Taiwan in days before and after the election, the most common sentiment expressed was along the lines of "I love Taiwan! I love my country!" Many of those interviewed were especially proud of the rapid gains women have made in Taiwan. While all were happy to enjoy the benefits of this progress, few were especially interested in politics or anxious to push for greater social change. All of those interviewed were college students or recent college graduates. Like many of their fellow citizens, many of these young women were disillusioned about politics.

Many complained about the corruption and ineptitude of the outgoing Chen Shui-bian administration. Still, these women insisted they were optimistic about Taiwan's future and were confident that women would play an important role in shaping that future. This optimism is clearly the product of recent accomplishments. While Soong Mei-ling, the wife of longtime president Chiang Kai-shek, had played a prominent role representing the Republic of China abroad, especially in the United States during World War II, women did not occupy important government offices until relatively recently. Annette Lu (Lu Hsiu-lien), as vice president for eight years is only the best-known of the women who have held important government posts.

Taiwan's constitution has guaranteed women 10% of the seats in the legislature since 1947. Most of those interviewed complained that this representational floor is now pointless. They hoped that the number of women legislators would eventually match the 49% female share of the population.

Several asserted that "since women are already perfectly capable of winning legislative seats on their own, this quota merely ends up serving as a patronizing crutch," according to Sharon Chiang, a recent political science graduate of Taiwan's National Chengchih University. Last January's legislative election placed Taiwan among the top twenty countries worldwide in terms of female political representation.

While they said they wanted more women in politics and working as government officers, however, none of the young women I spoke to were interested in pursuing such a career. They were engaged and reasonably well-informed. Most read newspapers online on a regular basis, follow television news, and routinely discuss politics with family members. A few of those interviewed majored in political science, law, or international relations in college, but even they rejected the idea of becoming politicians, government officials, or lawyers, mainly due to family or societal pressures. While they championed women's rights to run for elected office and to serve in government positions, they still noted that politics and government are still viewed as a "man's world."

Instead, they mostly seek careers in the private business sector since "their families and friends perceive the competition to be less fierce and the nature to be less corrupt in these private companies than in government posts," shared an English major at Chengchih University, who wished to withhold her name. "Bashing a fellow candidate during an election campaign, or even bashing one's fellow colleagues in the legislature, for example, is comparable to delivering blows and knockouts to a boxer's opponent. It seems to us Taiwanese people that, in politics, the more and harder you punch, the more likely you will be the eventual victor. And this just does not seem very ladylike to us," she explained. Several of the interviewed subjects also seemed satisfied that they could be successful at their jobs and not have to simultaneously worry about being in the public light at all times.

Perhaps because only a few of those interviewed had post-graduation work experience, none seemed concerned about women's labor and other rights. They said they had not encountered gender discrimination at school or at the workplace. Instead, they expressed pride at the improvement made in the status of women from one generation to the next. A twenty-six-year-old employee of ING Insurance) who asked not to be named noted, "Taiwanese women are living, working, and functioning extremely well right now, and that is why we do not have very many complaints. Women of older generations, such as our mothers and grandmothers, faced a kind of discrimination that we do not have to face today. We are lucky, and we know it. There is no longer this stigma of being a woman, and we know we are not inferior to men. As a Taiwanese woman, I feel capable and protected, and many of my friends feel the same way."

Though the young women I interviewed were not willing to enter the "man's world" of politics, they were proud of leaders such as Lu and Hsiao Bikhim, a Democratic Progressive Party leader and presidential advisor who has served as a legislator. And these women were following the election closely and were anxious to cast ballots. None, though, volunteered for one of the campaigns. Many of these young women favored the policies and promises of the Kuomintang (KMT candidate and eventual victor, Ma Ying-jeou, but overwhelmingly, those who favored him said they were primarily drawn to him because of his good looks and his kind personality.

Some Ma supporters were a bit shy and some were quite blunt, but each included comments about him being more "handsome, gentlemanly, presidential, and leader-like" than Frank Hsieh (Hsieh Ch'ang-t'ing), the Democratic Progressive Party (DPP) candidate. Most attributed the intensity of their support for Ma to his "emotional appeal." Hsieh:s young female supporters, on the other hand, argued that looks should not matter and that good leaders are better than leaders who merely look good. For these women, it was mostly Hsieh's passion for "everything Taiwanese" that attracted them to vote for him.

Additionally, many women pointed out that the DPP has traditionally been more generous to women in terms of appointing females to government staff positions. Bruce Jacobs, a professor of Asian Languages and Studies at Australia's Monash University, commented that Ma and the KMT are not the only ones who are making progressive change by elevating the public status of women. He added that "the DPP government, too, was committed to having women appointed to senior positions in the government," namely Lu, as mentioned before. Even more recently, with Tsai Ing-wen as the party's new chairwoman, the DPP continues to ensure that women are also very much an active part of both the local and national level.

Ma's March election and the January Kuomintang legislative victories will shake up the government. During the campaign Ma promised to appoint women to at least a third of the high-ranking offices in his administration. He also pledged to establish a gender equality commission to help elevate the status of women, create over a hundred thousand new jobs for women within four years of his inauguration, and allocate a budget for women-related policies as soon as he assumes office. In recent weeks since Ma's inauguration on May 20, he has already begun to act on some of these promises, already "signifying a considerable change from past KMT traditions of appointing males to be public officers," according to Meg Chiu of Taiwan Thinktank.

She went on to note the appointments of Chan Mignonne Man-Jung to Senior Advisor of National Security Council and Lai Shin-Yuan to Director of Mainland Affairs Council as examples of recent additions of women to his cabinet. If fully implemented, such measures should do much to strengthen the status of women and their engagement in vital decision-making. None of these promises, however, seemed decisive in winning the support of young women. Generally confident that their own lives and career prospects would be better than their mothers, these women were proud of Taiwan's democracy and happy enough to participate as voters.

8

Women's Political Participation in Indonesia

The UN Convention on the Elimination of all Forms of Discrimination against Women (CEDAW) was adopted by the UN General Assembly in 1979. Today, after more than twenty years since the signing of the Convention, more than 170 countries have ratified the agreement. The Convention provides the basis for realizing equality between women and men by ensuring women's equal access to, and equal opportunities in, political and public life, including the right to vote and to stand for election. Governments agreed to take all appropriate measures, including legislation and temporary special measures, so that women can enjoy all their human rights and fundamental freedoms. However, these measures have not been put into practice in many countries around the world. Indonesia ratified the UN Convention on Political Rights for Women under former President Soeharto in 1968. CEDAW was ratified in 1984.

The Habibie government later ratified the Optional Protocol of the Women's Convention. In recent years the Indonesian government has also taken steps to adopt measures aimed at best practices in gender policies, in particular gender mainstreaming, which is an important strategy included in the Beijing Platform for Action. Presidential Instruction No. 9/2000 directs all sectors of the Indonesian government to implement gender mainstreaming. Despite these ratifications, there are many critics of the current government who are unwilling to pass new legislation or amend existing laws to meet the requirements of the Convention.

During 2001, the debate concerning women's political representation and participation in politics increased and dominated much of the political agenda, being fueled by active and outspoken civil society organizations and activists. One of the critical issues was the adoption of a 30 per cent quota for women in the electoral process. The ongoing and sometimes controversial debates on gender and democracy were the result of three factors in Indonesia's recent past. The first is the historical and continuous under representation of Indonesian women in all levels of decision- making. In the national parliament, women constitute 9.2 per cent of the total members of parliament, which is less than the 12.5 per cent in the previous parliament.

The second factor is related to the current political reform. The transition to democracy has created increased opportunities for women and other sectors of society to express their views and to formulate and articulate their demands for greater gender awareness and sensitivity in government policies, legislation and in electoral politics. The third factor is related to the economic crisis in 1997 which triggered an increased demand for representation of women in all levels and in all aspects of political life. The crisis led to a lowering of women's living conditions, prompting women to take a stand to voice their needs and defend their rights.

All these factors have created an environment in which civil society organizations, NGOs, activists, politicians and international agencies have been able to articulate and collectively affect the discourse and the direction of government policy regarding the inclusion of women in Indonesian public life. Since 1998, International IDEA has provided strategic advice to national actors in government and civil society on options relating to the electoral system and on the administration of election management bodies. In 1999 IDEA also began sponsoring initiatives to strengthen women's political participation, involving women members of the national parliament.

Through a dialogue with dynamic and progressive groups in civil society, parliament members, political party members and academics, IDEA developed a gender track in Indonesia during 2002. The gender activities focus on women's political participation, with the main aim of strengthening women's participation within Indonesian politics. The gender track therefore seeks to stimulate a dialogue between different groups of society, nationally as well as internationally, to increase the knowledge among the groups working with gender issues, including parliamentarians, political party members and the general public at the national as well as provincial levels.

As part of the 2002 activities, International IDEA's gender track included an Asian Study Visit of Indonesian politicians and activists to India, Thailand and the Philippines in August, with the aim of sharing knowledge and experiences, but mainly to increase the dialogue between the participants and their counterparts in other countries. The Asian Study Visit also aimed to increase networking and exchanges between the Indonesian participants themselves. A total of 15 women and men took part in the Asian Study Visit, representing key sectors of the government, political parties and civil society. Furthermore, participants were included from different provinces in Indonesia, including East, Central and West Java, West Nusa Tenggara, South Sulawesi, and North Sumatra.

The Asian Study Visit was followed by a National Conference on Women in Politics in Jakarta in September 2002, in partnership with the Centre for Electoral Reform (CETRO). The objective of the National Conference was to share the newly gained knowledge from the study visits with other Indonesians, but also to act as a forum to gather national, provincial and international experiences on the issue of increasing women's political participation. The turnout at the National Conference was high, with approximately one hundred participants ranging from politicians, NGO activists to academics and members of the media.

There was an exceptionally high level of interest among the groups working in the field of gender and politics, as well as among the general public. The activities aimed to create action plans highlighting priority areas of work, identifying key strategies and stakeholders in the continuing struggle for gender equality ahead of Indonesia's election in 2004. The National Conference and Provincial Workshops provided dynamic, progressive and productive discussions among the participants and the expected outcomes were reached. This report provides an overview of these discussions, the problems identified, the strategies developed and the stakeholders involved in ensuring an effective increase in women's participation in politics in Indonesia.

The discussions are summarized according to the themes identified above, drawing on the information that was gathered during the Asian Study Visit, the National Conference and Provincial Workshops. The report will therefore provide a brief overview of some of the issues highlighted in the gender political debate in Indonesia during 2002. It also aims to serve as a background document for ongoing discussions and for planning future work in the field of increasing women's political participation in Indonesia.

INCREASING WOMEN'S POLITICAL PARTICIPATION THROUGH CONSTITUTIONAL AND ELECTORAL REFORMS

Increasing the number of women in politics was a highly debated issue in Indonesia in 2002. The discussion focused mainly on the 30 per cent quota to be implemented in the electoral or political party law. There is a near consensus among political activists, women in political parties, academics, and the NGO community for the need to increase women's political participation in Indonesia. There are several reasons why this issue is the subject of increased debate in Indonesia. Firstly, women continue to be under-represented in elected positions in Indonesia both at the national and local levels, with approximately 9.2 per cent of the seats in the

National Parliament (DPR), 5.2 per cent at provincial level (DPRD I) and even a lower number at district level (DPRD II). The second reason is related to the difficulties in Indonesia's transition to democracy.

The transition provided for an opportunity to demand an increase in women's representation. Many politically active women's NGOs started to strive for and to enhance women's political awareness. Political institutions were therefore put under pressure to consider gender issues as an essential part of the democratisation process. During the year 2002 gender issues received wide public attention in political debate in Indonesia as the 2004 drew nearer. Problems such as: the implementation of quotas for women in various political institutions at different levels, issues regarding the impact of the general election systems for women and also the implication of the increasing representation of women for political parties were widely discussed.

The economic crisis in 1997 affected the lives of women and children adversely. Some of the consequences of the crisis were higher mortality rates among mothers and infants, worsening health conditions among children, increasing numbers of women migrant workers, an increasing school drop-out rate, and a higher unemployment rate. These consequences have led to a heightened awareness for the need to devise a more gender sensitive political agenda. The presence of more politically engaged women is a prerequisite toward a more gender equal society.

In short, the need to increase women's political representation in Indonesia came from the realization that political priorities and agenda setting had to be changed and that the traditional political system was not able to achieve this. Only if women take a higher profile and assume more positions in the public sphere will they be able to prioritize and secure different social and economic values which are to their interest. Increasing women's political representation is about increasing women's effectiveness in influencing policy decisions that will secure the rights and entitlements for women, the community, and allocate resources to improve the quality of human security.

OBSTACLES TO WOMEN'S POLITICAL PARTICIPATION IN INDONESIA

The political factors include lack of support from political parties. More specifically, the participants thought that the Indonesian political system and the political parties were not gender sensitive. This resulted in a disregard of women and issues related to them. The topic of the electoral system was discussed with great interest at a time when the provision concerning women in relation to the election law was being debated in parliament. The types of systems discussed during the workshops and conference were: the majority system, the proportional system and the mixed system. The participants viewed the proportional system as most favourable for women, provided that a number of safeguards were instituted.

Even though these were issues that had been tackled in several workshops and were of great interest, a further discussion of this issue may be considered as knowledge among the participants varied across sectors. Another factor affecting the political system is the perception of women primarily as housewives rather than as citizens or political actors. This view limits the chances for women to be active in the political arena. The way political parties operate is seen to be one of the biggest obstacles to women's participation. Many of the participants believe that the nomination and recruitment of women in political parties is often restricted. The political structure is built upon a highly exclusive 'old boys network'.

The leadership within this structure is dominated by men. Furthermore, the lack of transparency in leadership selection gives few opportunities for women to position themselves as viable candidates. Personal loyalty, nepotism, corruption or collusion was cited by the participants as some of the ills confronting the current political system. The unwillingness of political parties to include a women's agenda was mentioned as an obstacle. The lack of women's participation in politics, particularly in political institutions, alludes to underlying ideological and psychological factors.

The participants in all the workshop events underscored the importance of these factors. The women participating themselves were reluctant to take leadership roles as they viewed political parties as being an arena where masculinity prevails. The conflict-ridden party conventions, where physical violence sometimes occurs, the prolonged internal struggles for positions and power, were deterring to them. They preferred to stay away from such politicking. The lack of a support system and support base for women and women's groups was also emphasised as a great hindrance to women's participation. Also, no organisation has the capacity to take an overall role in coordinating the establishment of this support base.

This lack of support also affects the quality of women's work in political institutions as well as the sourcing of women recruits. Moreover, the lack of coordination between different groups working in the field of gender also affects their levels of preparedness for the upcoming election, where an important prerequisite is the identification of women candidates. Many questions concerning the pool from which women candidates may be recruited were asked in the national conference and workshops. Political parties summarily mentioned that 'it was difficult to find "qualified women" at all levels for nomination'.

In contrast to the view taken by political parties, women activists and participants point out that there is in fact, an abundance of qualified women who have the commitment and willingness to run at all levels. What is missing is the political will and desire from parties to nominate women. These women also point out that almost all political parties have women's divisions. In addition, political parties also have affiliated organizations from which they can recruit women. For example, the National Awakening Party *(Partai Kebangkitan Bangsa, PKB)* have Women of the National Awakening Party *(Perempuan Partai Kebangkitan Bangsa, PPKB)* as its women's wing, and the *Fatayat NU* and *Muslimat NU* as its affiliate organizations; the United Development Party *(Partai Persatuan Pembangunan, PPP)* has Wanita Persatuan as its women's division; and, the National Mandate Party *(Partai Amanat Nasional, PAN)* also has the *Perempuan Amanat Nasional (PUAN)* and *Aisyiah* as its affiliate organizations.

Apart from women's divisions and affiliate organizations, women candidates can also be recruited at the grassroots level. These women may not yet be members of political parties but already have the commitment and willingness to work for women's empowerment and willingness to take up party positions. Many NGOs such as the Movement toward Education of Women Voters *(Gerakan Pemberdayaan Swara Perempuan GPSP)*, the Indonesian Women's Coalition for Justice and Democracy *(Koalisi Perempuan Indonesia untuk Keadilan dan Demokrasi, KPI)*, the Network of Women and Politics *(Jaringan Perempuan dan Politik, JPP)*, and Women's Solidarity *(Solidaritas Perempuan, SP)*, work for women's empowerment.

These NGOs have an extensive network and their activities cut across provincial and district levels in many areas in Indonesia. But their participation depends on the political parties' willingness to recruit these 'potential women' from outside their respective traditional bases. Other potential sources of recruitment are professional organizations of lawyers, doctors, teachers, business women, accountants, economists, and the like. These groups make up potential target bases that political parties may tap into. Women belonging to these groups possess 'qualifications' in terms of skills, good education and economic independence. The discussion on quotas led to a passionate debate at both the national and provincial levels.

This discussion has dominated the area of gender in Indonesia in the year 2002 and has attempted to elaborate two kinds of quotas for women. One kind of quota targets actual candidacy by political parties and another targets the manner of how seats are to be filled in parliament. Many of the participants held the view that quotas established by law aimed at ensuring that a certain percentage of seats in parliament would be held by women as being the paramount goal in the 2004 elections. The group was however divided in their approach toward the achievement of this goal. One group stressed the importance of quotas stipulated by law as the most effective way of achieving women's representation.

Another group held the view that quotas do not really create real political space for women in parliament because in the end they will create a ceiling. Instead, this group espouses the adoption of an informal, and therefore, more flexible quota. Although a consensus on 'the right way for Indonesia' was not eventually reached in the workshops, the participants took the opportunity to engage in a lively discussion. Participants observed that these obstacles that work against women being elected to parliament are not unique to Indonesia.

Participants who had the opportunity to visit India, Thailand and the Philippines have noticed similar problems in these countries. In their opinion, learning from the experiences of these countries may facilitate the achievement of greater women's political participation in Indonesia. The workshops in Makassar and Medan identified similar obstacles but with regional variations. An obstacle noted by participants in Makassar relates to the socio-cultural barrier of patriarchy, reinforced by a religious perception that circumscribes the role of women in society.

These perceptions are based on interpretations of the Qur'an, the Hadith, and teachings of Islamic scholars that reinforce the view those women belong to the domestic, and not to the public sphere. This partially explains women's perceived lack of interest in being politically involved. In Medan, the low representation of women is linked to poverty and the lack of education. These are some of the key factors explaining the absence of women in all levels of elected offices in North Sumatra. The workshops also examined what kinds of strategies might to be employed to substantially increase women's political representation in Indonesia.

The discussions among the participants revolved around lessons learned from an IDEA-organized study visit to India,

Thailand and the Philippines. The discussion focused on the possibility of introducing an affirmative action program by establishing a quota to increase women's political participation. The discussions also explored ideas about giving assistance to women so that they may gain relevant experiences which will hopefully enable them to compete for leadership positions within parties and electoral seats.

Although Indonesian women already have voting rights and the Constitution enshrines equality between men and women, it is widely recognised that a gap exists in practice. One step toward gender equality proposed by the participants is to lobby for quotas in special commissions and to press for the inclusion of similar quotas to be included in the draft bill on elections which may be considered by political parties as part of their legislative reform package. Quotas are introduced in order to ensure that women acquire a minimum share of seats in the legislature.

Rules that establish quotas in political parties and government institutions aim to assist women to overcome the barrier of under-representation in these areas of decision-making. In order to be effective, the adoption of affirmative action programs and the establishment of quotas have to be accompanied by definite timetables with clear targets. India was an example cited by several participants who observed that the target of reaching 33% of seats to be reserved for women at the district level (*panchayati raj*) is made possible by the 74th Amendment to the Constitution in 1989. Clearly, finding ways to make the system conducive and supportive of women entering politics cannot be separated from the aim of substantially reforming the Indonesian electoral system.

After discussing different options, participants agreed that an open list PR system is most desirable and that there is a need to lobby members of parliament to include this system in the electoral law. There is also a need to continue discussions and to expand the present network to include women in rural areas. Although there was a great interest in discussions about different types of electoral systems, general knowledge about these systems is limited. Specifically, very little is known about how different systems work and how differences among systems hold different implications for women's representation. For instance, different electoral systems, nomination and recruitment processes and the size of district have strong influences on the opportunity for women to be nominated and elected.

These differences in mechanism were however, not deeply examined in the national conference and regional workshops. The role played by political parties in nominating women in the electoral process should not be underestimated. The adoption of a closed list PR system allows political parties to determine the rank ordering of candidates on party lists for election, and in this process women may be placed in 'electable' positions on the lists. However, even if quotas were to be adopted in the closed list PR system, without corresponding changes in the party mechanisms, such as rules that assure the naming of women as board members or appointing them to key positions in the party hierarchy, then it will still be difficult to achieve an increase in women's political participation. Many participants were uninformed about a government proposal submitted to the Parliament that seeks to establish an open list PR system.

The argument presented by the government is that Indonesia's transition to democracy requires a new election system that combines popular representation as well as accountability. Although the Mixed system (a hybrid between Majority and PR systems) is considered most desirable, implementation would entail a long period of preparation. Given time constraints, the government has come to the conclusion that Indonesia would not be ready to implement a Mixed system (MMP) or a Majority system in 2004. The pragmatic alternative is that of an open list PR system. Unfortunately, the discussion on the impact of an open list PR system on women's representation did not get much attention. Participants were more focused on the goal of adopting quotas through the election law and political party law.

To sum up, participants mentioned several points to be considered in the electoral system debate and the possibility of introducing a quota law. The most crucial issues to be addressed in these laws should be:

- Women-friendly criteria in recruitment of members to political parties.
- Transparent, measurable and accountable criteria for election to party leadership positions.
- Affirmative action policies in the election of party leaders.
- Affirmative action policies in nominating of MPs at the national and local levels.
- Adopting an election system with proportional representation rather than an election system with a dominant first-past-the-post, single-member district features.
- Introducing 'zipping' methods to insert women alternately with men in the lists of candidates for MPs on the ballot paper.

There is also a need to build networks and caucuses among political party members, parliamentarians and civil society activists. Indonesia may learn a valuable lesson from Thailand where political parties are made to be accountable to their constituents. These two actors are able to work closely together in their efforts to improve the status of women through changes in public policy and legislation. This cooperation has resulted in a Constitution drafted in 1997 through a democratic process involving the citizens.

This momentum in citizen involvement was seized by women activists in their struggle to enshrine gender equality in the constitution. The Thai experience points to the need for Indonesia to reform its political parties. New systems to select candidates and new mechanisms in policy-making that assure transparency and accountability have to be devised. There is also a need to develop networks of mutual support which may act as a strong base for collaboration among women in Indonesian society.

This could be done either through a main body or a network of women's caucuses that may serve as a voice calling for greater recognition of their role in the political arena. Strategies for changing religious interpretations on the role of women were also discussed. The participants highlighted the importance of engaging religious leaders to discuss and dialogue around the issue of gender equality and its implications for traditional interpretations of religious texts. Enlisting the cooperation of the media is another strategy of importance raised during the discussions. The media should be encouraged to cover events that highlight gender issues. Women should also realize the importance of using the media to push their agenda, by appearing in talk shows, serving as resource persons, commenting on issues and writing articles.

An action plan was developed from inputs gathered during the course of the national conference and provincial workshops. The aim of this action plan was to outline possibilities for further work and to pursue greater levels of effectiveness among groups that focus on gender issues. The idea behind this exercise was to gain an understanding of what is needed and expected from all groups represented and to identify individuals who may serve as coordinators for upcoming activities. The discussions on women's political participation in Indonesia during 2002 focused on how to increase the number of women holding positions in political institutions.

This focus was apparent in the national conference in Jakarta and regional workshops in Medan and Makassar. The strategies proposed in both venues of discussion were intended to open up opportunities for increased women's participation particularly in the upcoming 2004 elections. What results have been achieved through these efforts and strategies? Despite strong protest from women's groups and a number of legislators who had demanded the adoption of a 30 per cent quota for women, the political party bill was nevertheless endorsed in November 2002.

The legislators who protested included Eka Komariah Kuncoro of the Golkar Party, Ida Fauziah from PKB, Chodijah

Soleh from PPP, Nurdiati Akma from PAN, Ahmad Farchan Hamid of PAN and Samuel Koto of PAN. Their protest drew applause from women activists from the balcony of the assembly hall. Later on female legislators joined the women activists to urge the special committee deliberating the bill to include a specific clause mandating a quota of 30 per cent for women in the recruitment of candidates at all levels of party leadership.

Following are some of the lessons learned:

- *A critical number of women in parliament is important to ensure the passage of the bill.* With only two women in the special committee that deliberated the political party bill, it was almost impossible to win support for proposals pushing for a quota.
- *Women's issues need to be represented by women.* Given the low number of women in decision- making bodies, and the reluctance of men to take up 'women's issues', women need to be present to articulate their demands.
- *Political processes for the passage of bills in the parliament do not always follow procedures.* The agreement on article 13 (3) of the Political Party Law on gender equity was reached during the break when no women were in the room.
- *Networking is very important inside and outside parliament in order to achieve common goals defined by women activists, women legislators and members of women caucuses.* The quota proposal, for instance, had to be closely monitored, required constant lobbying by women's organisations. Doing otherwise ultimately results in its dismissal from the agenda.
- *The media plays an important role in the advocacy of issues.* Pressure from the media can work effectively. Political parties and members of parliament are concerned about their image in the media and therefore tend to support popular issues.

Enlisting the help of the media can therefore sway the actions of political actors. Vigilance is of utmost importance. Workshops on women's empowerment need to be continued, strategies have to be defined and redefined according to the exigencies of the political milieu. The road to women's empowerment in Indonesia may be fraught with delays, disappointments, and setbacks, but the ultimate goal of gender equality must be constantly articulated. Women's representation in the National Parliament is approximately 9.2 per cent. The percentage of women's representation in local parliaments is even lower and stands at approximately 5.2 per cent. South Sulawesi is the most populated and developed province in East Indonesia, while North Sumatra is its demographic equivalent in West Indonesia.

STRENGTHENING WOMEN'S POLITICAL PARTICIPATION

Discussing the issue of strengthening women's political participation in Indonesia requires viewing it in context of the current transition to a more democratic political system. Democracy attempts to secure political equality for all citizens, including marginalized and minority groups. Although women in Indonesia demographically constitute the majority, they are a silent majority - marginalized politically, socially, culturally, economically - largely absent from the decision- making processes. For example, women's representation in the National Parliament (DPR) decreased from 12.5% in 1992 to 9.2% in 1999.

The impact of this decline is that laws and regulations enacted and implemented as well as the prioritisation of national and local development programs neither reflect principles of political equality and social justice, nor the interests of women. The need to increase the number of women in politics and to strengthen their power-base were two critical issues raised in the UN Conference on Women held in Beijing in 1995. The Indonesian government's active participation in this conference resulted in several workshops, seminars, and conferences for women political party members and women parliamentarians sponsored nationally by the Indonesian State Ministry for the Empowerment of Women.

The objectives of these activities were to strengthen women's networking and to lobby for the inclusion of gender issues, as well as quotas for women in legislation. The increased political participation of women both locally and nationally will influence the nature of Indonesian democracy, for all citizens. To move 'Beyond Numbers' means looking beyond simply increasing the number of women participating in the political arena, to address the extent to which women can succeed in politics, looking at the impact that women have when they participate in the political system, monitoring how the political agenda is developed, and observing the issues that are being raised through their involvement.

This issue concerning women's empowerment has not yet reached the same level of discussion as the topic of increasing the numbers of women in parliament. However, the discussions that took place during the events of the conference and workshops have taken us a step forward in raising awareness. Problems Identified In the discussions it was apparent that women from different socio-cultural, economic, and regional backgrounds encounter different problems. Similarly, women representatives from various levels of government (national, provincial, and municipal) face different obstacles.

Furthermore, women from different economic classes, urban and rural origins, ethnic and religious backgrounds, have specific problems and obstacles to overcome, and therefore require specific solutions. Prof. Farida Nurland, Head of the Gender Research Centre at the University of Hasannuddin, Makassar, South Sulawesi, has identified the following problems and obstacles: first, Indonesian culture is both feudalistic and patriarchal; second, society has adopted a very conservative understanding and interpretation of various religious teachings; third, state hegemony is still dominant, which is reflected in state institutions which perpetuate a patriarchal culture at all levels.

It is clear that at the national and provincial levels, the patriarchal culture and the political system negatively affect women who try to assert their right to political participation. In traditional Indonesian society, women are not encouraged to take active roles in the public domain; their talents and skills are recognised only in the private domain of the household. This dichotomy is often still maintained even in the present Reform Era. Indonesian women therefore face obstacles at two levels.

Over and above their struggle against patriarchal culture, they have to overcome discriminatory and gender-blind practices in the electoral process, in legislative bodies and also in political parties. These cultural norms are so deep-seated that they have been internalised by most Indonesian women. This has made them psychologically unprepared for political participation. Many women have developed a sense of inferiority and believe that they do not have the requisite skills for political issues. This has caused women to adopt a passive approach to politics, many perceiving politics as being negative, preventing women from developing and identifying strategies for themselves. In addition, the act of political campaigning is not seen by many as an appropriate activity for women.

The issue of women's 'dual role' as mothers and housewives, and as members of the labour force was highlighted by many participants. This reality constrains many women, limiting the time they can allot to political activities. Stereotyping of women creates other problems. For example, women who focus on their careers are often judged for going against the norm. They have to excel in both roles in order to be perceived as 'successful' women. The practices in political parties and organizations do not recognise and accommodate the 'dual role' of women. For example, important political decisions are frequently made during marathon meetings held from night to dawn when it is virtually impossible for many women party cadres to attend because of household responsibilities. In addition, mechanisms for women to support women hardly exist.

There is a lack of coordination not only at different levels (national and provincial), but also across groups operating in the same field of interest, geographic area, and political levels. The absence of unity through coordination and networking results in a weakened position for women in asserting their rights. Furthermore, the inability to mobilize across groups and at different levels lessens women's chances to win in elections. More specifically, within political parties, there are several obstacles or barriers confronting Indonesian women who try to advance themselves and increase their effectiveness and influence in the party system.

First, the level of political socialization of women is low; few women are active as party cadres. Second, leadership in political parties tends to be male, and in turn they tend to nominate male candidates whom they believe have a greater potential to win. Third, there is a tendency to select female candidates who are closely connected to men in power. Fourth, general elections are costly and require access to funds. Few women have independent resources to commit to this. Political parties rarely assist women candidates in raising funds. Fifth, women's lack of mobilization and inability to support each other places them in a vulnerable and disadvantaged position when they need to take an active stand in asserting their rights.

The strategies identified during the national conference and provincial workshops focus on a combination of governmental action through legislation and civil society activism (the matrix in the end of this ch sums up the activities and strategies planned at these events to be conducted by the groups represented). The first strategy involves political socialization through political education. It is necessary to provide training in organizational development to women candidates, to train women's groups to highlight gender issues, and to establish networks among women's groups in civil society, political parties, the parliament, and the media. The second strategy concerns strengthening the position of women who already hold public posts by giving them training in effective lobbying, successful campaigning, and identifying resource persons.

Increasing institutional capacity by investing in skills development for staff members, capacity building, and expanding the support-base of elected women. Suggestions were made to conduct these activities through collaborative activities among women parliamentarians, party members, academics and activists. The third strategy underscores the importance of providing assistance to political parties which are committed to the promotion of gender equality through their platforms and internal political structures. This assistance should come in the form of training programs and financial assistance or incentives through election management bodies.

The fourth strategy explores the development of a database to identify women with leadership potential at the national and local levels. The purpose of this database would be to profile MPs and potential candidates from political parties, as well as leaders from the executive, judicial, and legislative branches, and individual personalities from women's political caucuses, civil society organizations (CSOs), and other groups. This database would identify key persons who could be involved in the campaign to strengthen women's political participation, as well as women who may be recruited in public life. The fifth strategy aims to initiate programs that help develop political awareness and expand knowledge among potential female cadres who are not yet active in the public sphere.

The media was identified as one of the key players in the task of educating the public and spreading information on gender equality. The sixth strategy seeks to develop and strengthen the networks among women members in political parties, parliament, CSOs, and media. The cooperation of the media should be enlisted in the goal to present women as credible political actors. The last strategy relates to the overall structure of politics. The participants stressed that women's empowerment should pervade not only formal structures of politics, but also people's organisations, social movements and other civil society groups.

Along with implementing an action plan designed specifically to increase women's political participation, it is important to secure broad changes in the political system. This could be done through internal political party reforms to achieve higher levels of transparency, justice and gender equality. These broad movements towards greater democratization should also factor the importance of establishing real autonomy in the various political, legal, and social institutions of Indonesia such as political parties, parliament, the Supreme Court, and the mass media. These institutions must be insulated from political pressure.

Only then can public trust be gained. It is particularly important for women as a constituent group to trust the political system to be able to participate in its processes. In this context, there are several recommendations to be made on how to go beyond numbers in strengthening women's political participation in Indonesia: First, it is important to focus on political parties, in assisting them to become more gender- sensitive in order to increase the number of women within party ranks and to provide them with equal opportunities to participate in decision-making.

Concretely, this would include making changes in the way party meetings are scheduled, in order to accommodate the dual role played by women in the domestic as well as public spheres, and in providing assistance in campaign finance and in developing leadership skills. Second, there is a need to cultivate a critical mass of CSOs committed to improving the status of women, and to help them develop a feeling of shared causes with women in politics.

Ways of doing this work could include increasing the number of cooperative activities among groups, strengthening the networks between CSOs and women in politics, and assisting these groups in influencing government through the parliament and political parties, taking appropriate affirmative action measures to fast-track women's political empowerment, strengthening the link among international organizations with CSO components, and assisting CSOs in organizing citizenship training for both women voters and candidates.

Third, using existing cultural and religious institutions such as religious women's organizations like Fatayat, Aliyah, etc., in order to facilitate socialization in communities, is highly recommended. This approach is especially most appropriate among rural people to increase their awareness and consciousness of the importance of women's role in political life. Fourth, an important focus related to increasing women's involvement would be to conduct work related to village affairs in order to influence the decision-making at this level and to encourage the emergence of grassroots pressure aimed at higher levels of government.

Training women cadres at the village level increases the prospects of women playing a greater role in regional representative councils and later, also at the national level. Fifth, recommendations were also made to organize women's groups so that they may be able to respond to the needs of the community in the areas of reproductive health, provision of clean water, and sanitation, and link these initiatives as part of a broader strategic effort to increase the political participation of women. Sixth, there is a need to encourage CSOs to organize public debates, advocacy campaigns to promote women's political participation, and to provide organizational management and campaign training, and avenues for campaign finances for the women who become members of social and political organizations.

To summarise the recommendations, political participation should be assessed not only in terms of representation in national and local parliaments. Participation in political parties and in national and local political campaigns must also be considered. While there are many efforts being made to increase the critical mass of women in politics, the efforts to strengthen the quality of women's political engagement are also significant. These efforts depend on a multi-strategy approach over time that links ministries, parliamentary secretariats, political parties and CSOs. In the current transitional period, this is a key challenge that has to be faced by Indonesians, both women and men, who truly believe in democracy and social justice for all.

CREATING LINKS BETWEEN CIVIL SOCIETY AND POLITICAL INSTITUTIONS

Despite their majority in numbers and the contribution they have made in society and the economy, Indonesian women are underrepresented in existing political institutions. In the national parliament, women currently constitute only 9.2% of the total members of parliament, a decrease from 12.5% in the previous period. Historically, women's representation in the legislature has always been below 10%. The highest rate of representation was achieved between 1987-1992, when women constituted 13% of the national parliament. The numbers are even lower in the local legislatures where women make up less than 5% of provincial parliaments and less than 1% for district level parliaments. In the executive branch, the situation is not much better.

Although Indonesia has a woman president, currently, the cabinet only has only two women ministers: the Minister of Trade, and the Minister for Women's Affairs, which is a ministry without portfolio. Traditionally, women ministers only held 'soft' posts such as that of Women's Affairs and of Social Welfare. Historically only three women held posts outside these soft offices: there was a Minister of Labour during the Soekarno presidency, a Minister of Public Works during the Wahid presidency, and currently a Minister of Trade during the Megawati presidency.

Moreover, women's representation in top decision-making positions in all government ministries is also very low. Although women make up the majority of public servants in large and vital ministries such as the Ministry of Education, the Ministry of Health and the Ministry of Home Affairs, they mostly occupy mid to lower level bureaucratic positions. Most of the high echelon are occupied by men. The same situation prevails at the local level offices where there are only three women governors and three women district heads. Indonesia ratified the UN Convention on the Elimination of All Forms of Discriminations against Women in 1984, but to date, both the government and Parliament have yet to pass new legislation to implement the Convention or to adjust existing laws to meet the requirements of the Convention.

The lack of public pressure on the state to adopt measures in keeping with the Convention is a reflection of public ignorance about the Convention as well as the indifference of the nation's political elite towards fulfilling its obligations under international law. Implementing the Convention tends not to be regarded as a politically rewarding initiative by the political elite. The political elite, both at the national and local levels, tends to scoff at recommendations to adopt affirmative action policies to increase women's political representation. They tend to view these policies as fostering reverse discrimination against men and worse, as a zero-sum game targeted to 'take over' political institutions from the hands of men.

Many also believe that affirmative action policies will reduce the quality of male participation in exchange for the quantitative achievement of increasing women's political participation. The under representation of women in political institutions can have dire consequences on the lives of women in Indonesia. Most policies or legislation that directly affect the lives of women are mostly made by men who have neither empathy nor understanding of the experiences of women. In certain sectors such as health and labour, this can have grave implications for women.

One example is that Indonesia still has the highest maternal mortality rate (MMR) among ASEAN countries-an appalling condition given Indonesia's more advanced status compared to Cambodia and Laos, two of the poorer ASEAN members. Yet to date, there has not been a specific policy targeted to deal with the issue by the Ministry of Health, such as allotting a specific budget line for the improvement of pre-natal health as well as to improve natal and post-natal care for poor women. Another urgent issue is the plight of women migrant workers who often undergo physical abuse such as maltreatment and unsafe travel and working conditions. Recently, the issue of migrant workers dominated national headlines when Malaysia, one of the biggest host countries of Indonesian migrant workers, deported thousands of Indonesian migrant workers-mostly women.

The workers were placed in temporary shelters in Nunukan, East Kalimantan where unsanitary conditions, shortage of food, and meager health support prevails. Despite high media attention and the outpouring of public sympathy and aid, the government, was slow to respond and until this date, no specific guidelines have been produced to prevent such a simular situation. Another example of lack of support for women within the legislature is reflected in the rise of support for the implementation of a conservative interpretation of the *shari'a law* in several provinces in Indonesia. In the Province of Aceh, the protracted war with the separatist movement finally forced the central government to pass a law allowing the province to implement *shari'a law*.

The substance of the law became controversial as early drafts indicated that many of the provisions will limit the participation of women in public life. In other provinces, the renewed popularity of *shari'a law* also prompted local legislatures, which have virtually no women members, to consider the passage of night curfews for women-ostensibly aimed to reduce prostitution. Vigorous protests from women's organization have, to date, prevented such regulations from being passed. However, with very few women in legislatures to prevent such provisions from being proposed again, it is likely that similar initiatives will come up in the agenda of legislatures in other provinces.

Achieving women's political representation at the local levels, especially at the district level, has become critical with the advent of regional autonomy. Greater authority and powers are now granted to the district government and legislatures making them the most strategic policy-making institutions at the local levels. Given that most of the policies dealing directly with the lives of women and children are made at the local levels, it is alarming to see that this is where women are mostly under-represented. As a rule, the media can play an important role in increasing public awareness and generate public pressure on the state.

This has been true as can be seen in the case of pro-reform agendas supported by the media during the transition. However, certain women's issues have not made significant inroads into mainstream media. In general, the media tends to view women's issues as being too limited and narrow to deserve more coverage. The problem is compounded by the fact that most editorial board members of mainstream media take the same negative position of the political elites on the issue of affirmative action. In this context, it is therefore important that all parties committed to strengthening women's political participation make a concerted effort towards increasing women's representation in political institutions.

Civil society organizations (CSOs) working on women's issues as well as women's studies centres in many public universities have an in-depth understanding of the issue and are therefore better positioned to take the lead. Many CSOs focusing on women's issues have made significant achievements in advocating their respective causes such as eliminating domestic violence, improving the status of women migrant workers, ensuring women's reproductive rights, and dealing with the plight of women refugees in conflict areas. However, at the policy level, the response to these advocacy efforts has been dismal.

Most of these CSOs tend to emphasize increasing public awareness of their specific causes and directly try to provide temporary solutions without determining long-term policy alternatives. One of the reasons for this is that there is a lack of significant partners in government who the CSOs can engage and lobby for long-term solutions. The very few women who are in government and the legislatures both at the national and local levels, are politically too weak to adopt a strong stance on women's interests. Their small numbers make it even more difficult for them to constitute a formidable faction within the legislatures.

There is a general distrust of public institutions, including the legislatures, which is an obstacle towards developing cooperation and partnerships between actors within the CSOs and within public institutions. Social organizations are reluctant to cooperate with parliamentarians and other public officials because of the long tradition of CSOs performing the role of opposition against state authority in Indonesia. This stance was adopted during the authoritarian regime of Soeharto. State officials, including parliamentarians and political party leaders, also tend to share a similar distrust and suspicion towards CSOs. Many hold the assumption that CSOs are generally radical and opposed to any government policy.

It is also important to add that Indonesia is still in the midst of a very difficult political transition from authoritarianism to democracy. It is a very daunting task for women's organizations to push for their agenda against high-profile items such as anti-corruption, human rights, financial sector restructuring and anti-terrorism. In this context, the struggle to achieve political representation for women is an uphill battle.

A well-defined and well-planned strategy is needed to foster effective measures to achieve significant representation for women. In principle, there are several problems that can be identified and need to be dealt with in order to achieve greater political representation for women:

1. Political parties show little understanding for the need to recruit more women and have little commitment to enlist more women into their ranks and appoint more women to decision-making positions within the parties.

Most women who join political parties assume regular membership positions. Even if appointed or elected to leadership positions, they only occupy minor decision-making posts such as that of the secretary or organizer of the party's women's wing. The leadership of most political parties assert that their recruitment policy does not specifically discriminate against women. However, if one looks closely at some of the criteria for membership, for leadership positions, or for nomination as MPs, implicit discrimination against women does exist. For one thing, most parties establish 'organizational experience' as one of the criteria for membership or for leadership positions. For most women, this is a barrier.

Most women in Indonesia do not have documented experience in organization compared to men because their participation in public life is severely limited by marriage and family life. Usually, older women or those whose children are relatively grown up can devote more time outside their homes to participate in organizations, such as religious or neighbourhood associations. If these are the objective qualifications required, then it is difficult for women to compete with their male colleagues to occupy leadership positions, let alone be nominated as MPs. There is also no concerted strategy to attract more women into political parties.

Women are seldom encouraged to join political parties, and there are no programs to socialize and train women party members to become highly skilled and qualified party cadres. Existing organizational activities arranged by political parties shows a lack of consideration for women's needs and interests. This is also the reason why, as most party leaders claim, there is no abundant supply of qualified women to occupy leadership positions in their parties or to be nominated as MPs. This is so despite the fact that educational attainment of women has risen significantly in the past decade. However, many women are not interested in joining parties partly because of the implicit discrimination in the recruitment criteria, as well as a certain stigma that society places on women in politics.

2. Participants also highlighted the importance of establishing a legal basis for 'affirmative action' policies in order to gain significant inroads for women in existing political institutions, notably the legislatures. The problem is how could affirmative action policies be passed when most of the members of the legislatures are men who generally view 'affirmative action' as discrimination?
3. The problem is especially acute among the political elite who make crucial decisions that affect the lives of women as well as among members of the media who more often than not stigmatize public participation by women.
4. There are no concerted efforts by actors who are committed to the cause of women's rights in crafting an effective strategy to increase women's political representation.

The problem is two-fold: first, disagreements remain among women's organizations or NGOs on whether an increase in women's political representation is the key to alleviating general discrimination against women. Secondly, even if there is an understanding for the need to increase women's political representation, CSOs tend to work separately and are reluctant to collaborate with politicians in political parties and the legislatures. To address the above-mentioned problems and challenges, there is an urgent need to devise a concerted and effective strategy to increase women's political representation:

1. *Meeting of minds among CSOs with an interest in women's issues*

   Prior to planning strategies, it is important for CSOs to meet and discuss the issues at hand, in order to determine the approaches and strategies to be taken. Differences in strategies and viewpoints should be tolerated and viewed as enriching the division of labour among the participating CSOs. This coordination meeting should also involve regional CSOs. The meetings may also be replicated at the provincial levels so that strategies most appropriate to local conditions may be determined by the groups themselves.

2. *Identify women with leadership potential*

   There is a need to establish a database of women with leadership potential at the national and local levels, with the help of CSOs and NGOs.

3. *Strengthen the capacity of women to occupy leadership positions*

   Organize workshops with a specific curriculum devised to strengthen women's leadership qualities especially their ability to work in public and political organizations. Women need to be trained to be aware that they will be working within a political environment that is generally hostile to their inclusion. The curriculum may be drafted to address this specific context, and will include specific case studies or situations likely to be faced by women.

The capacity-building programs should include the following:

- Drafting of curriculum and training manuals to address the specific context in which women's political participation must be increased and strengthened.

- Training of trainers to encourage women's political participation.
- Establish criteria for training participants.
- Conduct capacity-building workshops with participants who are members of political parties, parliaments, the academic community, CSOs, and government institutions.

4. *Draft legislation allowing affirmative action policies*

The most strategic legislation that influences women's political participation is those that pertain to political parties and elections.

5. *Assertive lobbying of Parliament*

A well-planned and effective lobbying effort must be established by CSOs, NGOs and MPs if real change is to be achieved. Steps to be prepared for lobbying are among others:

- Carefully select lobbyists with a good understanding of the parliamentary process, familiarity with important MPs and leaders of the Parliament, and who have the ability to negotiate with parliamentarians on an equal footing.
- Identify key allies in the Parliament, and establish a strategic partnership with these allies by providing them with support in terms of written arguments, reports and other documents needed to strengthen their negotiations within the Parliament.
- Identify key opponents in the debates, and study their basic arguments in order to prepare counter arguments in a subtle and diplomatic manner.
- Study both the 'official' and 'unwritten' legislative calendar in order to enable close monitoring of the legislative process. Also, investigate all changes made in the venue of legislative meetings, especially closed meetings among leaders of factions in the Parliament.
- Prepare compromise points or 'worst-case scenario' positions that are acceptable to all.

6. Establish a caucus or strategic network among protagonists

Cross-sector networks should be established to provide more stable alliances that would make the movement stronger and continuous. These networks may be established among 'protagonists' from the parliament, CSOs, academics community, religious organizations, and the media. This network should establish regular strategy meetings and maintain contact among its members. This caucus should also be established at the provincial, and if possible, at the district levels to strengthen the movement.

7. Media campaign

Media campaigns can be used as effective tools during the legislative process. The media campaign can serve the following functions:

- Increase public awareness on the issue of women's political representation.
- Rally public support for gender equality policies.
- Exert pressure on the Parliament to pass gender equality legislation.

Media campaigns should be run both at the national and local levels through print and electronic media (especially radio), and by producing campaign paraphernalia such as posters, banners, stickers, and buttons. Other effective media campaign strategies include holding public discussions with large numbers of participants in big cities and to link them with high-profile events that draw media attention. It is also important to approach the editorial board members of the mainstream media organizations in order to get support for coverage of the issue.

The National Conference and the Provincial Workshops provided a forum for productive and sustained discussions and dialogue among the major participants on the issue of increasing women's political representation in the Indonesian legislature. In the context of the transition from an authoritarian to a democratic political system since 1998, these discussions and dialogues are crucial not only for Indonesian women but also for the positive evolution of Indonesian democracy. The dynamic interaction at both the above events focused on three major themes: increasing women's political participation through constitutional and electoral reforms; looking beyond the question of numbers on how to strengthen women's political participation, and creating links between civil society and political institutions.

The themes were discussed in the Indonesian context: the obstacles women face, the strategies identified for reform, and the development of an action plan to support the representation and political participation of women in the country. For ongoing discussions and planning regarding women's political participation in Indonesia, it is hoped that this report will serve as a reference point on lessons learned from recent experiences in working on the three general themes.

For future strategies and action plans to be successful, they should take into consideration several important factors. First, it is apparent that a critical number of women in parliament are required to ensure the passage of a particular bill through the parliament. Second, women are in the best position to represent the problems faced by Indonesian women in their lives. Third, women activists and women legislators should seek to work hard in their networking activities to achieve this. Fourth, public campaigns, both through print and electronic media should to be sustained in order to raise public awareness and to influence policy decision-making. The theme of looking beyond numbers to strengthen women's political participation indicates the importance of focusing on the internal organisation of political party structures in order for them to become more gender-sensitive and gender-oriented.

Francisia SSE Seda notes that the conference and workshop recommendations point to the need to build a critical mass of civil society organizations (CSOs) committed to improving the status of women and help them develop a common cause with women in politics. It is therefore crucial to increase the cooperation and networking between these different groups. The linkage between Indonesian CSOs and international organizations working on this specific issue can become beneficial in organizing citizenship training both for the female electorate and for female candidates to parliament. Existing cultural and religious institutions such as religious women's organizations can play a facilitating role in socializing local communities on the need for increasing women's political representation. Training of women political cadres at the village level increases the prospects of a greater political role for women in the local legislatures.

The linkage between women's initiatives to improve major community needs such as reproductive health, provision of clean water, and sanitation within a broader strategic effort to increase women's political participation needs to be established. CSOs also need to be more active in advocacy campaigns; further, the organizational capacity of women has to be increased. The challenge for the future is to have a multi-strategy approach over time that links the bureaucracy, parliament secretariats, political parties and CSOs in a joint long-term effort to increase women political representation in the legislature at all levels.

On the theme of creating links between civil society and political institutions, Smita Notosusanto stresses the importance of a close cooperation and a division of labour within the CSO community working on the issue of women's interests at the local, provincial, and the national levels. One strategy is to establish a caucus or network among the parliamentarians, CSOs, academics, religious organizations and the media in order to provide more permanent alliances that would strengthen and sustain the women's movement. Identifying women with leadership potential, strengthening the capacity of women to occupy leadership positions, drafting legislation to allow affirmative action policies are also strategies that need to be comprehensively developed for the long-term prospect of increasing women's political representation.

Assertive lobbying of Parliament and an informed media campaign are important strategies to ensure the successful passage of gender-oriented laws including laws or policy interventions on increasing women's political representation. After the National Conference and the Provincial Workshops were held, two major landmarks occurred related to Indonesian women's political representation. On 28 November 2002 and 18 February 2003, two bills were passed through parliament, respectively the Law on Political Parties and the Law on General Elections. However, the Law on Political Parties did not adopt the 30 per cent quota for women in the recruitment of the candidates at all levels and in leadership positions of political parties that was so vehemently demanded by the Indonesian women's movement.

It only specificies the importance of taking into consideration the principles of gender equality and gender fairness. Despite the minority report noting the protests of several female and male legislators from various political parties during the full plenary session, the Law on Political Parties was passed. While this was perceived as a defeat for the Indonesian women's movement, nevertheless the debate on the 30 per cent quota was a means to bring a gender issue into the political arena, in a way that it had never been done before. In fact, the inclusion of a gender consideration in the Law on General Elections is considered as a major breakthrough for providing the legal basis to increase women's political representation despite the lack of legal sanctions for political parties.

Article 65 (1) states that: "Each political party contesting in the General Elections may nominate candidates for *DPR* (National Parliament), *DPRD Propinsi* (Provincial Parliament), and *DPRD* Kabupaten/Kota (Local Parliament) for each electoral district with considerations on the minimum 30 per cent of women representation". For the first time in the history of Indonesian political legislation, a legal basis is provided for increasing women's political representation with a specific percentage stated within the article of the law. The challenge for both women and men inside and outside the political system who are committed to increasing women's visibility is how to ensure that political parties will implement article 65 (1) of the Law on General Elections both in the short and the long terms.

In this regard, the suggested recommendations and strategies discussed in the National Conference and Provincial Workshops are still highly relevant and significant. This will be an uphill struggle, but not impossible, if women parliamentarians, members of political parties, academics, activists, and the media are willing and able to work together. It is also important that this is done in partnership with men. This kind of inclusive and participatory decision-making will serve to benefit Indonesian society in its transition towards a more democratic future.

In Indonesia, women's participation, particularly in the political arena, has been formally guaranteed through the 1945 Constitution and the Broad State Guidelines outlined by the People's Consultative Assembly (MPR). The government has also stated its commitment internationally with regards to equal rights and the duties of men and women as stated in Regulation No. 7 of 1984 which ratified the Convention on the Elimination of all Forms of Discrimination against Women (CEDAW), and in Law No. 39/1999 on Human Rights, which states in section 46 that elections, parties, selection of legislative members and the selection system for the executive branch must guarantee the representation of women, also as outlined in Law No. 26/2000 on human rights.

Nevertheless, despite this legislation, the de facto participation of women is still quite low, and a great cause for concern. Data shows that at the national level, beginning with the period of parliamentary democracy, women representatives in the People's Representative Assembly *(DPR)* increased from 3.8% out of 237 legislators to 6.3% in the 1955 elections, to 7,8% out of 460 legislators in the 1971 elections, and reached its peak of 13% out of 500 members in the 1987 elections. This number has declined since then through the 1999 elections with 8.8% of the legislators being women.

At the level of the provinces, urban municipalities, and regencies, where the process of regional autonomy is being implemented, the number of women represented is alarmingly low, generally below 5% and actually 0% at the level of regencies and urban municipalities. With these figures in mind, the Ministry for Women's Empowerment has been focusing on increasing women's participation and involvement in the political arena in the following ways:

1. Improving the quality and quantity of women in strategic positions in political bodies as decision-makers and policy-makers through political education.
2. Socializing strategies for gender equality and justice sectorally through the Prioritizing Gender Requirement (PUG) strategy as described in Presidential Instruction No. 9 of 2000.
3. Socializing strategies for gender equality and justice to the public in order to create a society and culture that is more conducive for women to have a role in influencing national policy as underlined in the 1999 Broad State Guidelines, which is a guide for national policy as well as for the implementation of regional autonomy.

The need to improve the quantity and quality of women as decision-makers and as key figures in the process of drafting and coordinating policy based on their experience and knowledge, both in the formal as well as traditional sense, is a pressing issue, particularly at the legislative level. As we see, many concerns affecting women have emerged, such as violence, rape, exploitation and trafficking of women and children, the spread of drugs/HIV, pornography and the use of television to broadcast images that degrade our culture and values.

These conditions have been caused by socio-cultural and economic factors affecting the population who do not yet have a sense of the importance of equal rights for men and women-what we call 'gender bias'-as well as a political culture that is tied to regulations and laws that still allow human rights violations in the form of violence, discrimination and abuse of power to happen. The Broad State Guidelines for 1999-2004, which constitutes MPR Decree No. IV/MPR/ 1999, clearly states the need to guarantee the representation of women, in order to support a development process that is founded on justice.

The Guidelines have established the following policy directions:

1. Increase the representation and role of women in national life and in national culture through national policy.
2. Develop a national political system based on the people's sovereignty that emphasizes the principles of equality and anti-discrimination in all aspects of the national culture and in national life.
3. Increase political education to be more intensive and comprehensive in order to develop a democratic political culture that respects plurality, and to underscore the supremacy of the rule of law and of human rights based on *Pancasila* and the 1945 Constitution.
4. Implement a national legal system that fully recognizes and respects religious and traditional law and that revises the laws inherited from the colonial era and the other laws that are discriminative and that perpetuate gender inequality, and that are not consistent with reform demands, through legislation.

In keeping with the theme of this conference, *Strengthening Women's Political Participation*, the Ministry for Women's Empowerment hopes that it can produce programs and strategies that will accelerate the creation of fair and equal positions and conditions for women and men, particularly in the field of politics. A need can be seen for a kind of 'special interim action' or 'affirmative action' to increase women's representation by choosing candidates to serve in the legislature based on basic standards that are outlined and guaranteed through national legislation in order to increase the participation, role and position of women in the national and regional decision- making process.

Such action would be instrumental in creating development based on justice, through a democratic and non-discriminative process, that also respects the hopes and dreams of a plurality of voices. The experience gained from the study visit to India will help us understand and analyze women's efforts in the policy-making process in order to increase women's political participation through constitutional and electoral processes. From this we can also get a sense of how far cultural and patriarchal values persist in society and what can be done to eliminate them. Political participation involves an active role of the citizenry in the political processes of the state with the objective to bring about desired changes in the form of policies and decisions.

There are two kinds of political participation:

- Mobilized participation, and
- Voluntary participation.

The former is characteristic of authoritarian political systems, and the latter of open and democratic systems. Since the Indian system claims to be open and democratic, voluntary political participation seems to be a phenomenon which lends vibrance to the political culture of India. However, mere physical participation in formal political institutions like elections of political parties, social movements and demonstrations is not enough.

Even an expanded level of participation by way of increased numbers or percentages may not lead to the advancement of the cause of a social group. Many studies on the participation of women in the electoral process that look at voting or candidacy seem to mainly concern themselves with this type of statistical package. Equally simplistic have been the studies which deal with the participation of women in the executive, administrative, judicial and local governmental (*panchayati raj*) machineries. Obviously, the theoretical premise of these studies is that women would promote women, would be easily approachable and would be better in formulating and implementing policies for women. This may however, not always be true. Equally significant is the level of political consciousness, and in this case, also gender consciousness.

EFFORTS TO EMPOWER WOMEN'S POLITICAL PARTICIPATION

Culturally, the barriers for women in the Philippines to participate in political decision-making are almost the same as those in Indonesia. However, viewed from political culture, it is rather different. In the Philippines there exists a party that consistently pushes for the quota of 30 per cent for women in the legislature. Political parties in Indonesia, especially those having strong support among the masses in villages, do not push for this. Though the majority of the Indonesians are in villages and most of them are women, political parties in Indonesia do not see them as voters who need to be wooed. This matter is based on two assumptions.

First, the votes of the masses in rural areas very much depend on public figures who can be emulated. In this way, attracting their votes is easily assured by approaching them. Second, the political knowledge of women is deemed to be low in general and the votes of women still depend on the votes of men. Therefore in the campaign process, only a few political parties direct their campaign targets at women. The experiences of NGOs in the Philippines to devise strategies to integrate women issues into public policy-making, to organize women at the local level and to push forward their aspirations at the legislature, are also relevant in the Indonesian context.

Specifically, the efforts included in this framework are as follows:

1. Increasing women's involvement in villages in the context of influencing political decision- making in the village government in particular and at higher government levels in general through village discussions in an attempt to define problems and forward them to the Regional Development Planning Board, of the Regional Representative Councils (DPRD).
2. Organize women to respond to tactical needs (in the areas of reproductive health, clean water, sanitation, etc.), accompanied by efforts to establish women's organization at the local level as a strategic effort to improve women's political participation.
3. The organization of public debate, advocacy, organizational management, campaign training with gender-perspectives

among women who are members of social and political organizations.

INCREASING WOMEN'S POLITICAL PARTICIPATION

In discussions about electoral systems, two questions need to be asked: what electoral systems actually are and why are they important to the participation of different groups in society, including women? Electoral systems may be categorised into three broad families:

a. Plurality Majority
b. Semi-proportional
c. Proportional Plurality-Majority First-Past-the-Post (FPTP), Block Vote (BV), Alternative Vote (AV) and Two Round systems all belong to the Plurality-Majority system.

Single-member districts are used in the Plurality Majority system. In a First-Past-the-Post (FPTP) system the winner is the candidate with the most votes but not necessarily an absolute majority of the votes. The same principle applies to the Block Vote (BV) system but the difference is that the latter uses multi–member districts where voters have as many votes as there are seats to be filled and the candidates with the most number of votes fill the positions regardless of the percentage of the vote they actually achieve. The Alternative Vote (AV) and the Two–Round system try to ensure that the winning candidates receive an absolute majority (i.e., over 50 per cent). Each system in essence makes use of voters' second preferences to produce a majority winner if one does not emerge from the first round of voting.

Semi-Proportional System

Under the Semi- Proportional system, the Parallel system and the Single Non-Transferable Vote (SNTV) is applied. In the Single Non-Transferable Vote (SNTV), each elector has one vote but there are several seats in the district to be filled and the candidates with the highest number of votes fill these positions. This allows for the election of minority party candidates, for example, women's parties. In general, this system can increase and improve parliamentary proportionality. The Parallel system uses both the Proportional Representation (PR) lists and Plurality-Majority (PR, winner–takes all).

Proportional Representation

Reducing the disparity between a party's share of the national vote and its share of the parliamentary seats can be done by applying the PR system. Proportionality is often seen as being best achieved by the use of party lists where political parties present lists of candidates to the voters on a national or regional basis. It can be achieved just as easily if the proportional component of a Mixed Member Proportional (MMP) system compensates for any disproportionality which comes out of the Majoritarian district results. In the Single Transferable Vote (STV), voiers rank the order of candidates in multi-member districts.

Electoral system are shaped by the structure of society in terms of the ideological structure, religion, class hierarchies, regional conditions and the history of how democracy was established in the country (traditional or new democracy, the level of 'party seriousness', in terms of the number of members and the distribution of party followers). The next issue revolves around the constitution. The questions that emerge in connection with this is, does the constitution exist, and if it does, what are the advantages and benefits it can give to women in terms of opening the door to decision-making positions and equal rights for women in the legislature?

The Philippines practices a Semi–Proportional Parallel System which uses a combination of PR and Plurality-Majority districts which means that some members of parliament are elected by PR system (20 per cent) and the remainder by the PM system. In the Philippines, the reform of the electoral system is of critical importance for the following reasons:

a. In day-to-day political practice, people often argue that the easiest political institution to be manipulated for good or for bad is the electoral system.

b. People always translate the votes cast in general elections into seats in the legislature.
c. The choice of electoral systems can effectively determine who is elected and which party gains power.
d. System sometimes leads to coalition governments.
e. Systems can be used as a tool for conflict management within a society.

Constitutional Reform

Although the status of women in the Philippines is not solely determined by the Constitution, it is clear that legislation can obstruct or accelerate the achievement of full equality between women and men. The development of the legal status of women under Philippine law is evident in the history of the electoral law. It was only in the 1930s that women were allowed to exercise their right to vote and be elected. Under the 1987 Constitution, the status of women has changed. The role of women in nation-building is now expressly recognized.

Although the Philippines already has the above acts, according to the policy paper on promoting gender balance in political representation which was issued by the Center for Legislative Development (CLD), there are still political barriers. The electoral system and campaign finances are among the structural barriers to women's political participation. For example, Vicky Vega (a woman councilor from Angeles City) spent around 200,000 pesos during her campaign to become councilor. The amount of money needed to win an election is the single biggest disincentive for women to run for parliament as is also the case with men.

It is therefore not a surprise that most women who run successfully for public office are those who belong to wealthy, propertied families or who have legions of fans ready to support them in any way. In this instance, the single-member plurality system such as what the Philippines has is generally unfriendly to women. On electoral politics, the only provision of the 1987 Constitution that touches directly on women's political participation is that of the party-list system.

This provision is found in Article VI (on the Legislative Department) which states:

1. The House of Representatives shall be composed of not more than two hundred and fifty members, unless otherwise fixed by law, who shall be elected from legislative districts apportioned among the provinces, cities and the Metropolitan Manila area in accordance with the number of their respective inhabitants and on the basis of uniform and progressive ratios, and those who as provided by law, shall be elected through a party–list system of registered national, regional and sectoral parties or organizations.
2. The party list representatives shall constitute twenty per cent of the total number of representatives including those under the party list.

For three consecutive terms after the ratification of this Constitution, one–half of the seats allocated to party–list representatives shall be filled as provided by law, by selection or election from the labour, peasant, urban poor, indigenous cultural communities, women, youth and such other sectors as may be provided by law, except the religious sector. Twenty bills on the subject of 'increasing women's political representation' have been introduced.

One of the most significant was the Women's Empowerment Act which was the act seeking to reserve for women one-third of the following positions:

- Cabinet Secretaries;
- Undersecretaries and positions of comparable salary grade or at least one in every line department, government-owned and controlled corporations, government financing, institutions, state colleges, and universities and local government units;
- Assistant secretaries in every department; and
- Directors in every department.

However, only 29 legislators out of 215 supported the Women's Empowerment Act. Some of the points of disagreement on the act are as follows:

- Women should be appointed not on the basis of 'reservation' but on their qualification.
- The bill provided a ceiling rather than a beginning. It had no provision whatsoever to move towards gender balance, 50/50 in women's representation and participation. The number of women might be nailed down to 30 per cent which is a limitation rather than a jumpstart.

The Realities of Women in the Philippine Public Life

- The first reality pertains to sources of political power. The political system is based on wealthy political dynasties which use politics as a means to gain more wealth. It is elite and male-dominated with no clear party system.
- Candidates often rely on personality, popularity, charisma and the personal relations rather than capability.
- Voting is often based on pragmatism and immediate gains which leads to wealthy candidates always being reelected.

Many NGOs in the Philippines are engaged in negotiations and lobbies regarding requirement policy reforms: affirmative action, electoral system and campaign finances. One proposed policy reform is that of a quota for women of at least one-third (33 per cent) in all appointive and elective national and local decision-making positions in government by 2005 and when that has been achieved, to move towards gender balance and achieve 50/50 not later than 2015, the target date of the Millennium Development Goals laid down in the Millennium Summit in 2000. Another reality of the election process in the Philippine is massive fraud using the 3 Gs (guns, goons and gold-the use of violence and intimidation, and vote buying). Voting is often based on practically and immediate gains and the voters lack awareness concerning their rights and responsibilities.

How Can the Philippine Case be Applied in Indonesia

A look into Philippine political practices seems to reveal that many disadvantages still exist with regards to increasing women's candidacy since they have to finance campaigns which tend to be very expensive. Based on numerous studies of electoral systems, PR tends to be more favourable to women.

In PR systems, parties have the chance to compete for and win several seats, allowing them to go further down the party list where women usually are. Through PR, political parties can be pressured to balance the candidates by including women. Logically, if political parties have 30 per cent women candidates, then this will result in about 30 per cent women membership in parliament.

Although PR as an electoral system tends to be more favourable to women in terms of increasing their political representation, there are other contributing factors to consider such as the type of PR system, the political environment and local culture. Sometimes, PR systems that use closed lists where women's names cannot be stroked off or demoted are preferable to women. In Indonesia, we can introduce 'zebra rule' where 'every second seat is allotted to women'. A question should be addressed to political parties: how can women have access to the structure of parties?

In most political parties in Indonesia, women are still very rare in high decision- making spheres. Because of this condition, parties must declare pre-electoral commitments about the percentage of women they are fielding. Women are often discouraged to enter politics because of various costs they have to shoulder.

Many women who decide to join elections are forced by the prevailing political culture to spend huge amounts to compete with male candidates who in most cases have a solid financial base. There is a need in Indonesia to have a regulation which monitors and regulates the amount of funds that candidates are allowed to give to the party that supports them.

Many party leaders in Indonesia especially at the provincial, district and sub-district level do not realize that women can be an electoral asset. In order to increase the chances for women, the party has to incorporate a gender dimension by taking one or all of the following steps:

- Establish a committee on gender equality or a gender focal point with a mandate to scrutinize the party's policy in that connection.
- Reorienting the party's women's wing so that it promotes women's vision and secures support for women within the party and not just offering women's support to the party.
- Reviewing rules and practice for internal elections to ensure equality of access by women and men to the leadership positions in the party and to local and national elective mandates.

Points to Consider in Increasing Women's Political Participation

a. Promote awareness of electoral rules and regulations The rule and regulations of the electoral system as well as for candidacy should be clear and well articulated in the community, especially for women. By increasing the awareness and knowledge of women about electoral laws and changes in structure and process, automatically this will increase women's political participation.

b. Organizing women to be candidates Whatever the electoral system, women should be prepared to be candidates. Women need to organize themselves within and outside of political parties. Continuous awareness-raising activities such as leadership training/seminars are necessary to develop women's skills and knowledge to prepare them for their political career.

c. Organizing women's groups and strengthening networks Strengthening networks and continue to empathetically pressure various sectors. A resolute women's movement translates memberships into votes, which means major parties which are mostly male-dominated, will be moved to include women in their list of candidates.

d. Advocate for change in the structure of the party organization The number of men in strategic positions within the party is always higher than what women can achieve.

This means that men are always in the list of party candidates. Women should be allowed easy access to resources and accurate and up-to-date information which can act as inputs for making decisions and as evidence to push for gender-equal legislation.

In Indonesia today, political parties are predominant in political life and in the running of institutions. They can mobilize considerable support and logistics for electoral campaigning. This contrasts with the situation in the Philippines whereby the chances of independent candidates (including women) are determined by their own efforts in nominating themselves and raising funds and support, the greatest difficulty for women in Indonesia is how to obtain nomination through a political party. For this reason, the internal regulation of the party should state that a minimum percentage (e.g.30 per cent) of parliament candidates should be women.

Bibliography

Adburgham, Alison. *Women in Print. Writing Women and Women's Magazines from Restoration to the Accession of Victoria.* London: Allen & Unwin, 1972.

Arnold, Ethel M. *Literature for Ladies, 1830-1930.* Manhattan: K.S.A.C. Press, 1930.

Barrell, Joan. *The Business of Women's Magazines.* 2nd ed. London: Kogan Page, 1988.

Beetham, Margaret. *Victorian Women's Magazines : An Anthology.* Manchester: Manchester University Press, 2001.

Boston Women's Health Book Collective. *Our Bodies Ourselves.* New York: Simon & Schuster, 1976.

Braithwaite, Brian. *The Business of Women's Magazines: The Agonies and the Ecstasies.* London: Associated Business Press, 1979.

Braithwaite, Brian. *Women's Magazines: The First 300 Years.* London: Peter Owen, 1995.

Brody, Michal, ed. *Are We There Yet? A Continuing History of Lavender Woman.* Iowa City; Aunt Lute Company, 1985.

Burman, Barbara, ed. *The Culture of Sewing: Gender, Consumption and Homedressmaking (Dress, Body, Culture).* Oxford: Berg, 1999.

Coakley, Mary Lewis. *1907-Sex, Sisterhood, and Self-Delusion: What Happened to Women's Magazines?* New Rochelle: Arlington House, c. 1979.

Dancyger, Irene. *A World of Women. An Illustrated History of Women's Magazines.* Dublin: Gill and Macmillian, 1978.

Danky, James P., ed. *Women's Periodicals and Newspapers from the 18th Century to 1981: A Union List of the Holdings of Madison, Wisconsin Libraries.* Boston: GK Hall, 1982.

Doughan, David, and Denise Sanchez. *Feminist Periodicals, 1855-1984: An Annotated Critical Bibliography of British, Irish, Commonwealth and International Titles.* Brighton: Harvester, 1987.

Eskridge, Melissa J. *How the Psychology of Women Is Presented in Women's Magazines,* 1986.

Ferguson, Marjorie. *Forever Feminine: Women's Magazines and the Cult of Femininity.* London: Heinemann, 1983.

Friedan, Betty. *The Feminine Mystique.* New York: Dell Publishing Co., Inc., 1963.

Gough-Yates, Ann. *Understanding Women's Magazines: Publishing, Markets and Readership.* London: Routledge, 2003.

Grimstad, Kirsten and Susan Rennie, eds. *The New Woman's Survival Catalog.* New York: Berkley Publishing Corporation, 1973.

Hermes, Joke. *Reading Women's Magazines: An Analysis of Everyday Media Use.* Cambridge: Polity Press, 1995.

Hoffmann, Phyllis P. *Women's Magazines.* 1983.

Incantalupo, Patricia. *The Portrayal of Women in Sport Advertising in Two Women's Fitness Magazines,* 1992.

Johnson, Judy M, ed. *Spot Illustrations from Women's Magazines of the Teens and Twenties: 828 Cuts of Women, Family, Home, Garden, Etc.* New York: Dover Publications, 1989.

Mann, Robert S. "Women and the Newspaper." *The University of Missouri Bulletin,* no. 2640.

Millum, Trevor. *Images of Woman: Advertising in Women's Magazines.* London: Chatto & Windus, 1975.

Ramet, Adèle. *Creating a Twist in the Tale: How to Write Winning Short Stories for Women's Magazines.* Plymouth: How To Books, 1996.

Shevelow, Kathryn. *Women and Print Culture: The Construction of Femininity in the Early Periodical.* London: Routledge, 1989.

Sievers, Sharon L. *Flowers in Salt: The Beginnings of Feminist Consciousness in Modern Japan.* Stanford: Stanford University Press, 1983.

Waller, Jane, and Michael Vaughan-Rees. *Women in Wartime; the Role of Women's Magazines 1939-1945.* London: Macdonald Optima, 1987.

White, Cynthia L. "Growth between the Wars: 1920-1938." In *Women's Magazines 1693-1968.* London: Michael Joseph Ltd, 1970.

White, Cynthia L. *Women's Magazines 1693-1968.* London: Michael Joseph Ltd, 1970.

Winship, Janice. *Advertising in Women's Magazines, 1956-74.* Birmingham: Centre for Contemporary Cultural Studies, University of Birmingham, 1980.

Winship, Janice. *Inside Women's Magazines.* New York: Pandora, 1987.

Yackey, Lena Millicent. *Contributions of Women's Magazines to Homemaking Problems on Food.* New York, 1930.

Index

A

Addressing Gender, 28.

C

Campaigns, 11, 48, 130, 132, 205, 206, 212, 214, 239, 261, 270, 271, 272, 284.
Celebrations and Commemorations, 163.
Changes in Linqu, 234.
Charitable Organizations, 164.
Citizenship, 144, 260, 272.
Civil Liberties, 169.
Civil Society, 91, 109, 123, 124, 134, 148, 150, 190, 261, 265, 274, 281, 282, 286.
Consciousness-Raising, 223.
Consensus on the Local level, 83.
Constitutional and Electoral Reforms, 244.
Constitutional Reform, 281.
Contention on the National Level, 83.
Conversion and Mission, 163.
Cultural Barriers, 137.

D

Demographics, 166.

E

Educational Institutions, 164.
Educational Obstacles, 200.
Electoral Systems, 52, 55, 68, 73, 126, 194, 212, 213, 215, 221, 250, 251, 279, 281, 284.
Empowerment of Civil Society, 125.
Empowerment of Women, 5, 135, 137, 255.

F

Family Code, 100, 167.
Female Agenda, 99.
Feminization of the Labor Market, 114.

G

Gender, 7, 10, 12, 13, 14, 15, 16, 18, 19, 20, 21, 22, 23, 24, 25, 26, 27, 28, 29, 30, 31, 33, 35, 36, 37, 38, 42,

43, 44, 45, 46, 48, 49, 50, 52, 53, 55, 57, 58, 59, 60, 62, 63, 66, 70, 72, 74, 75, 80, 82, 83, 86, 87, 91, 92, 93, 96, 97, 98, 101, 104, 105, 106, 107, 108, 109, 187, 188, 189, 190, 192, 193, 254, 255, 257, 259, 260, 261, 262, 264, 265, 266, 267, 277, 278, 280, 282, 283, 284, 285, 286.

Gender Inequality in India, 78.

Gender Mainstreaming in Law, 102.

Global Under Representation, 35.

H

Hospitals and Service Projects, 164.

I

Impact of Women Politicians, 180.

Institution Building, 4.

L

Larger Role for Women, 236.

Lessons Learned, 138.

Limits of its Prioritization, 24.

Linchpin of Global Policy, 28.

N

Networking, 6, 9, 11, 243, 255, 257, 271.

O

Obstacles and Challenges, 94.

Occupational Obstacles, 201.

Official Life Story, 155.

Organizations, 14, 15, 19, 26, 27, 83, 85, 90, 97, 98, 100, 109, 115, 116, 118, 135, 156, 161, 179, 180, 206, 216, 242, 247, 248, 257, 259, 260, 261, 265, 266, 267, 268, 270, 271, 272, 279, 282.

Ownership Rights, 170.

P

Philippine Public Life, 283.

Physical Integrity, 169.

Policy Priorities, 173, 182, 184, 185.

Political Institutions, 128, 130, 175, 245, 246, 247, 253, 261, 262, 263, 265, 267, 271, 272, 277.

Political Participation, 38, 94, 100, 117, 119, 120, 122, 123, 124, 126, 127, 131, 133, 135, 172, 195, 197, 199, 234, 241, 243, 244, 246, 249, 250, 251, 253, 255, 256, 257, 259, 260, 261, 263, 265, 268, 269, 271, 272, 276, 277, 278, 281, 285.

Political Parties, 11, 48, 49, 51, 55, 65, 81, 83, 84, 97, 107, 121, 123, 124, 125, 129, 132,

133, 174, 192, 194, 205, 207, 208, 209, 210, 251, 252, 257, 258, 259, 260, 261, 266, 267, 268, 269, 272, 273, 274, 277, 278, 280, 284, 285, 286.
Political Representation in the Lok Sabha, 80.
Political-Electoral System, 105.
Politics in Philippines, 89.
Practices in the Ashrams, 156.
Proportional Representation, 8, 47, 49, 50, 52, 63, 68, 71, 73, 91, 212, 213, 216, 220, 252.
Prospects of Women, 92.

Q

Quo Vadis, 117.
Quota Criticism, 75.

R

Realities of Women, 283.
Reasonable Access to Education, 112.
Recruitment Process, 195.
Religious Legitimacy, 171.
Remnants of Colonialism, 96.
Reserved Seats System for Women, 71.

S

Sathya Sai Baba groups, 160.
Selection Process, 202, 207, 208.
Semi-Proportional System, 279.
Social and Cultural Obstacles, 196.
Structural Barriers, 137.
Successful Strategies, 137.

T

Teachings, 148, 149, 157, 158, 160, 249, 256.
The Biggest Barriers Faced, 137.

U

UN Goals Not Met, 97.
Unsuccessful Strategies and Efforts, 138.

W

Women Candidates, 8, 12, 39, 50, 61, 62, 66, 82, 83, 89, 221, 247, 248, 258, 284.
Women in Elected Office, 35, 38.
Women in Nation Building Law, 103.
Women in Philippine Politics, 91, 92, 96.
Women Who Win, 98.

